WORLD OFF TRACK

JARRET SCHECTER

TROLLEY

COUNTRIES TRAVELLED BY TRAIN

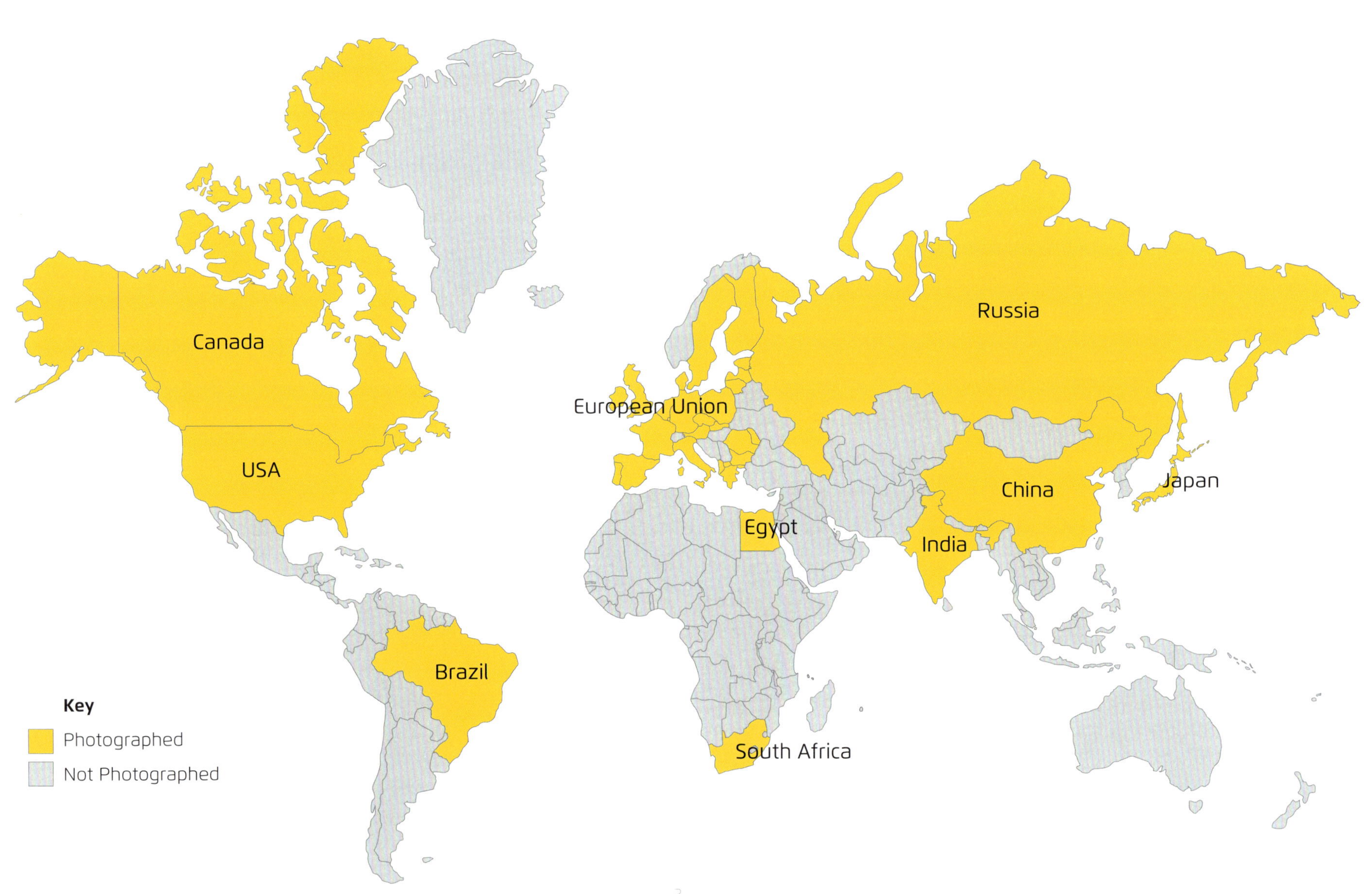

INTRODUCTION

Looking at a train traversing the 19th century landscape must have been an unprecedented and quintessential image of both promise and progress in a newly emerging, modern industrial world. Both a cause and effect of the Industrial Revolution, trains made of steel and fueled by coal, transported goods and people, and in turn were the symbol par excellence of speed, power, growth and freedom in a dawning new socioeconomic age of progressively-leaning capitalism.

Looking from a train window today less than two hundred years later, it is difficult not to feel collectively uncertain or even anxious. Quickly glancing at the past, Europe imploded on itself twice only to be replaced by a global superpower conflict, which subsequently was exchanged for ethnic strife, religious fundamentalism and other forms of conflict and authoritarianism. The past becomes the present, and in the alarming context of a population explosion, environmental degradation, amidst a neoliberal economic crisis among other ailments, we are presently left with nostalgia of what could have been and/or anxiety of what could be. In the present, the combination of a nostalgic past and an anxious future, leads us on a vague and indefinable search to collectively be somehow, correctly on track.

Looking not for an explanation let alone a cause, the following images taken through the train windows from the world's most powerful and influential nations, might pictorially hint at the weaknesses and the possible remedies in a 'World Off Track'.

With respect to power, influence and hegemony within and between continents, the criteria used are 1) population, 2) size, and most importantly, 3) potential (including some combination of economic, political, military, and cultural potential to effect change). The countries included are the United States, China, Russia, India, Brazil, Japan, Canada, South Africa, Egypt and the new experiment in nationality and from the region that first brought the world the concept of the nation state, the European Union.[1] Although notable exceptions would be Mexico, Argentina, Nigeria, South Korea, Indonesia, Turkey and a few others, the above nations, who were built and are still being built by trains, amazingly constitute a great percentage of the world's land and population. With nearly 200 countries in the world, incredibly only the relatively few nations included in this collective survey comprise over 85% of the world's GDP, and a huge yet incalculable percentage of the world's future physical and psychological health. The images that follow are an attempt at taking a pictorial pulse of the world, that in many ways is visibly and sadly off track. Jarret Schecter

1 At time of publication all countries included are full members of the EU, except Serbia which is a candidate country.

California, USA

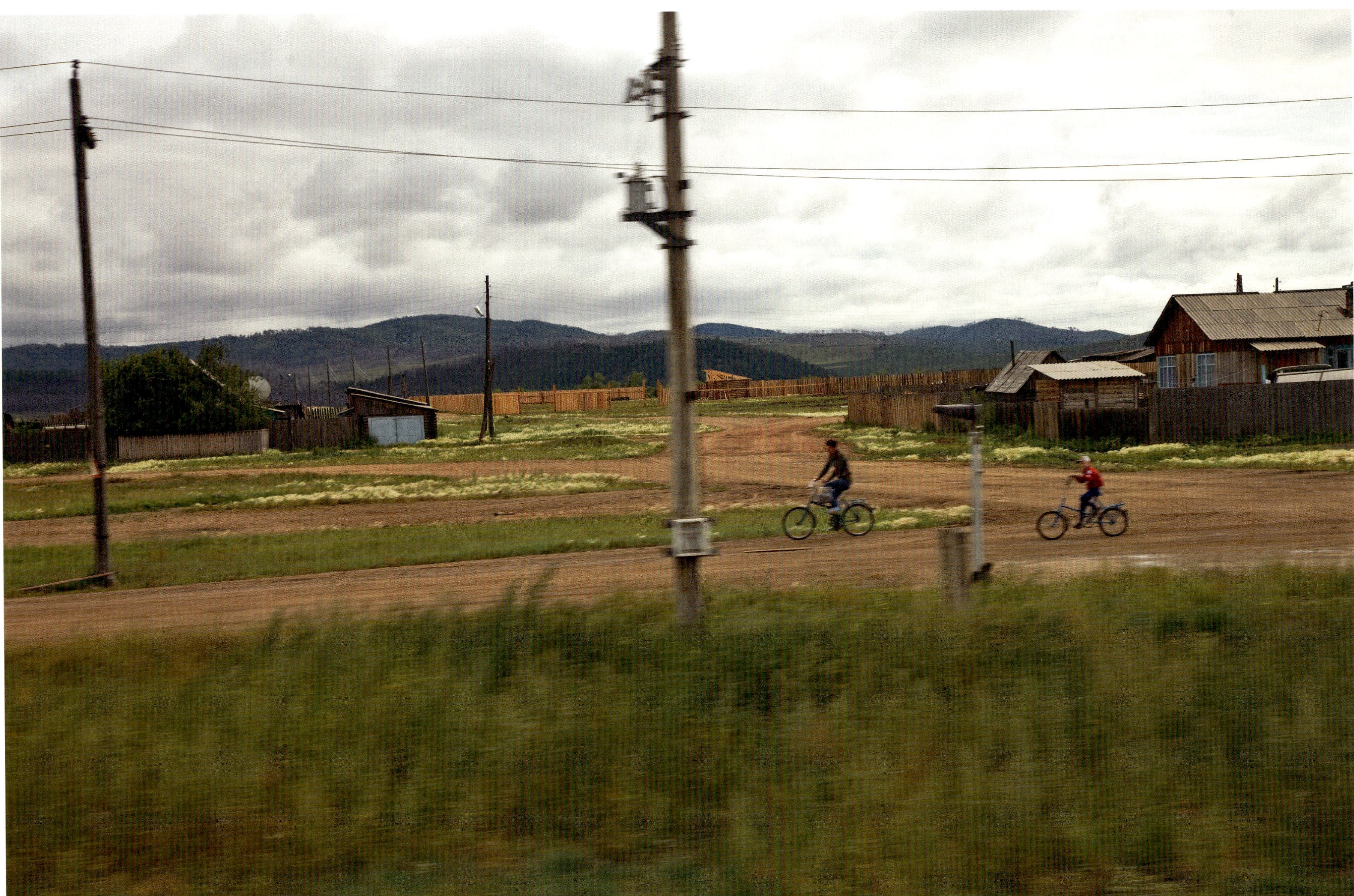

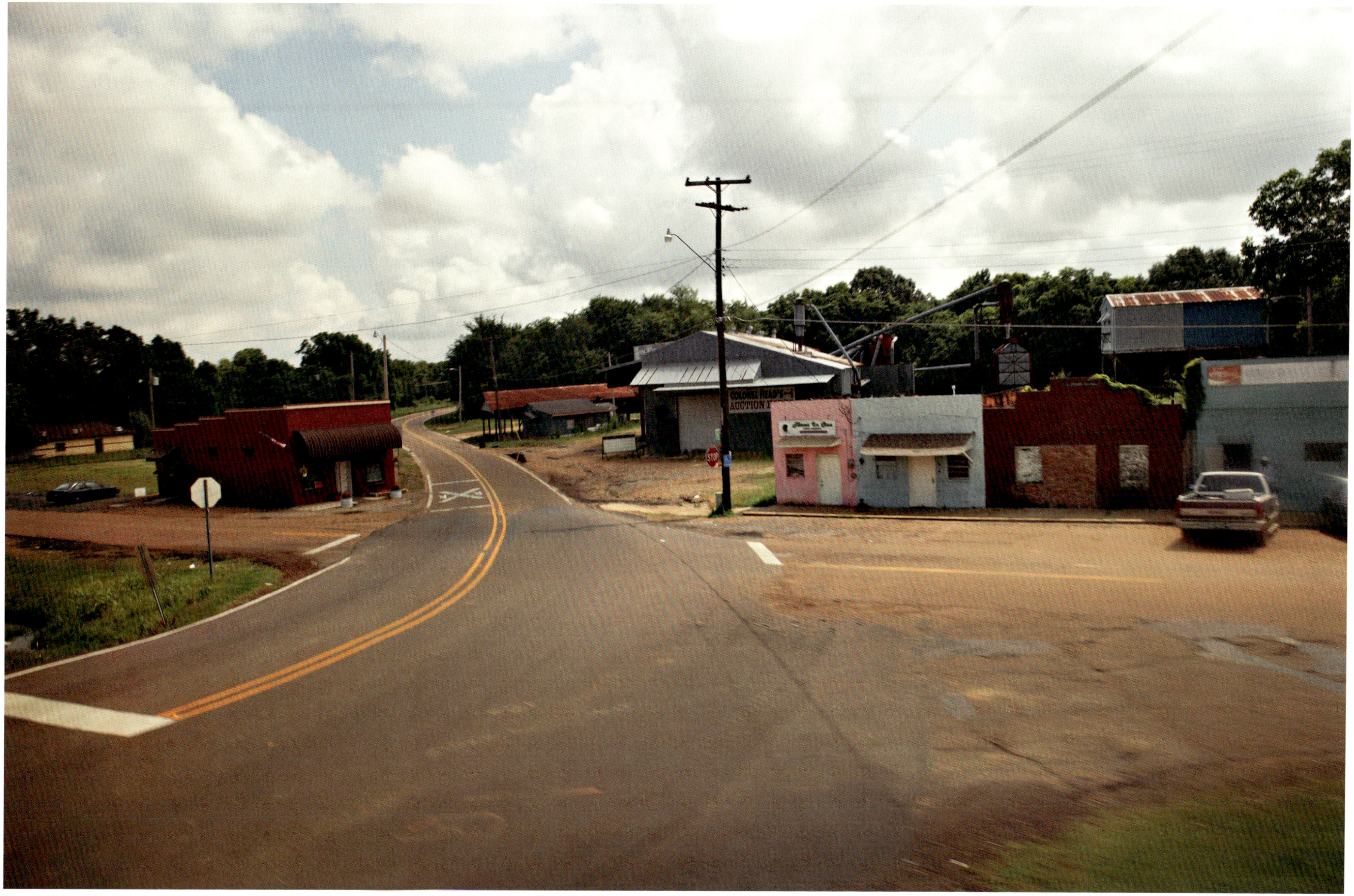

Alabama, USA

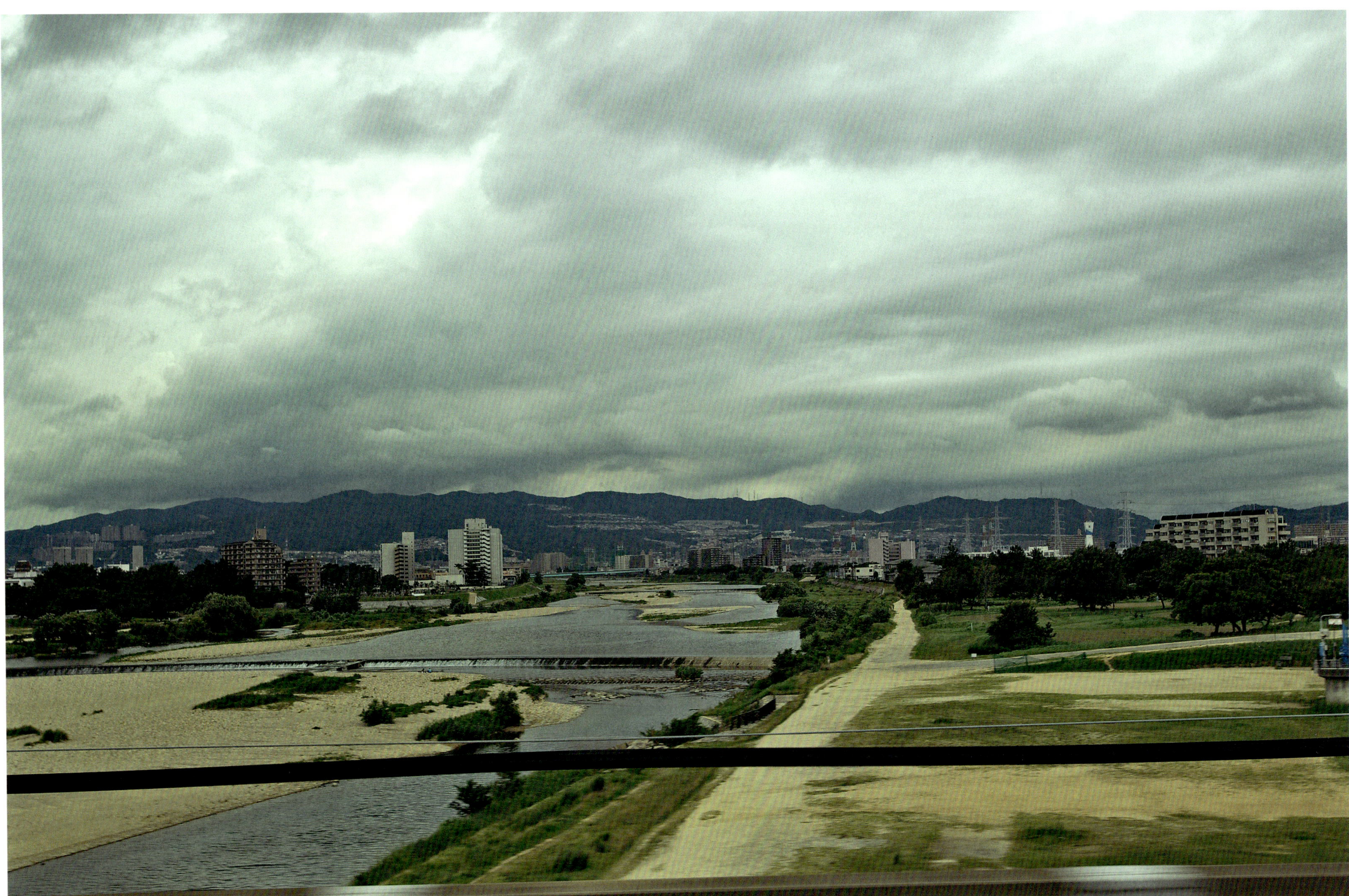

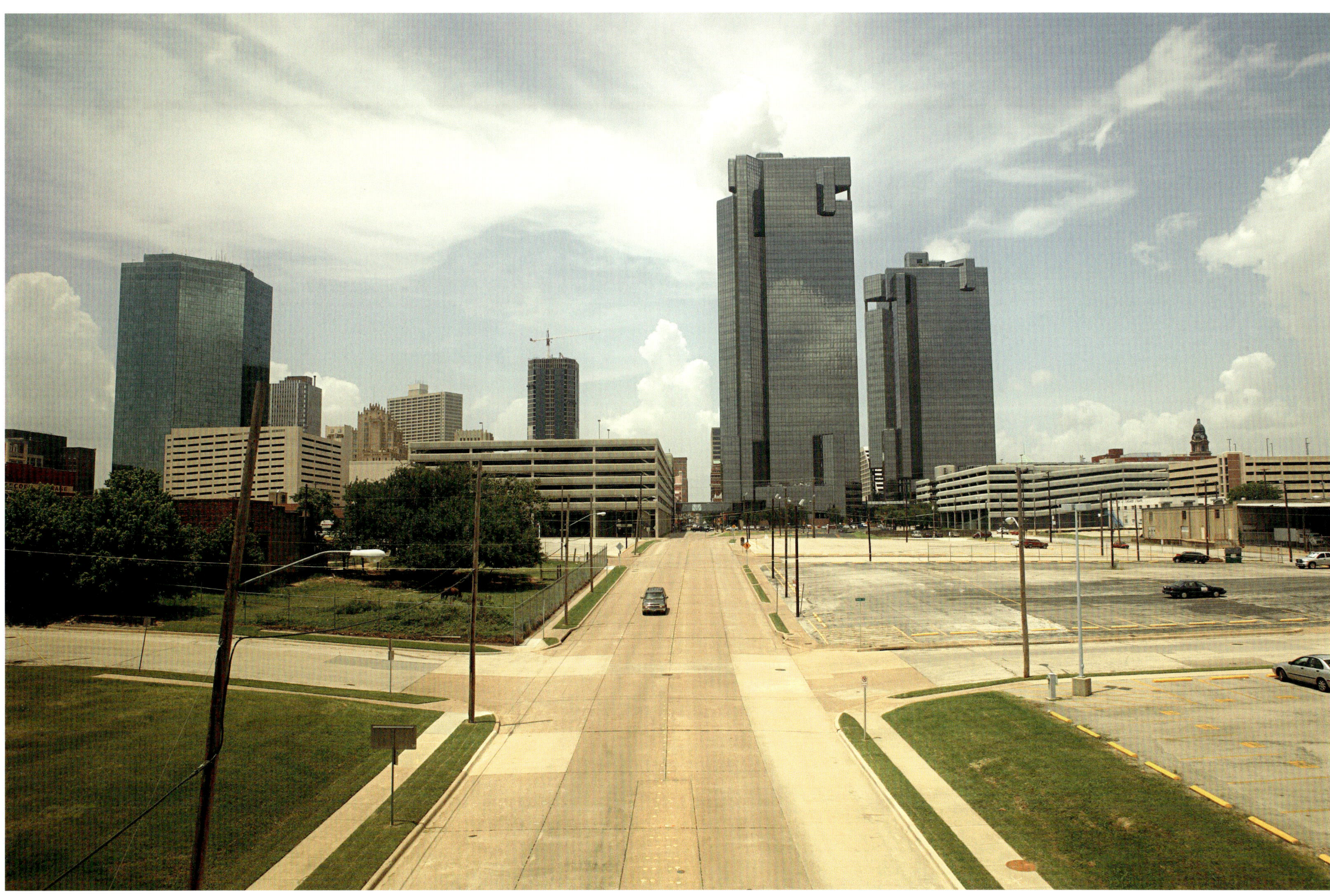

Fort Worth, Texas, USA

Brazil, with the 2016 Olympics in Rio and aware of its status as an emerging global superpower, is aiming to have a 40,000 km / 24,855 mile rail network by 2020. Although impressive, this pales in comparison to a country such as China, which as of 2011 already had a rail network length of more than 90,000 km / 55,923 miles.

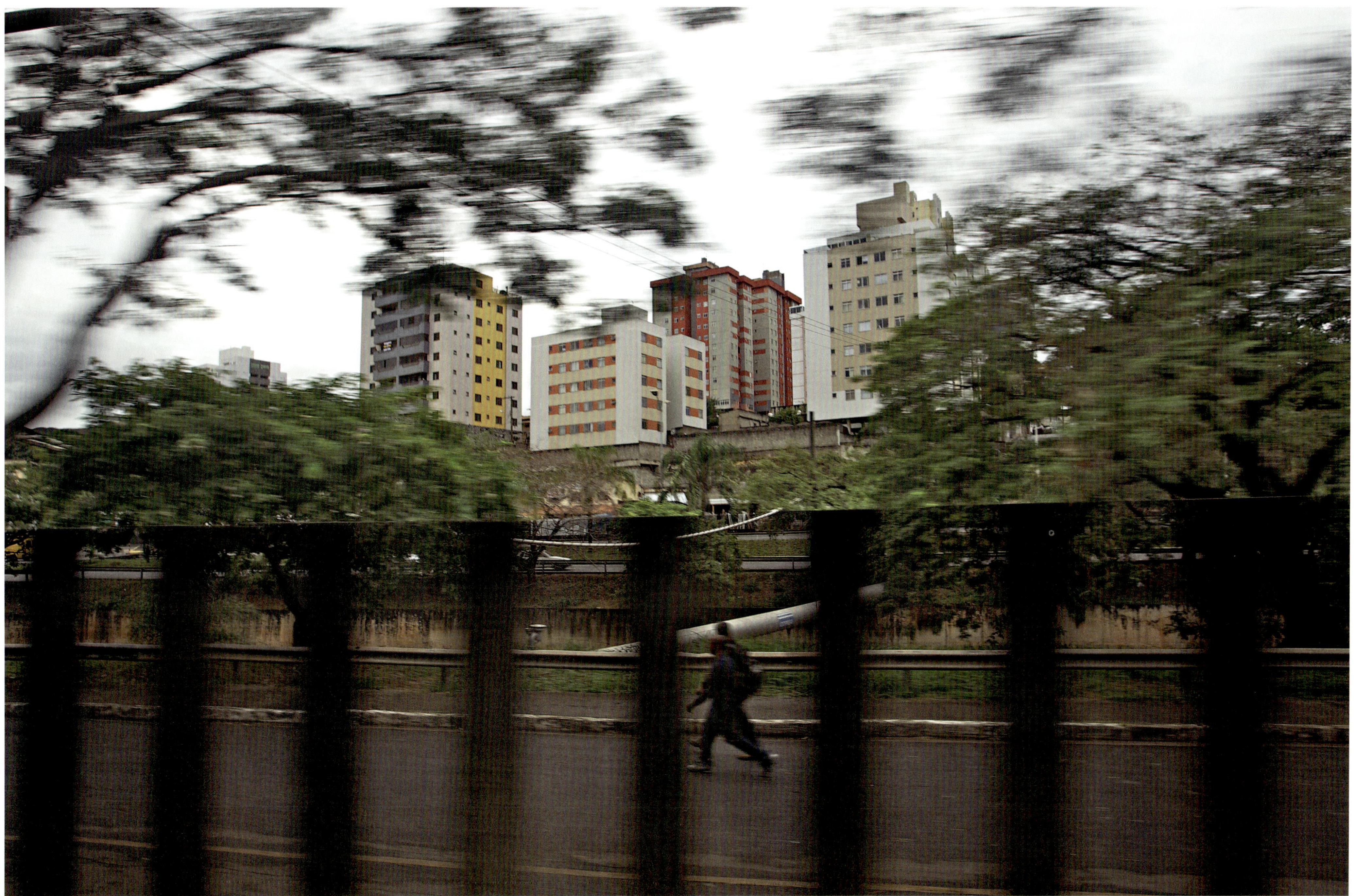

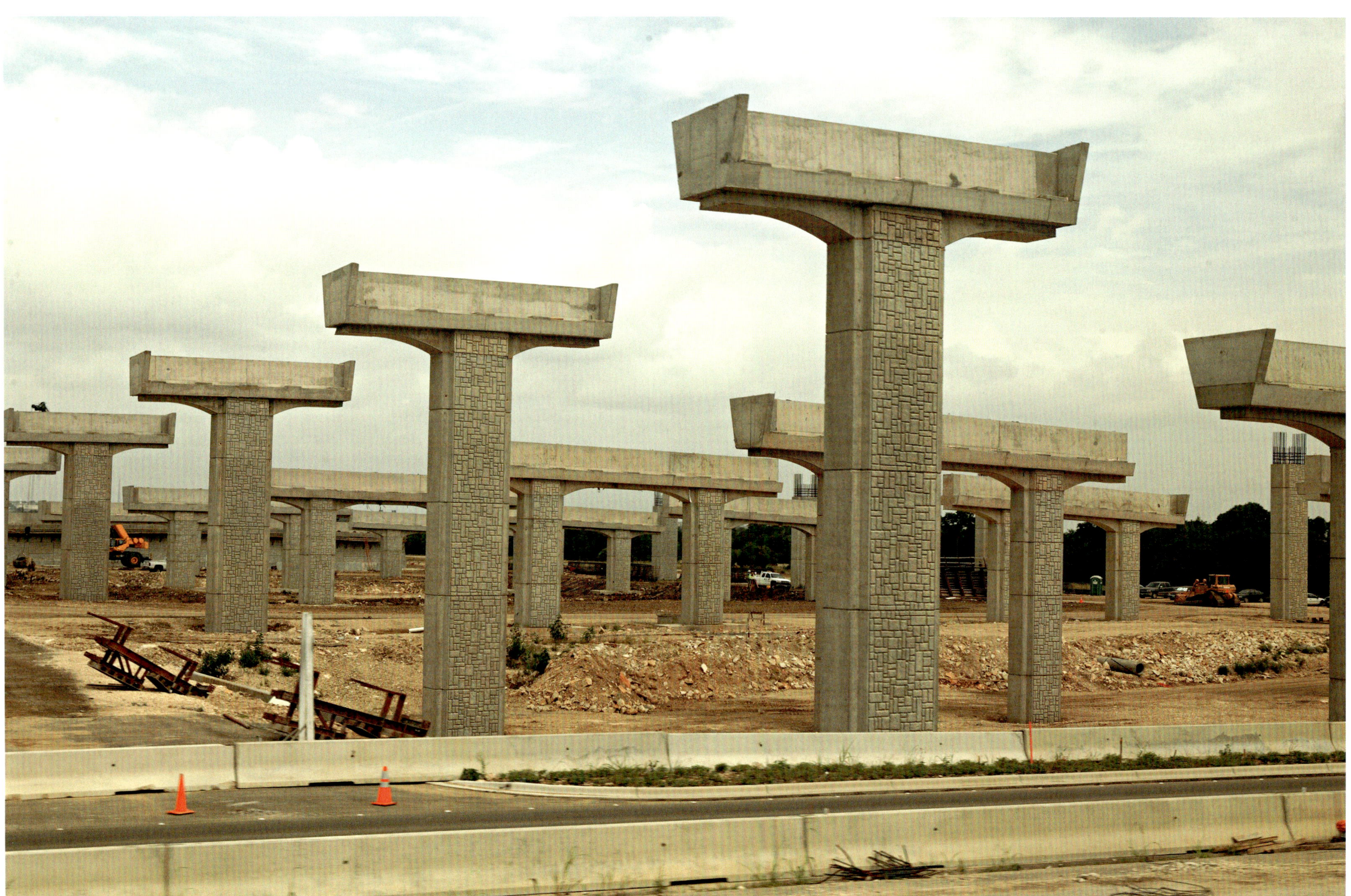
Texas, USA

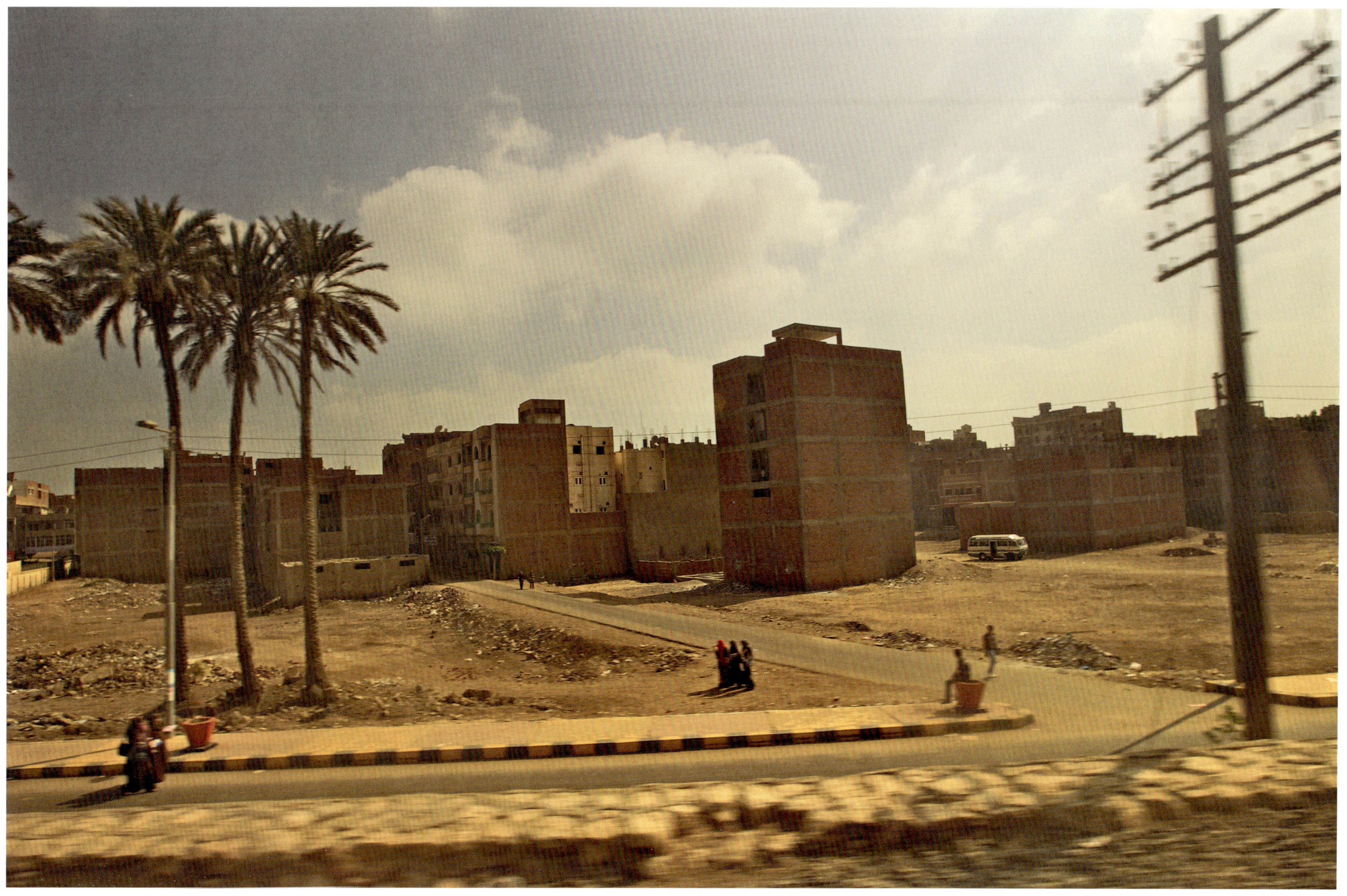
Egypt

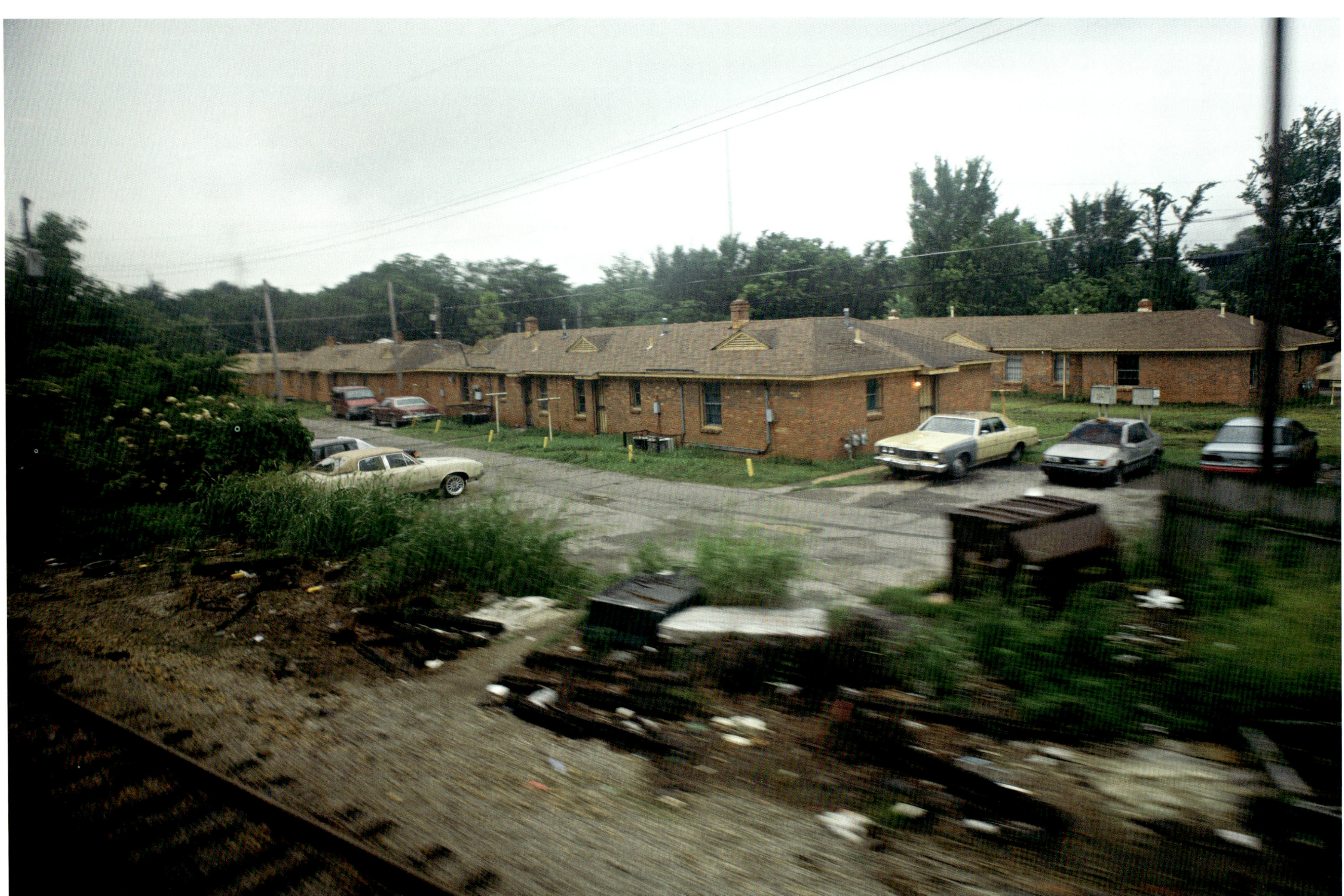

Memphis, Tennessee

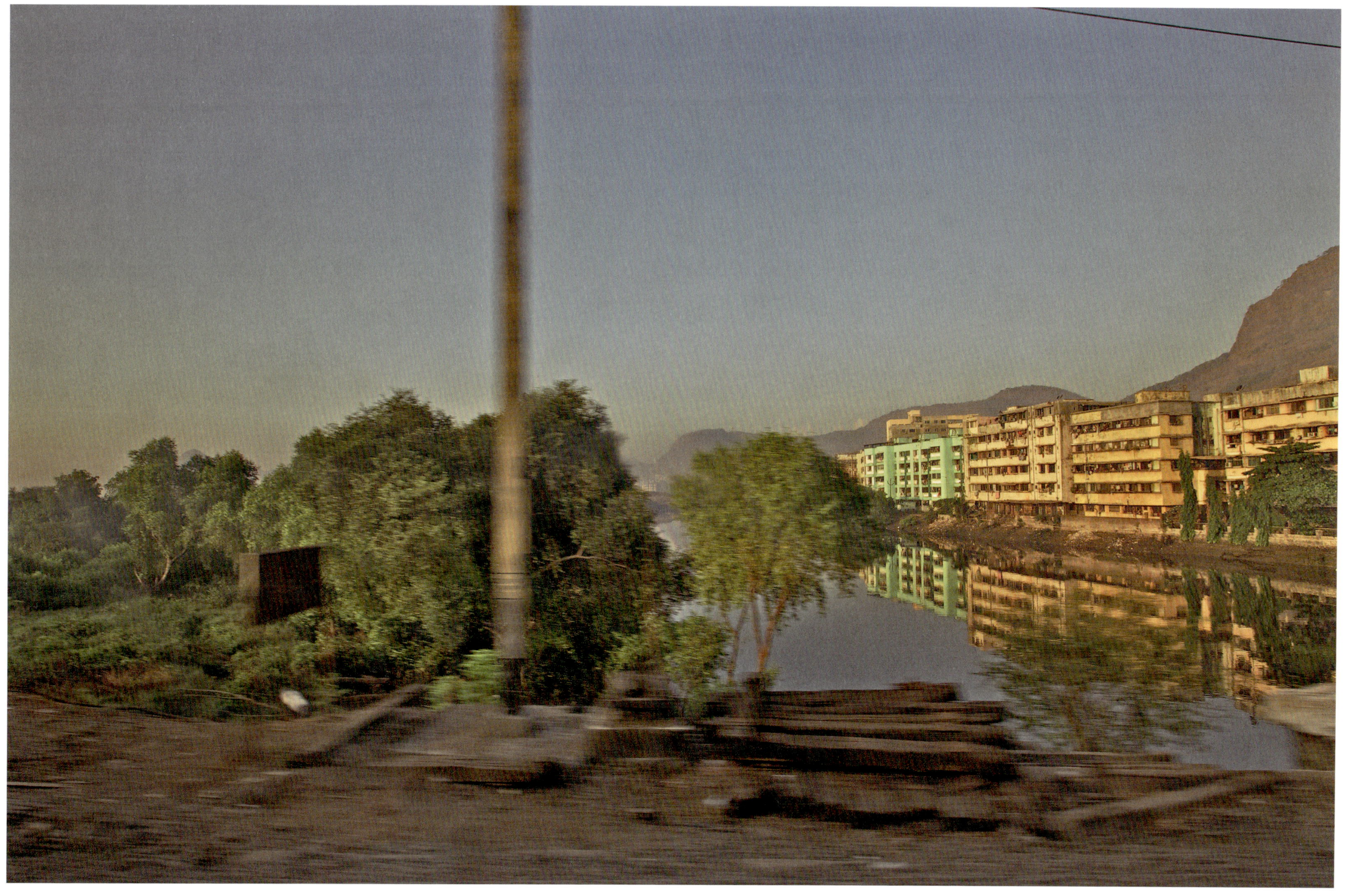

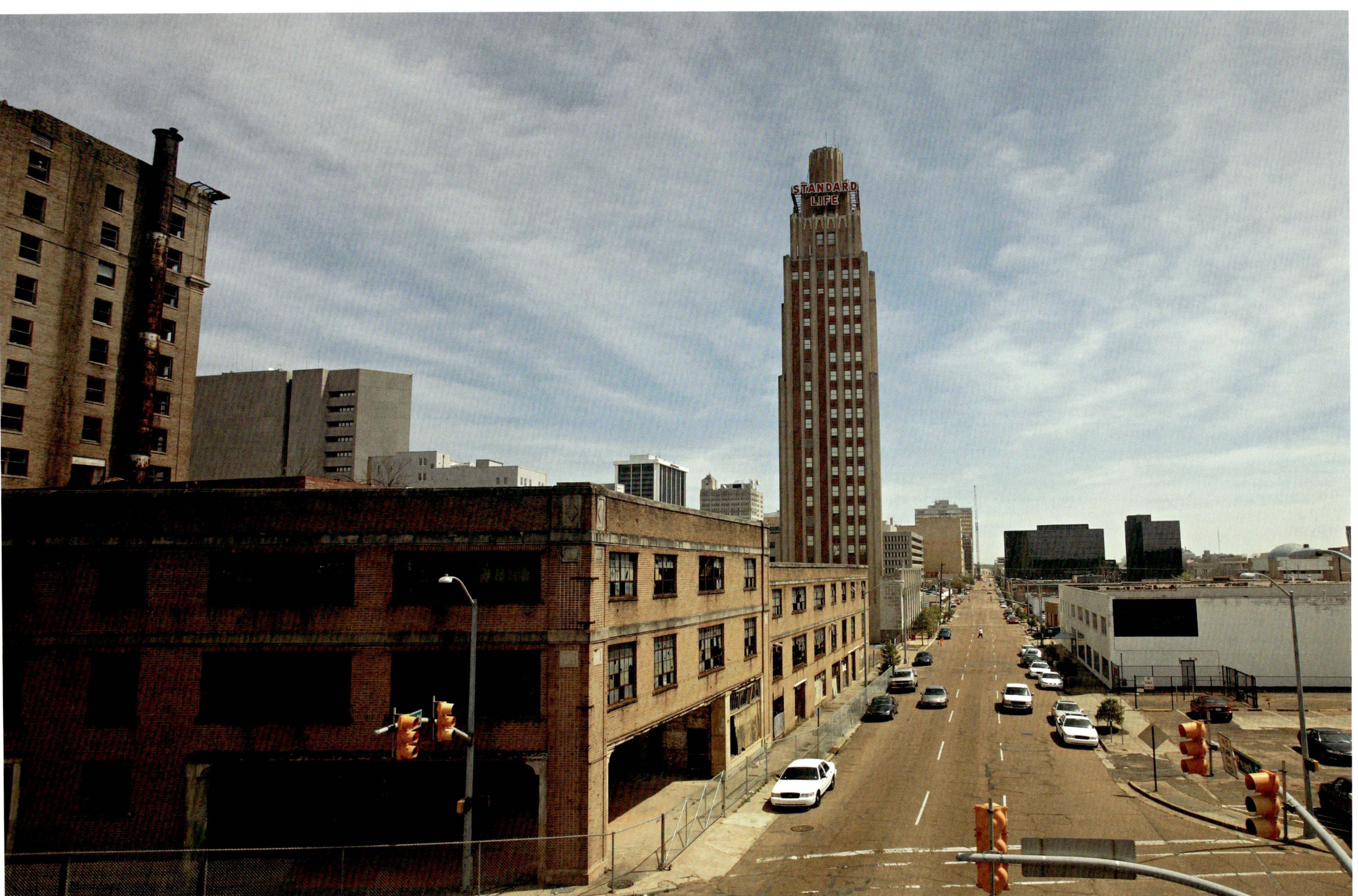

STANDARD
LIFE

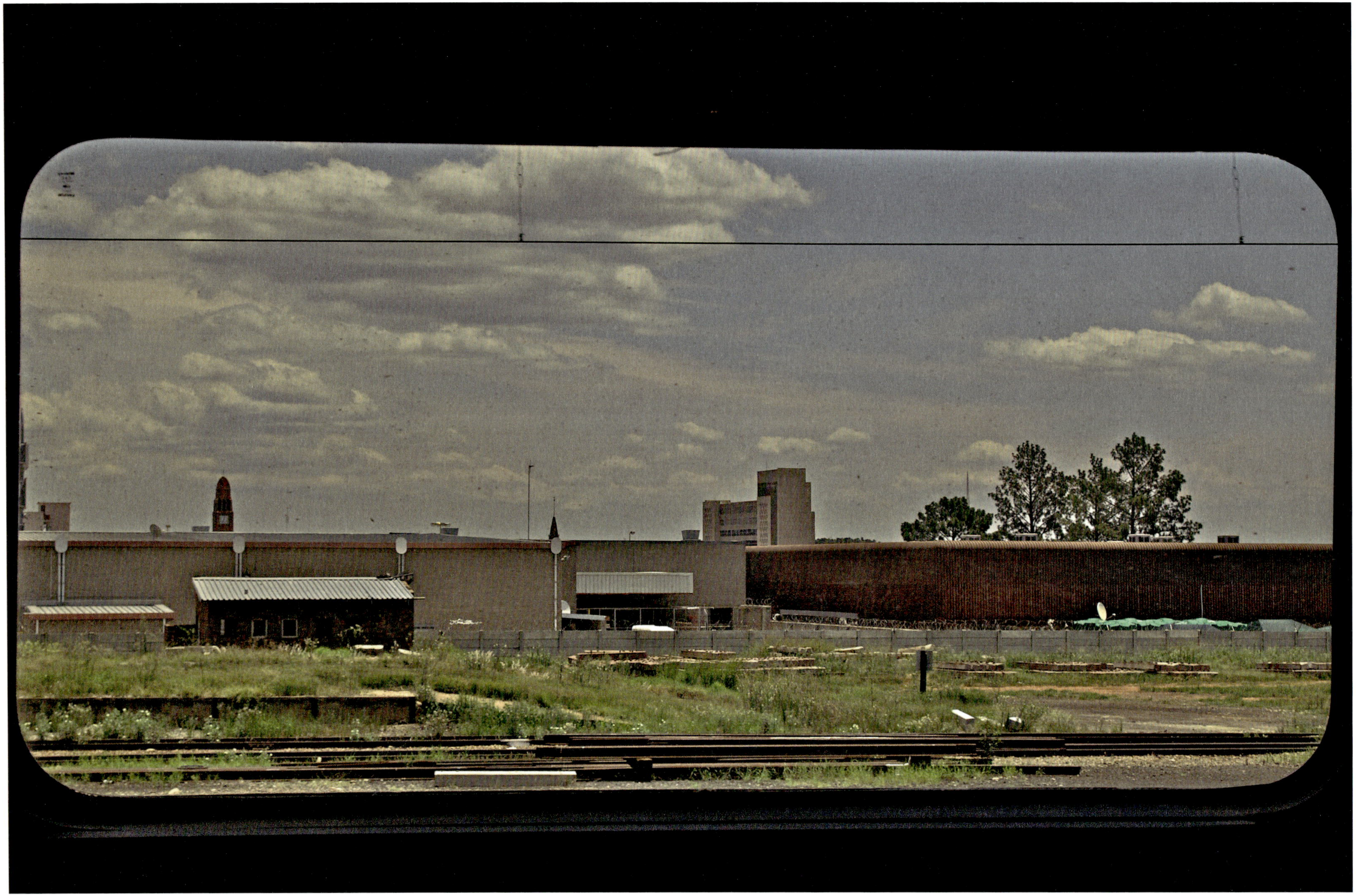

South Africa

Toronto, Canada

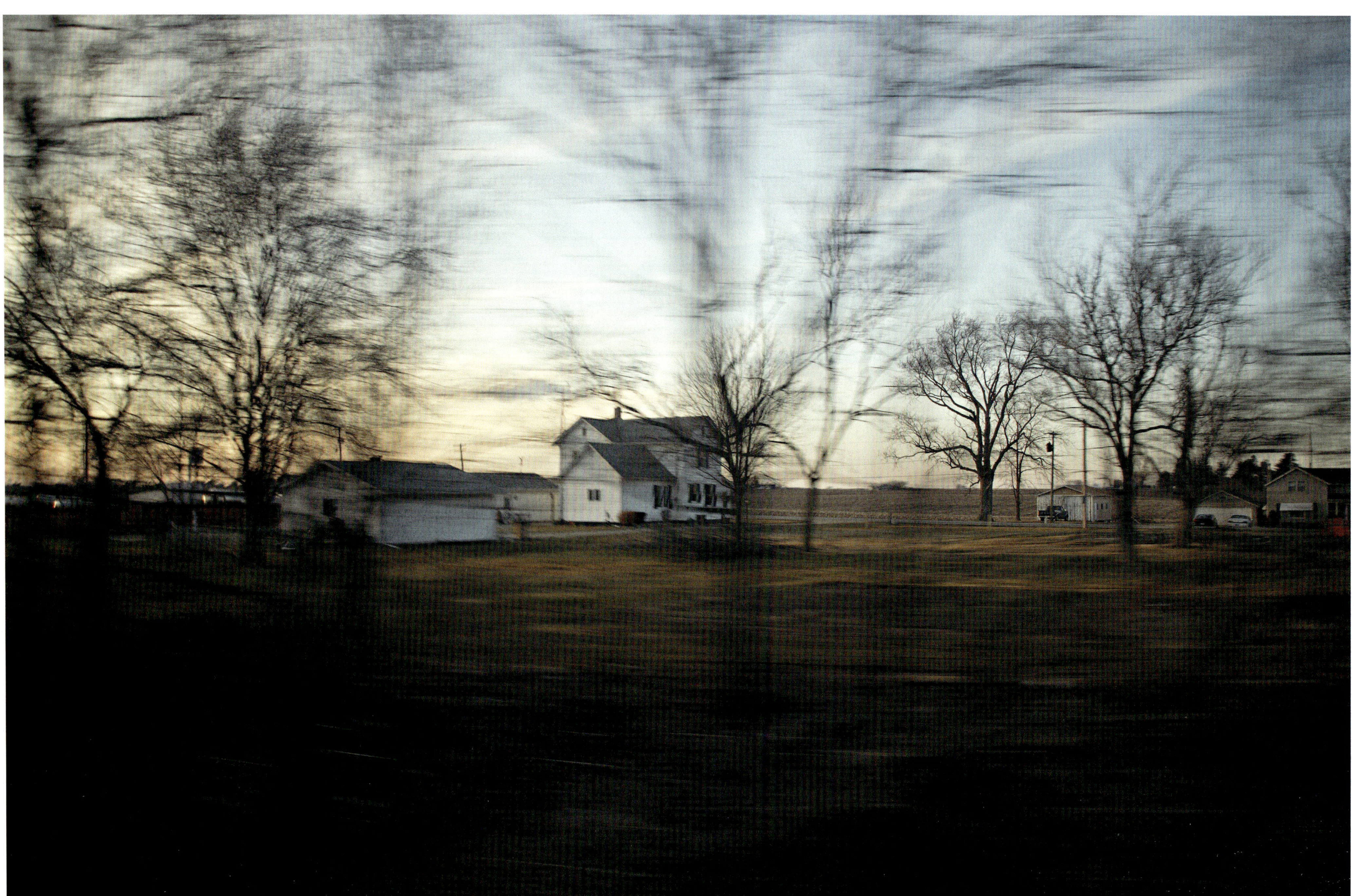

Illinois, USA

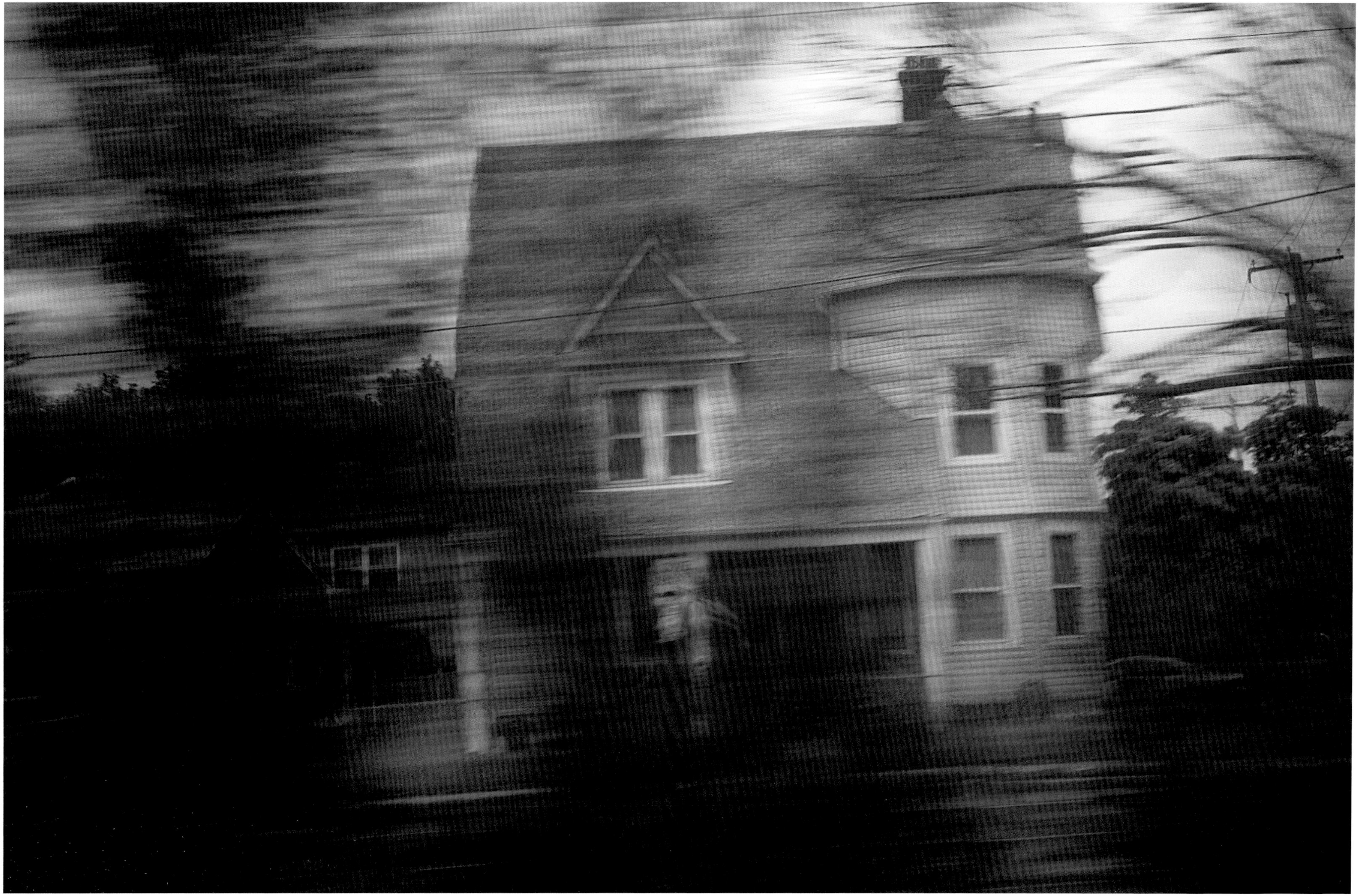

New Jersey, USA

Canada's railways conserve fuel, are environmentally friendly and reduce highway congestion. One train, on average, moves the same tonnage of freight as 280 big trucks.

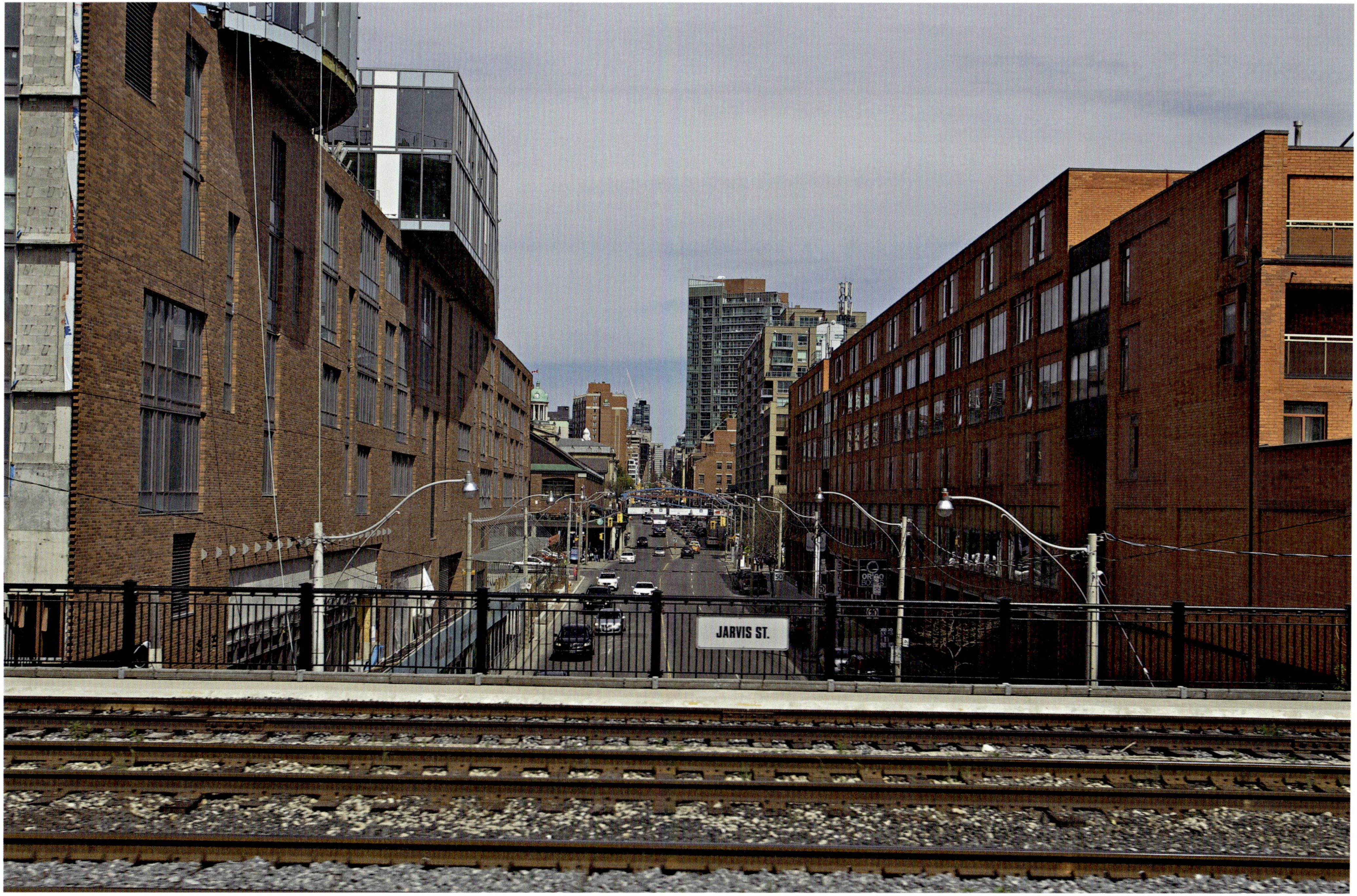

JARVIS ST.

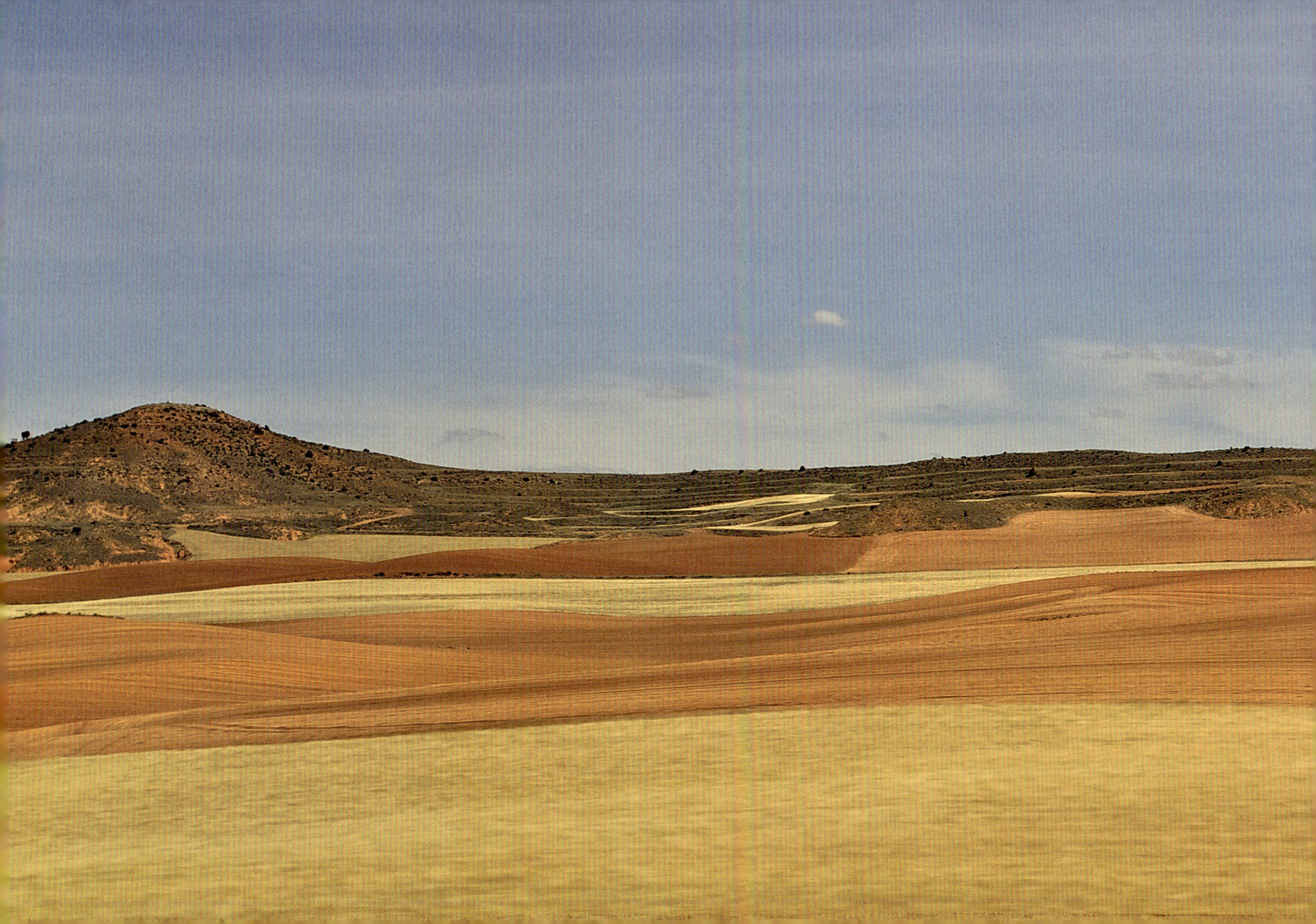

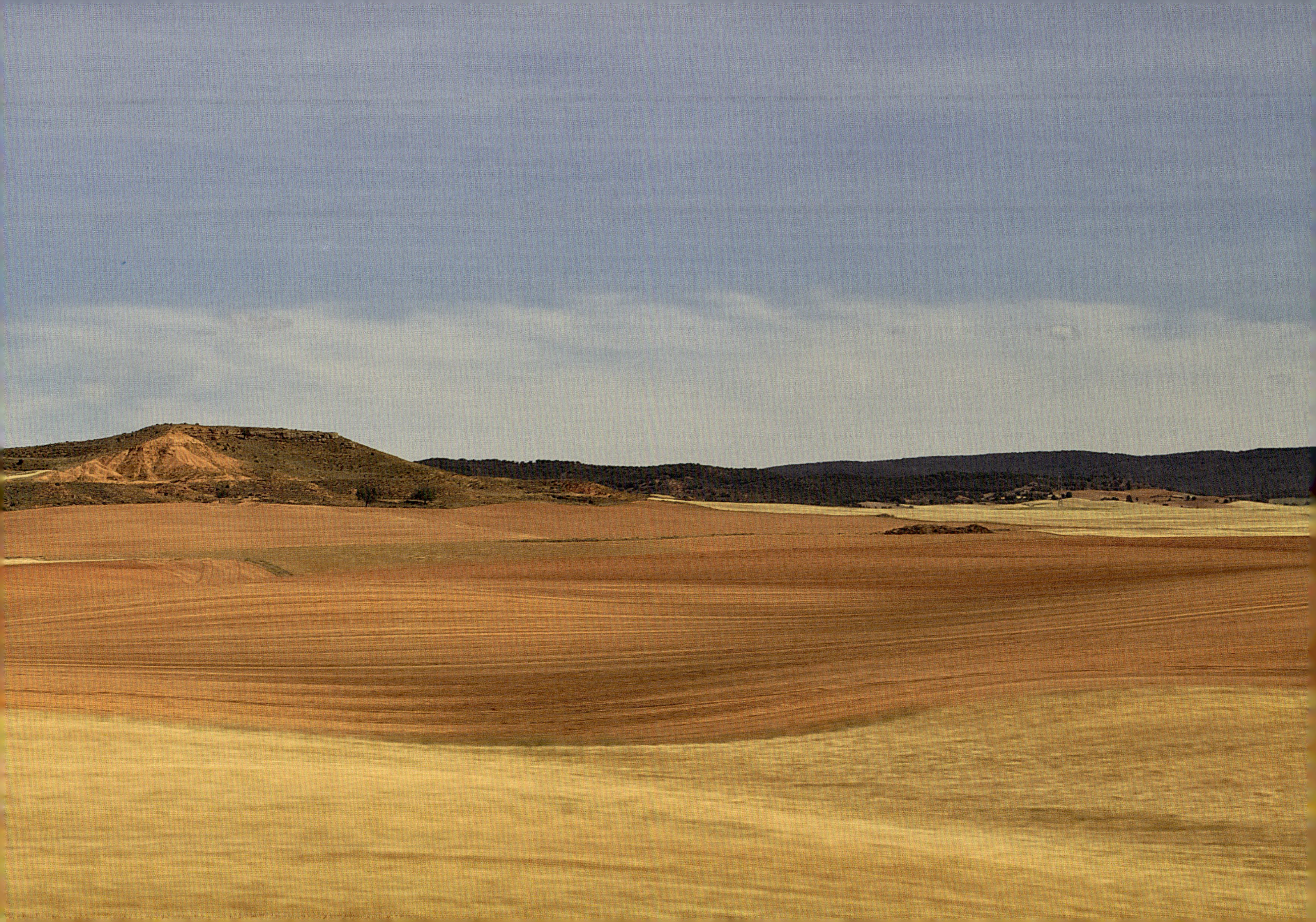

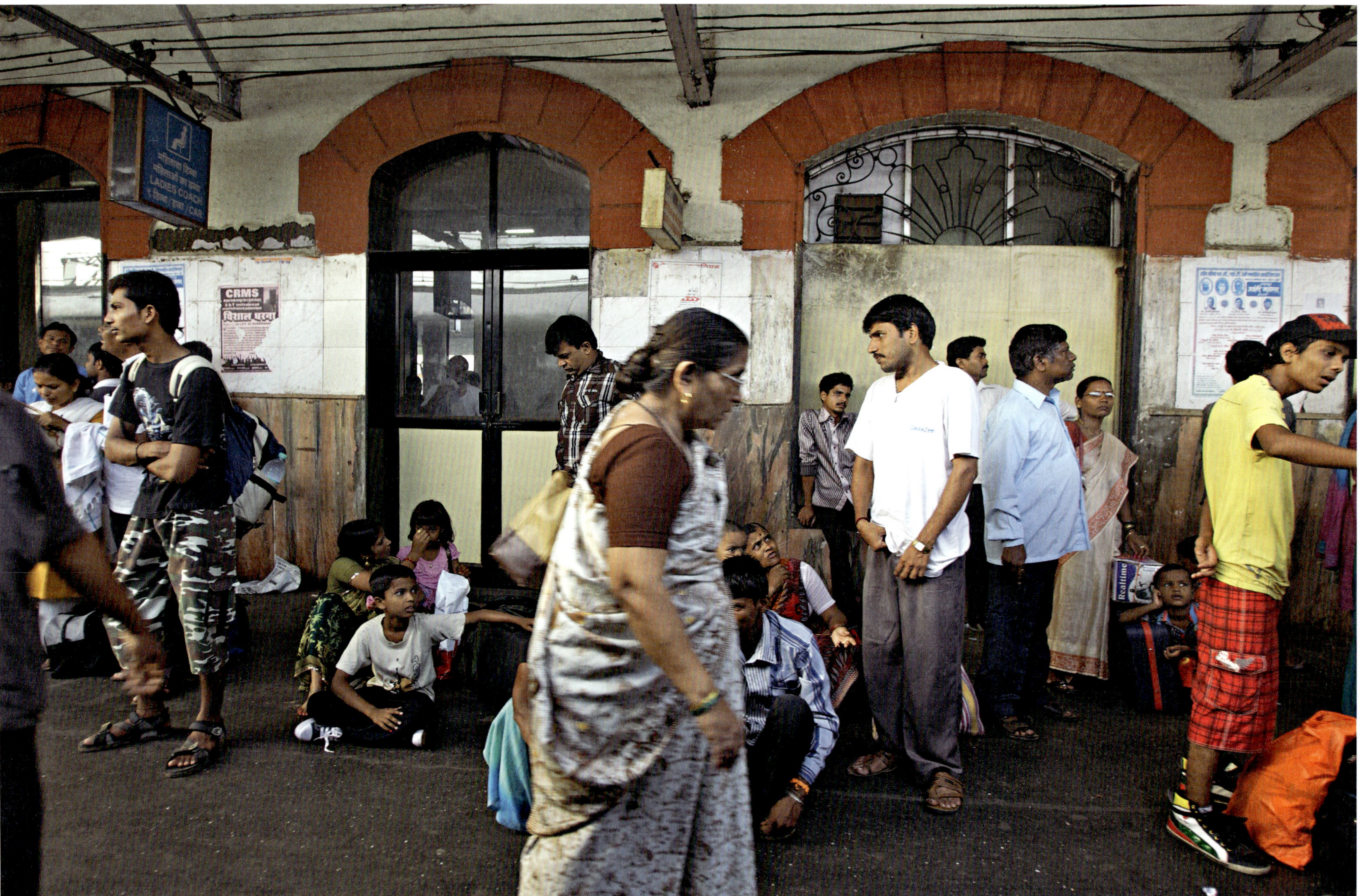

Indian Railways (IR) is known to be the largest railway network in Asia and the world's largest railway system under single management. IR employs about 1.6 million people, making it by number of employees the ninth largest commercial or utility employer in the world.

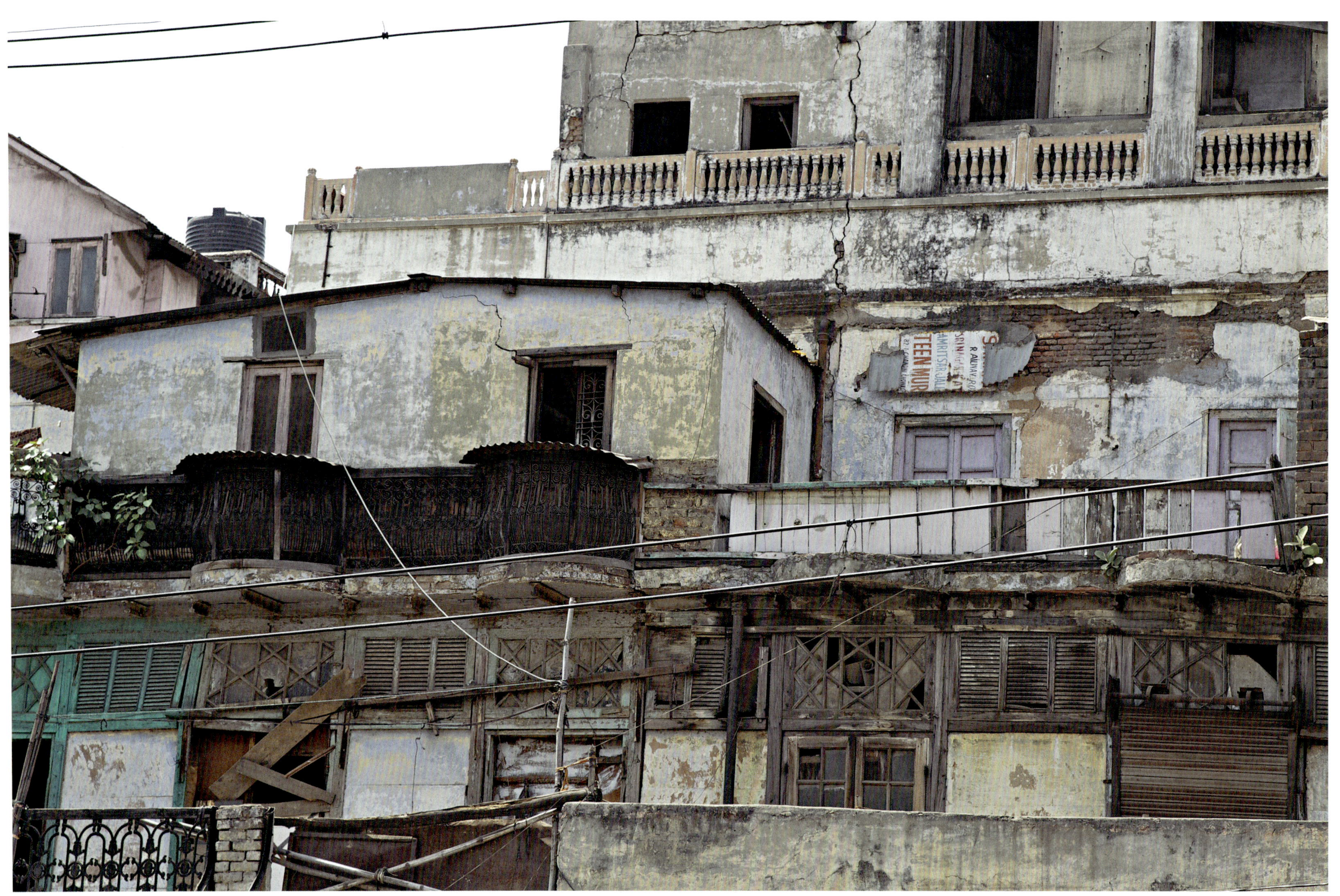
S
R. AILWAY. RO
SRINAGAR
AMRITSAR. JAL
TEEN MUR
82-1-CHANDNI CHOWK

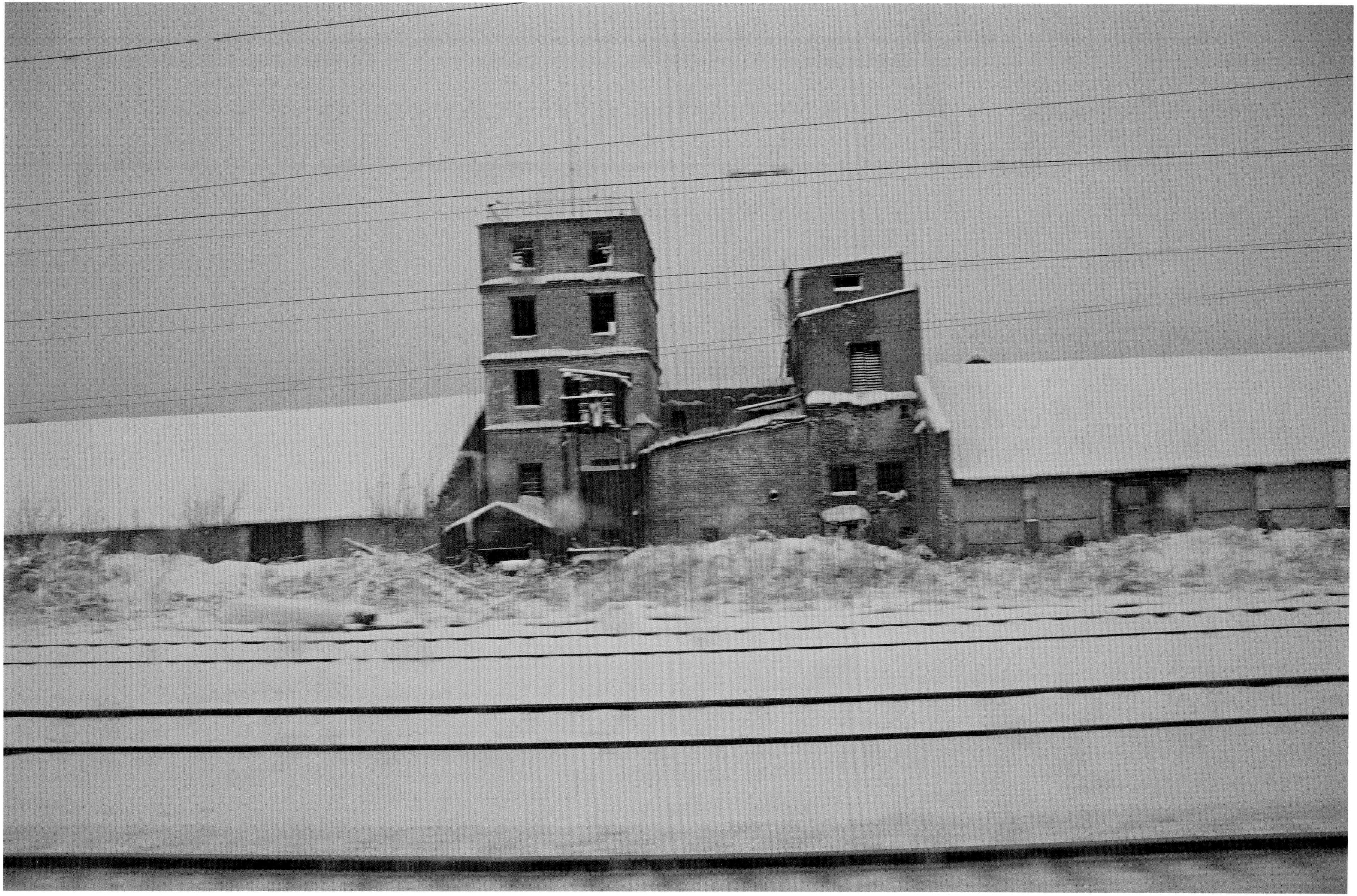

Russia

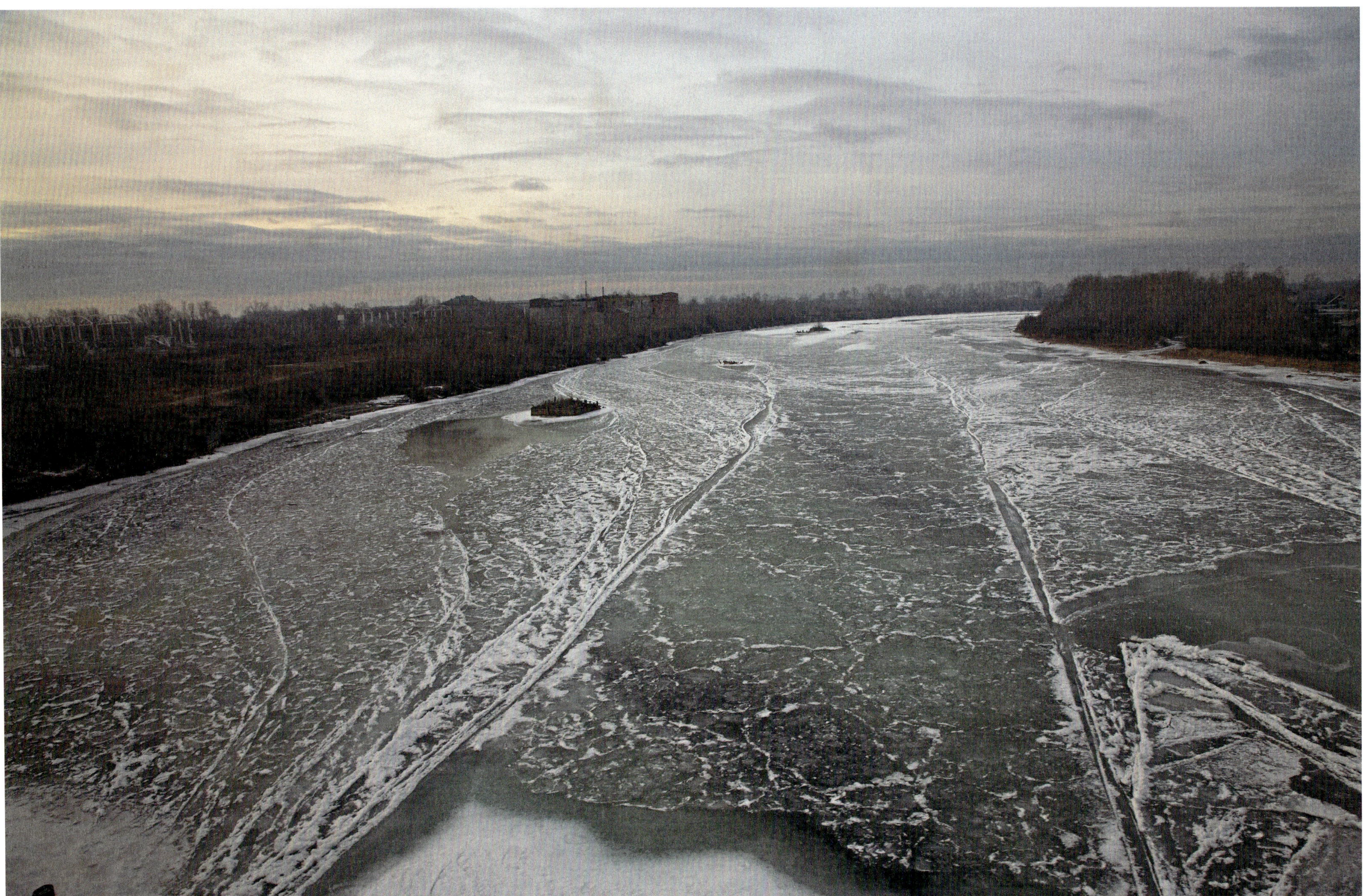

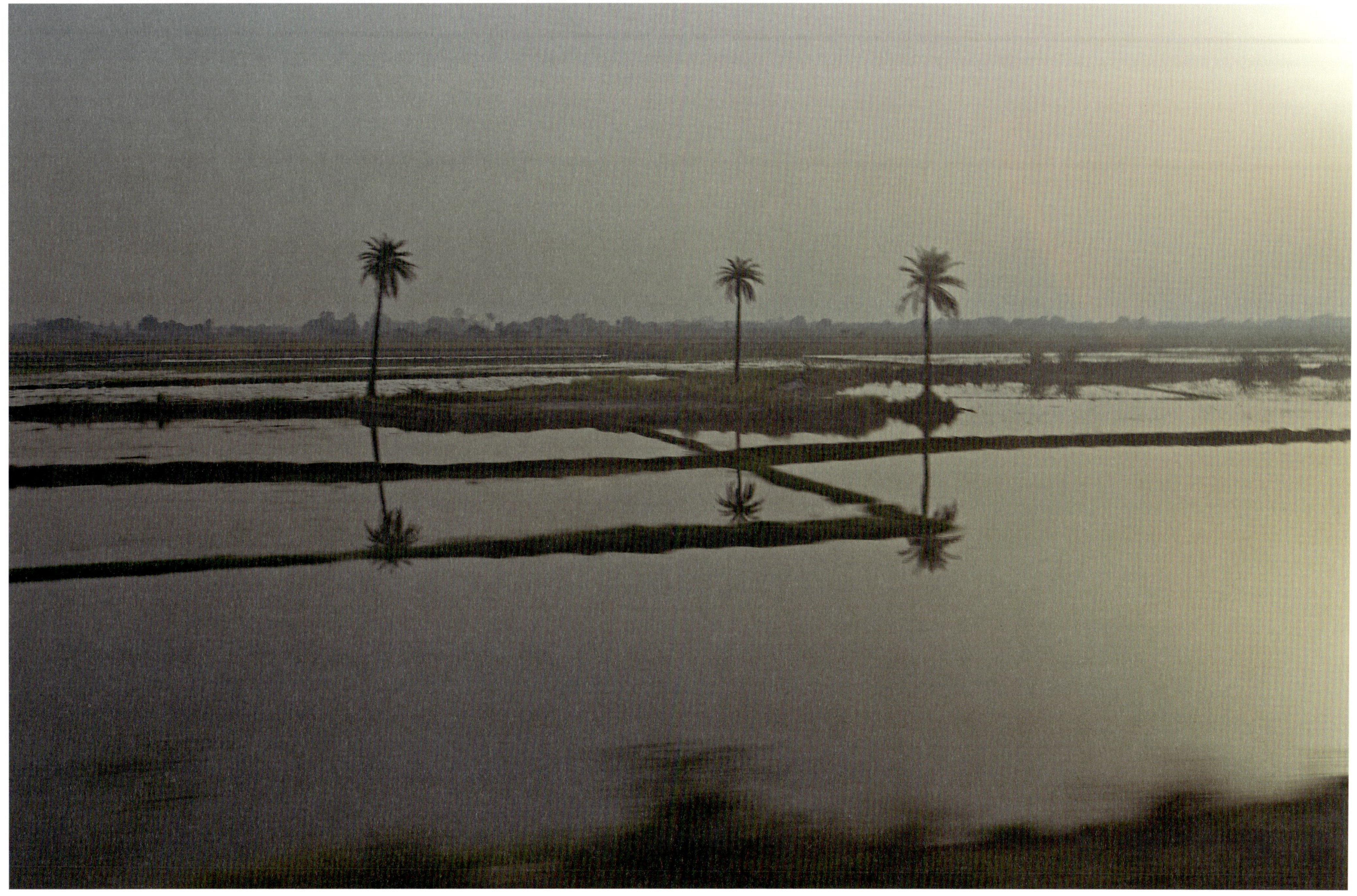
India

China is the world's most prolific railway builder. It adds around 6,000 km / 3728 miles of track a year.

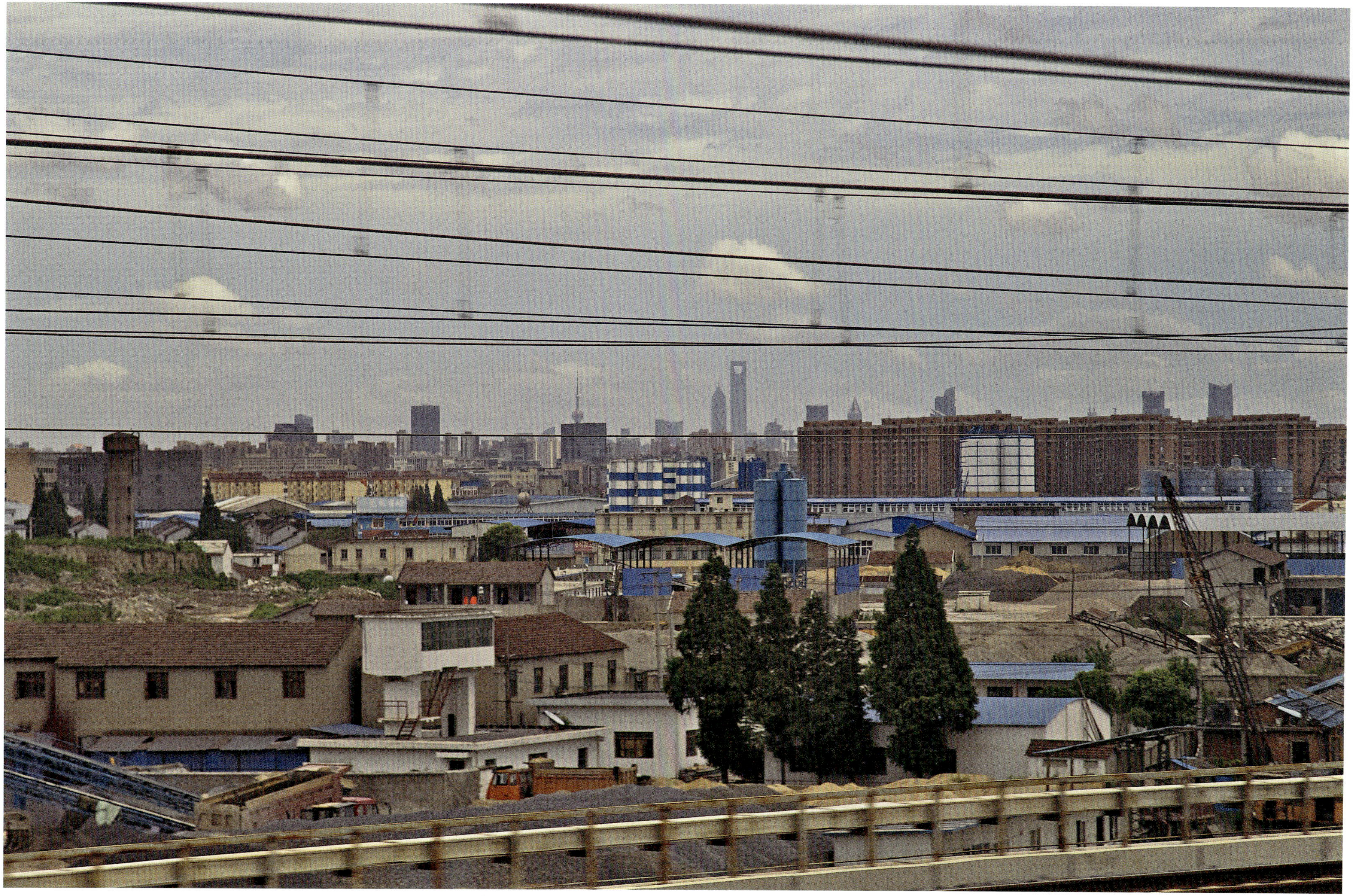

Shanghai China

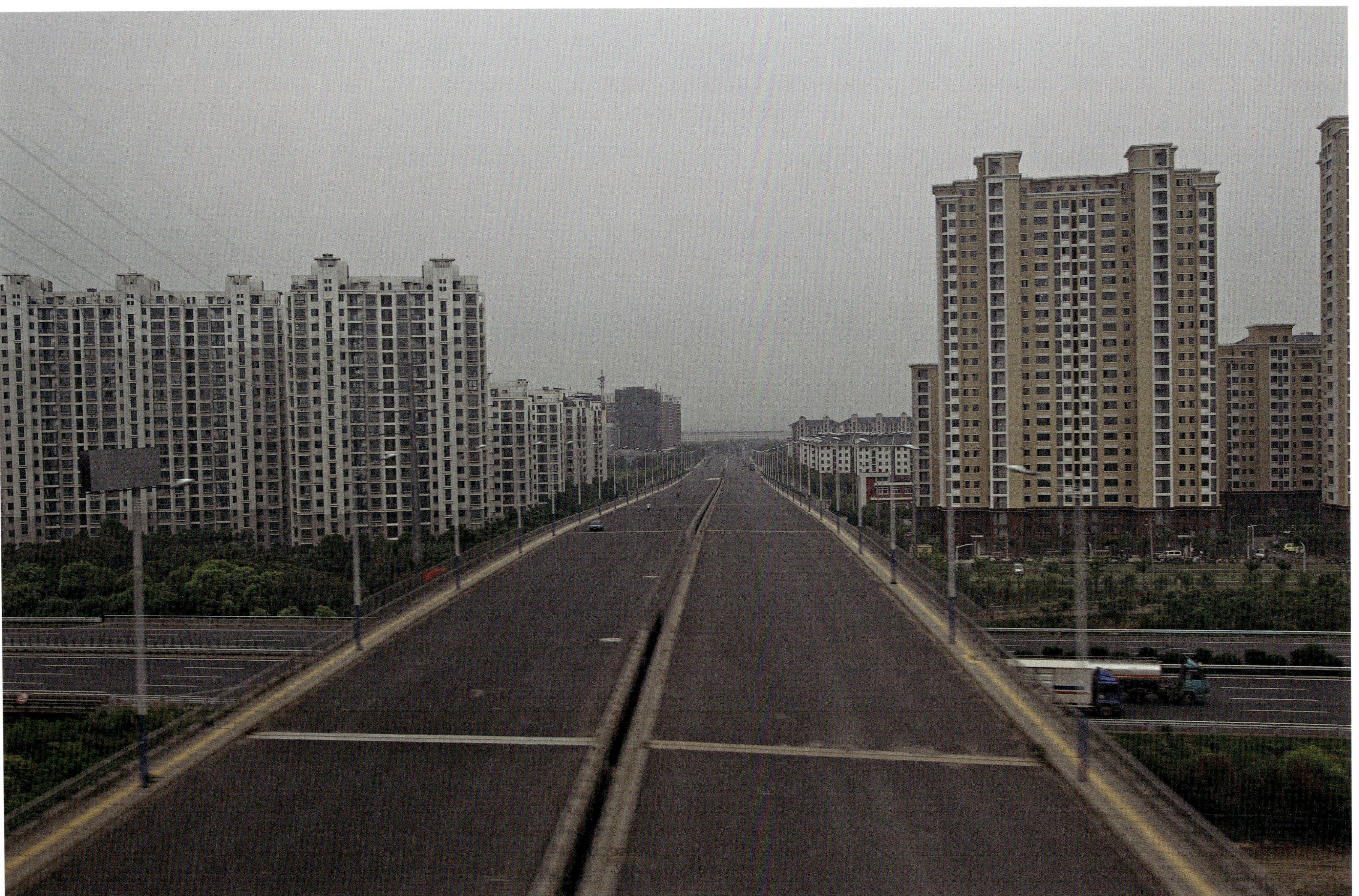

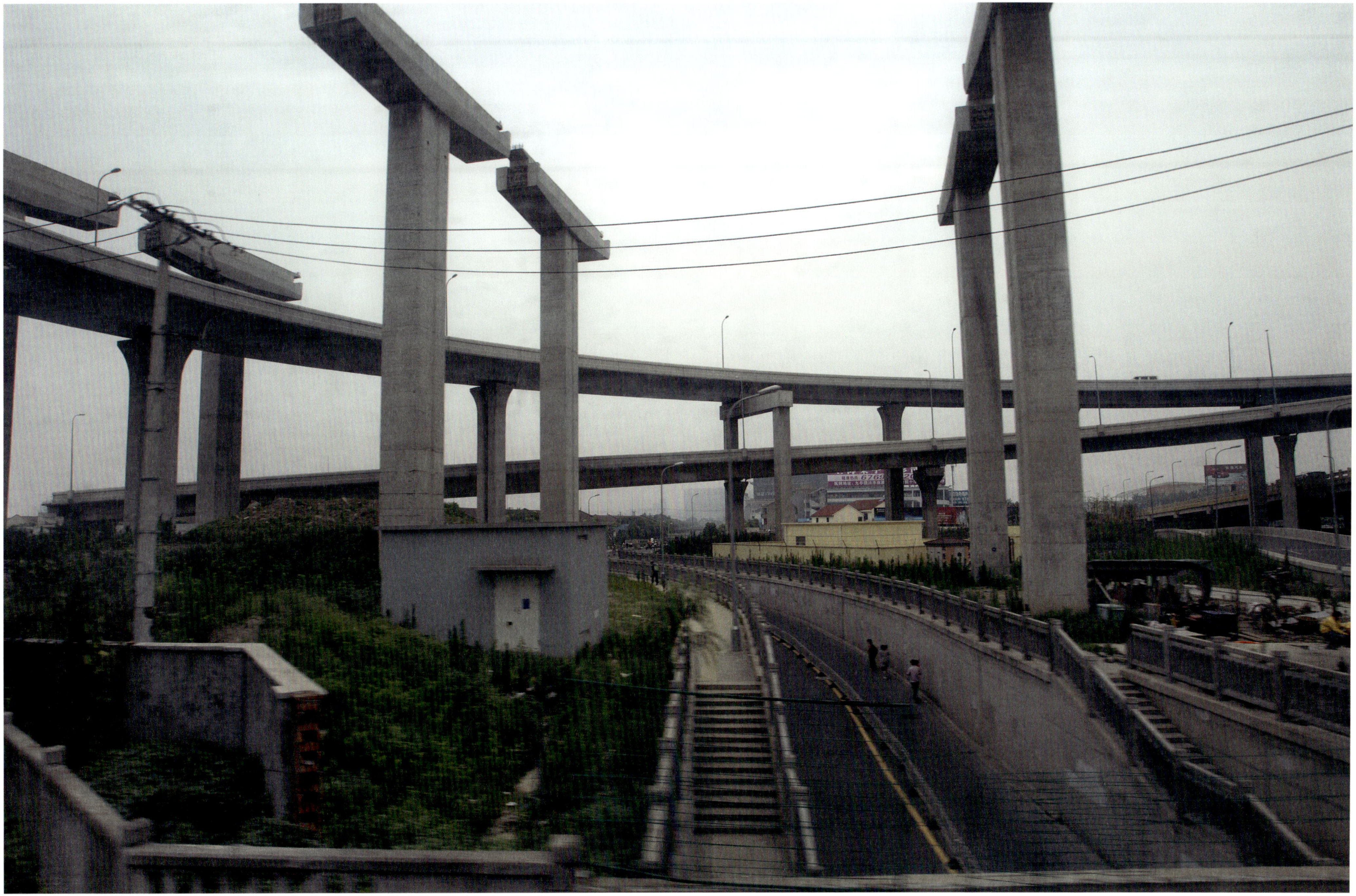

China

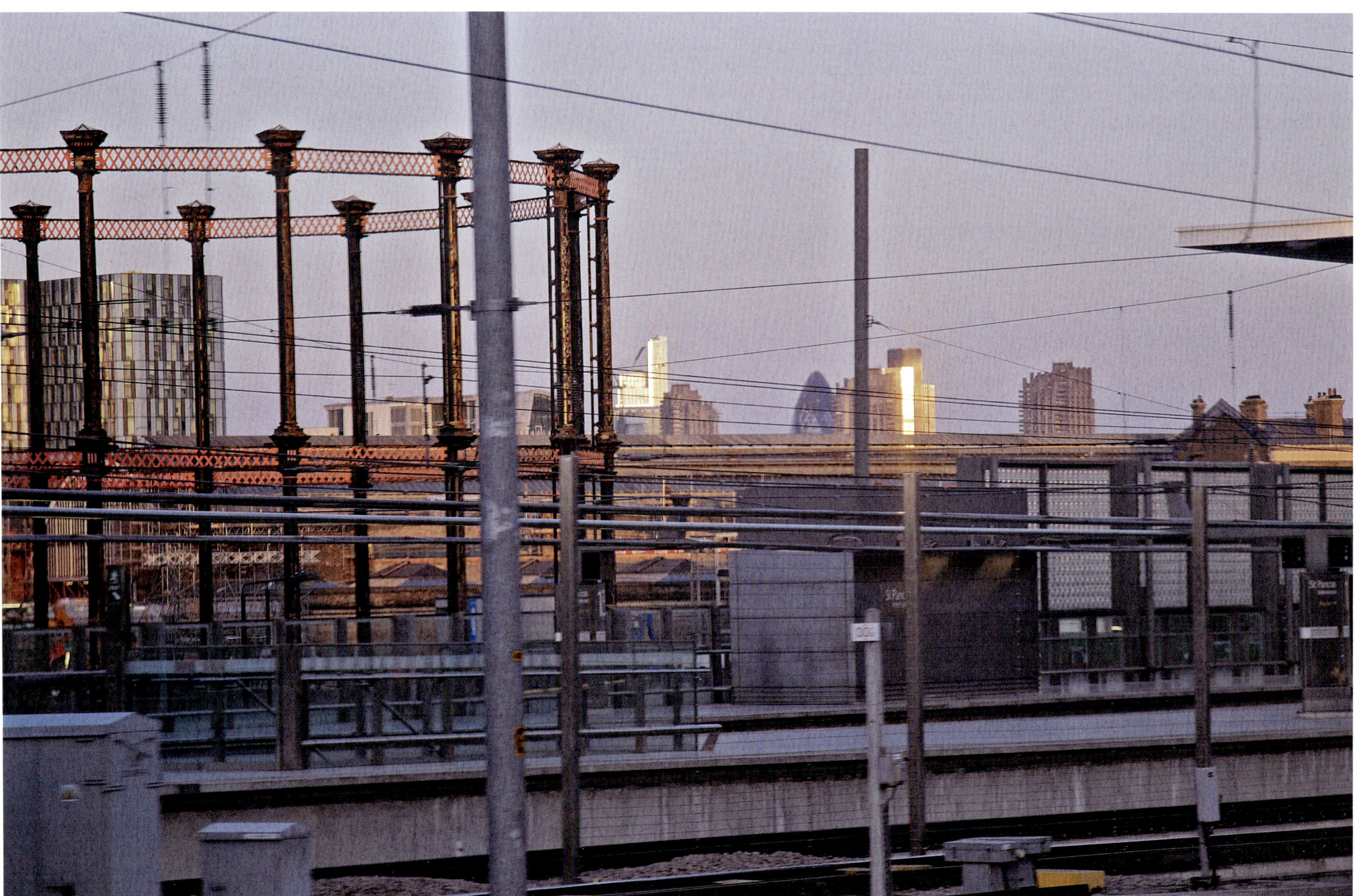
London, UK

Coinciding with the onset of the Industrial Revolution, the very first passenger train ran on March 25th, 1807 in the United Kingdom, from Swansea to Mumbles in Wales.

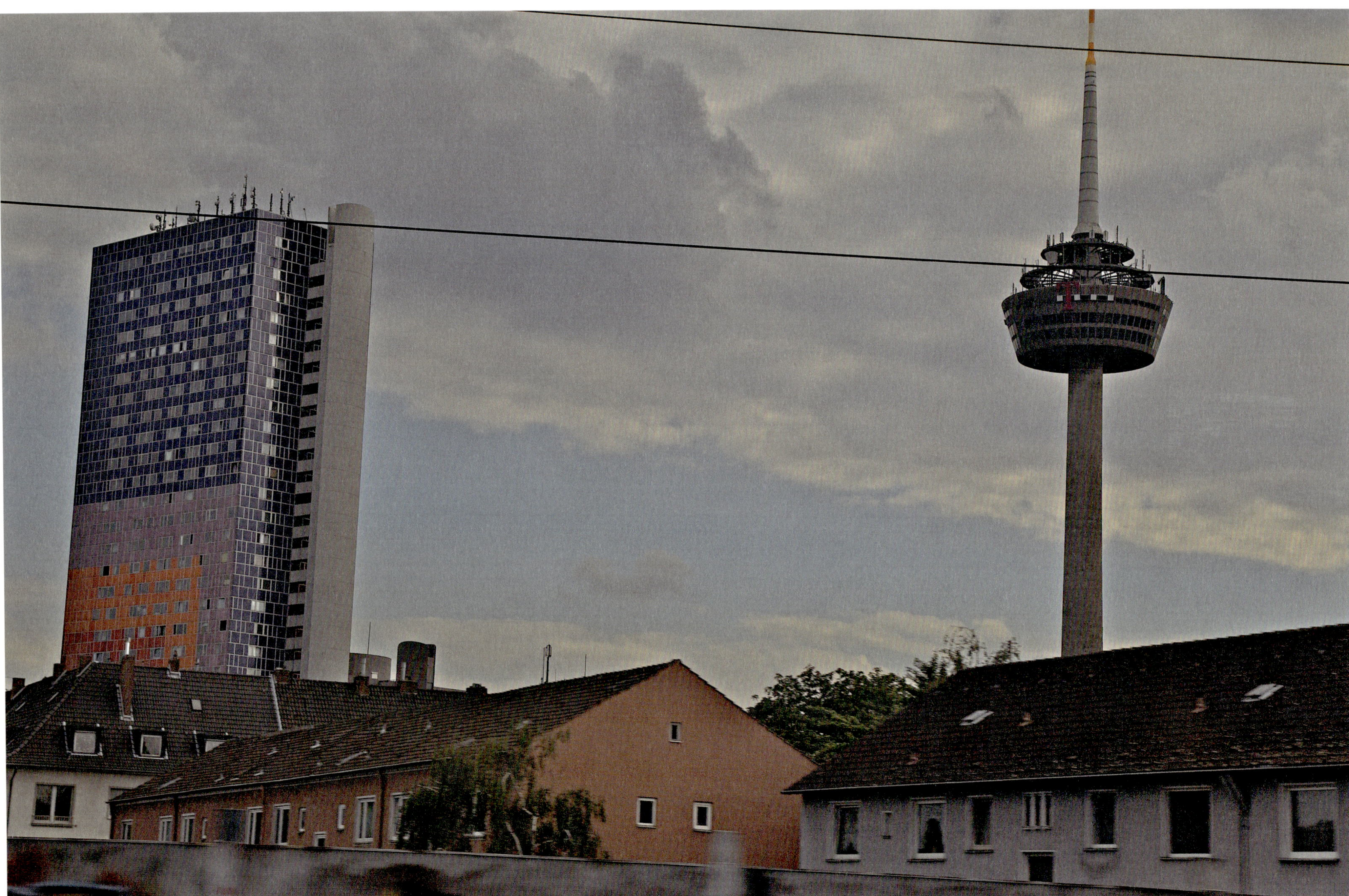
Hanover, Germany

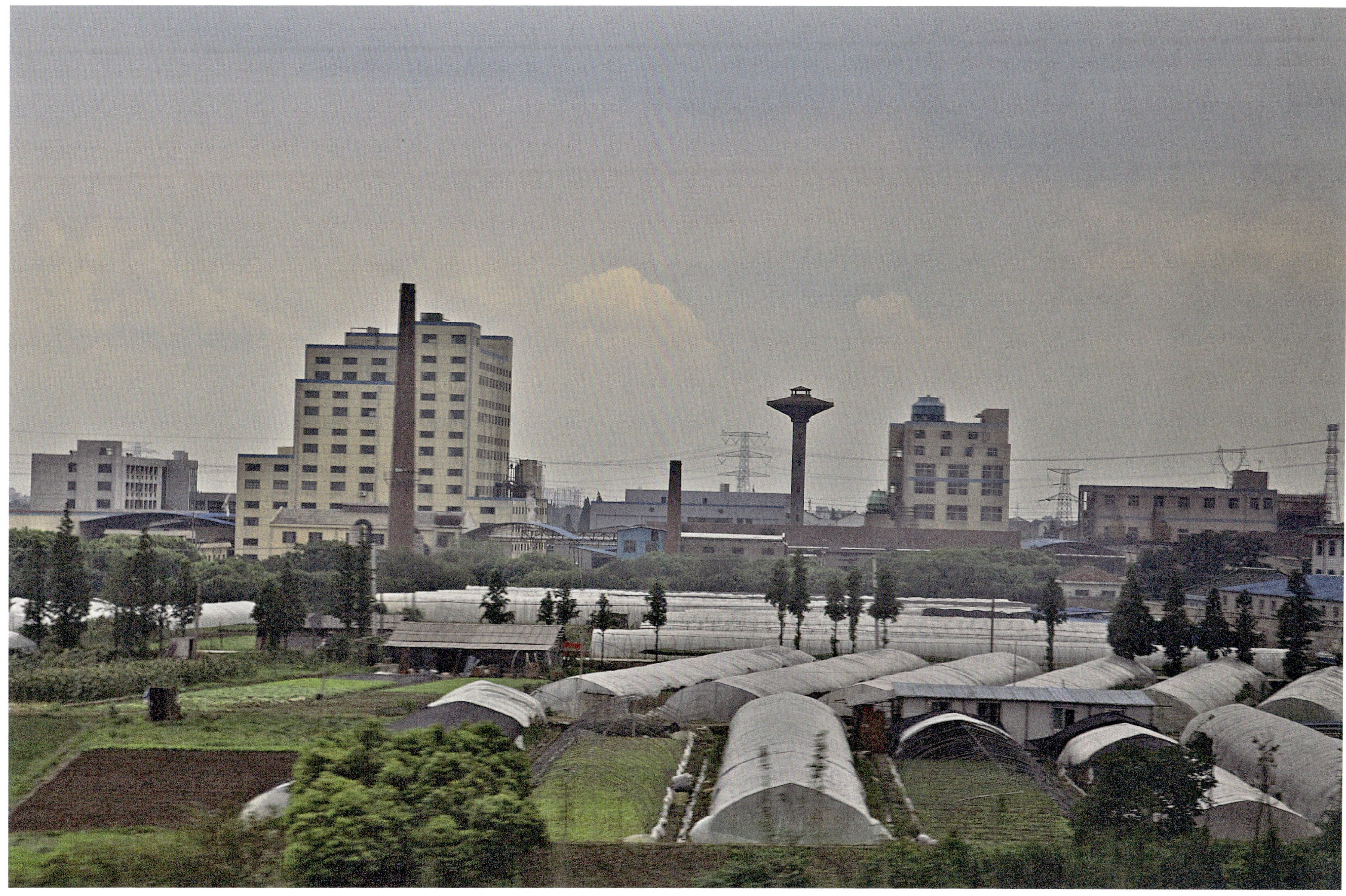

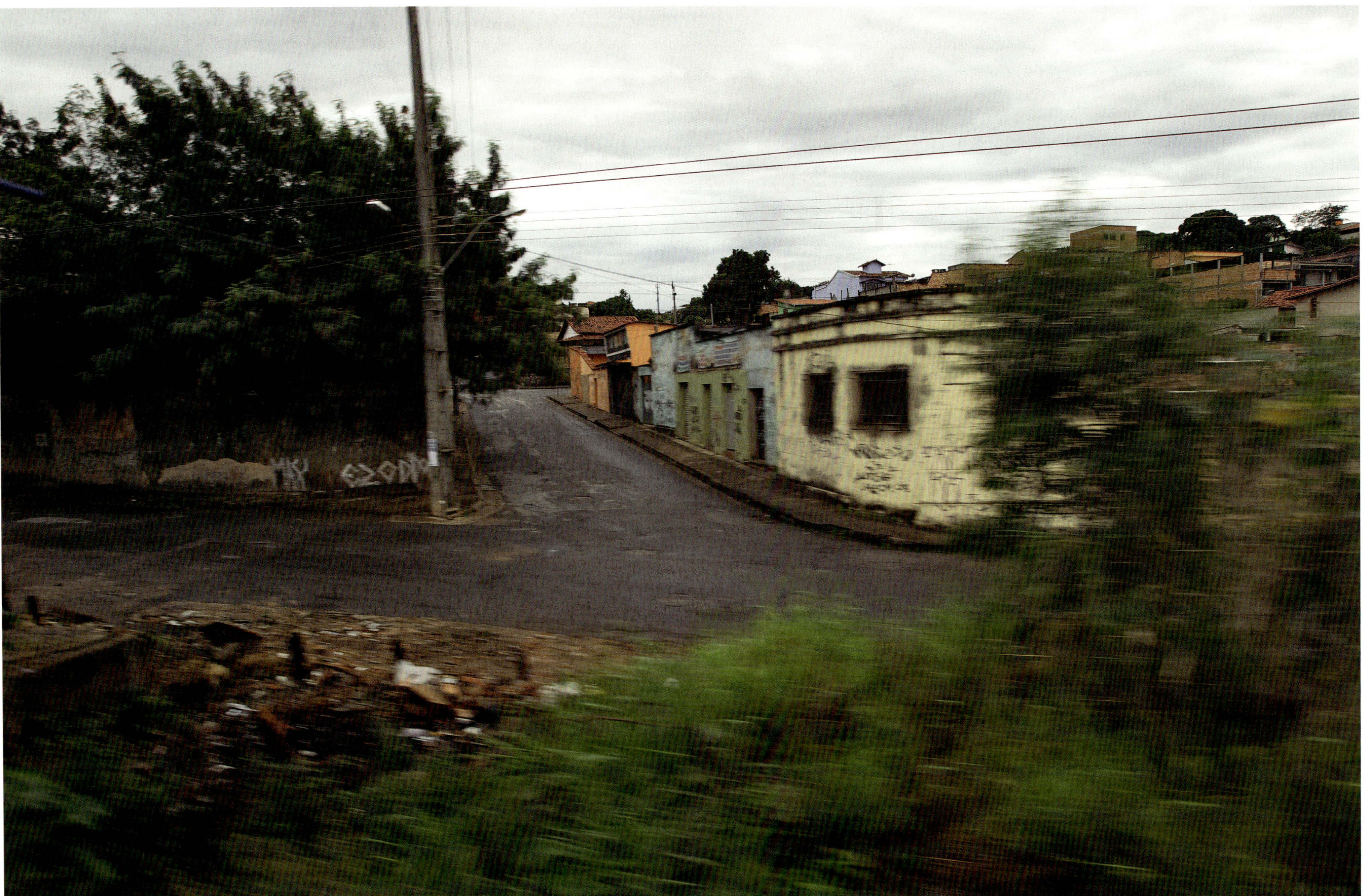

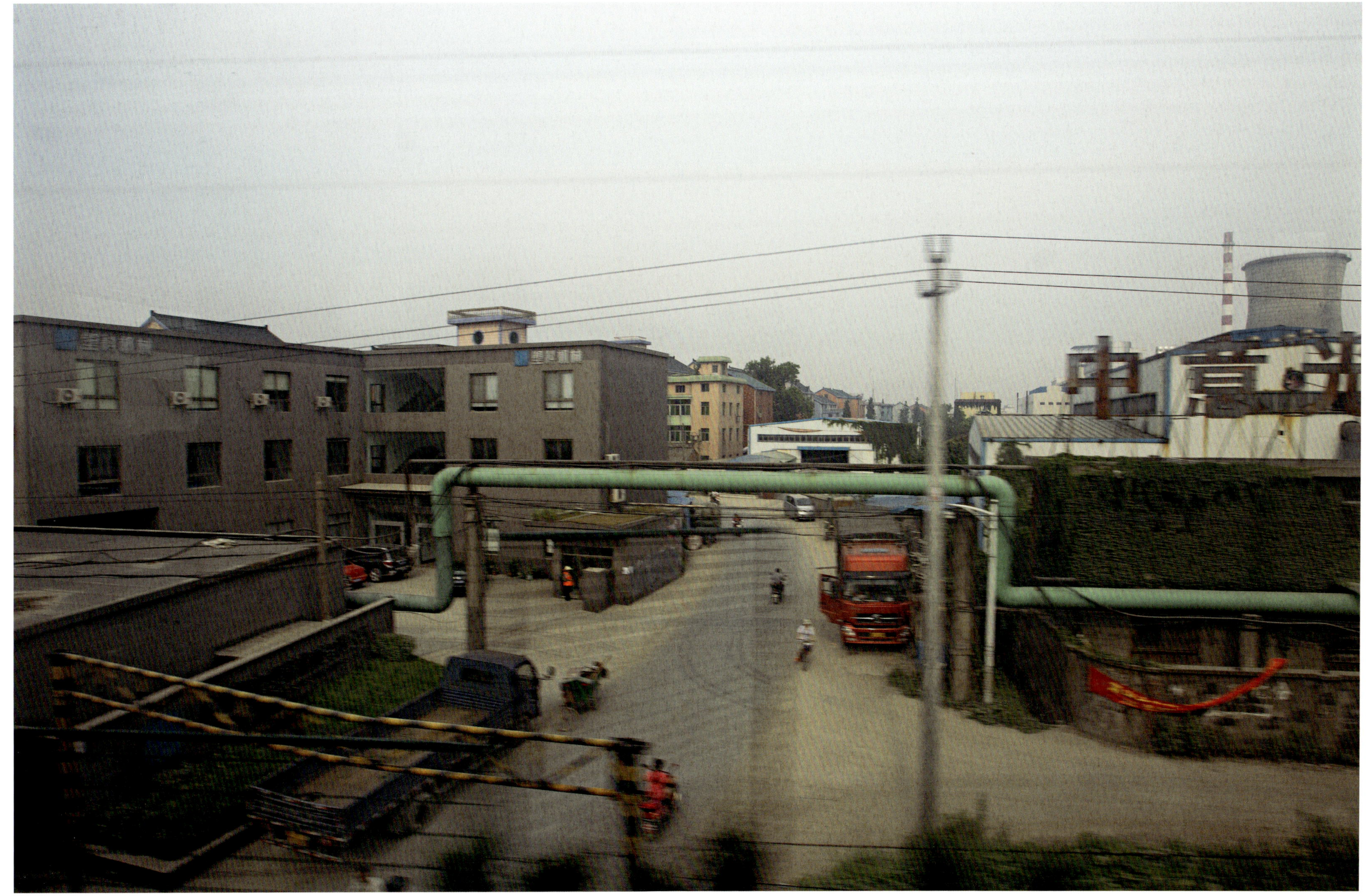

China

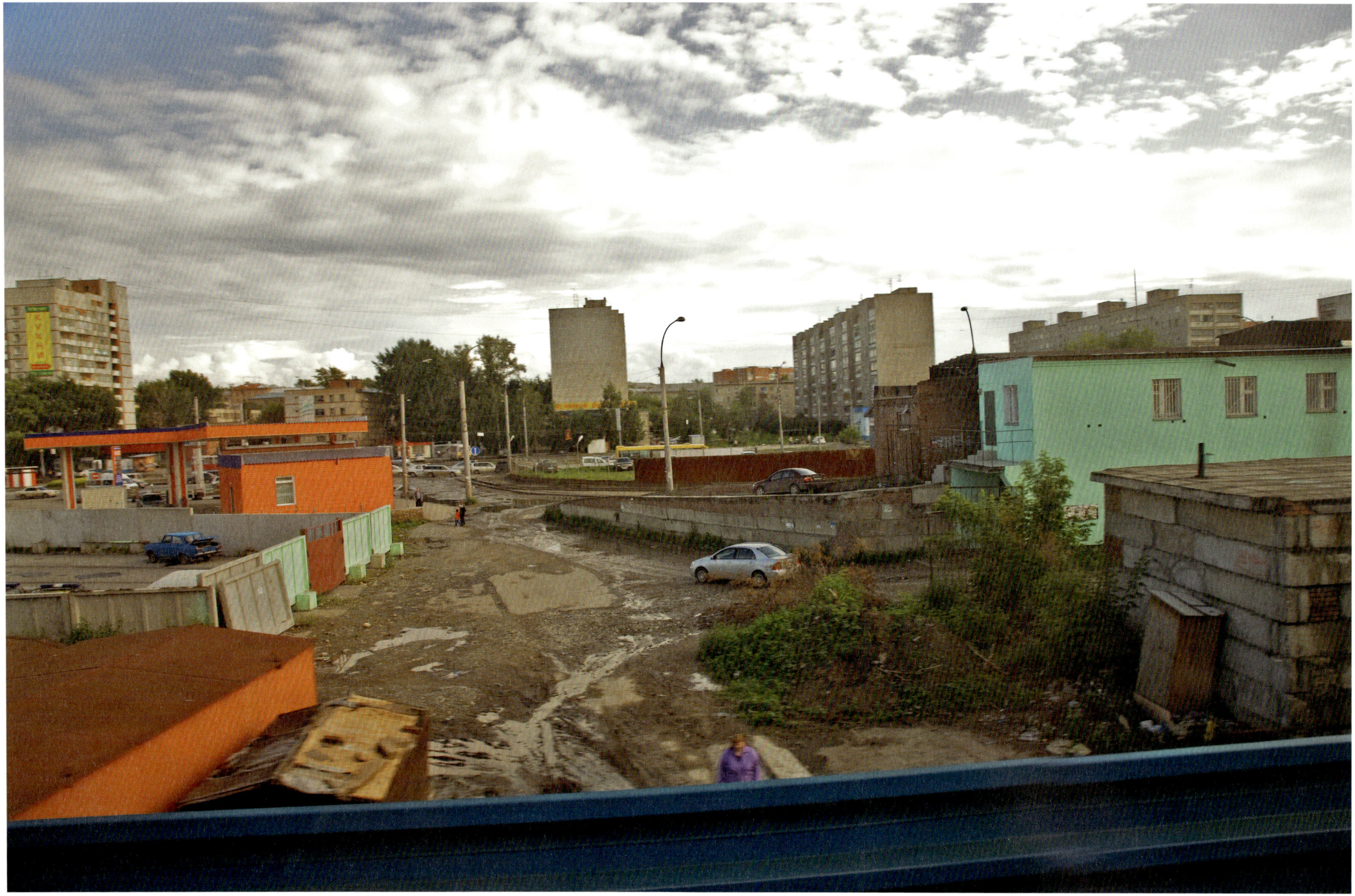

Following pages: Russia

The Trans-Siberian Railway in Russia is an epic rail journey covering a distance of 9259 km / 5753 miles — or almost a quarter of the earth's circumference. It was begun in 1905, largely corresponding with Russia's growth as a great world power, and connects Moscow in the West with Vladivostok in the East. Taking seven continuous days to complete, and including a total of 67 stops, it is the longest train line in the world.

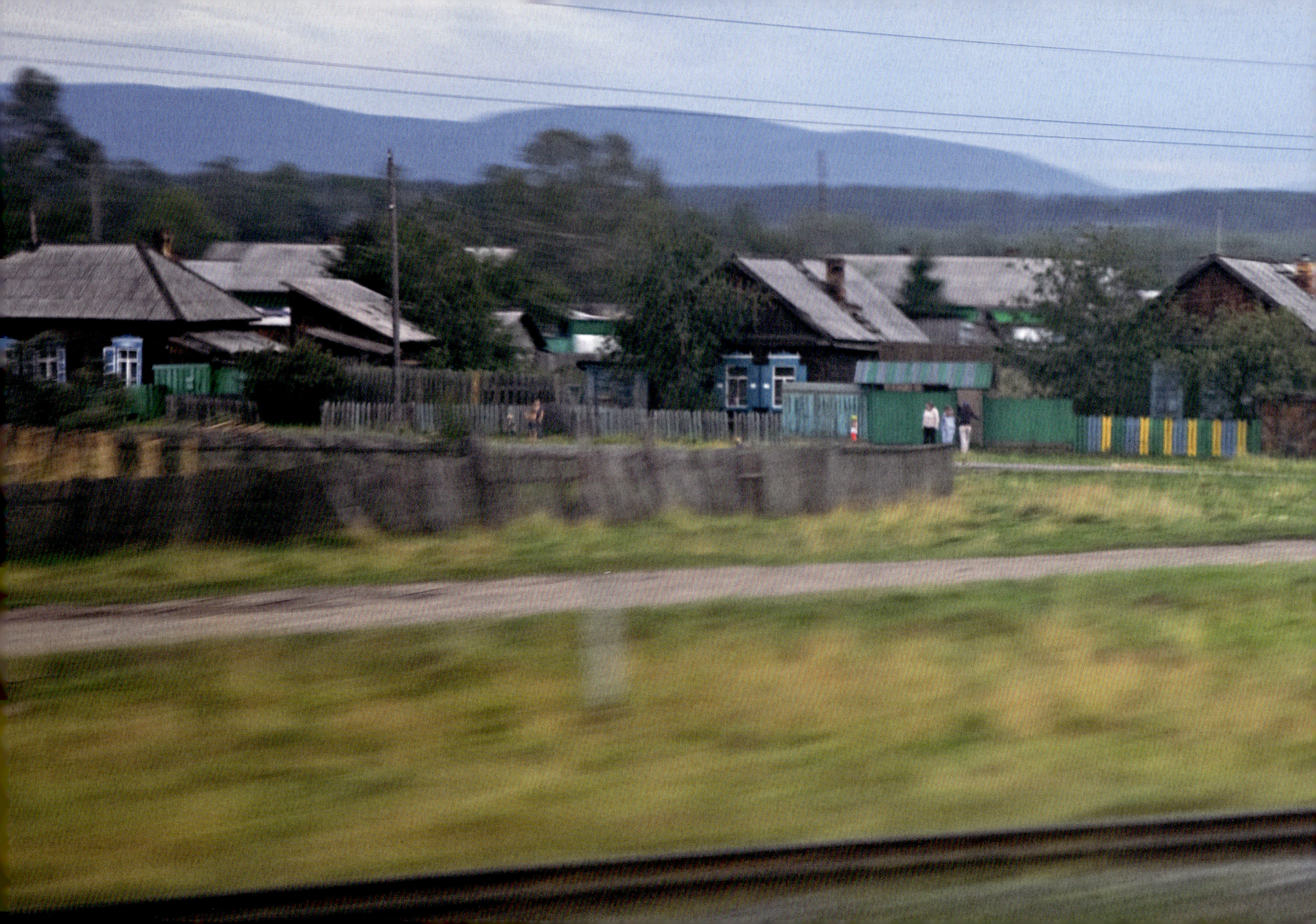

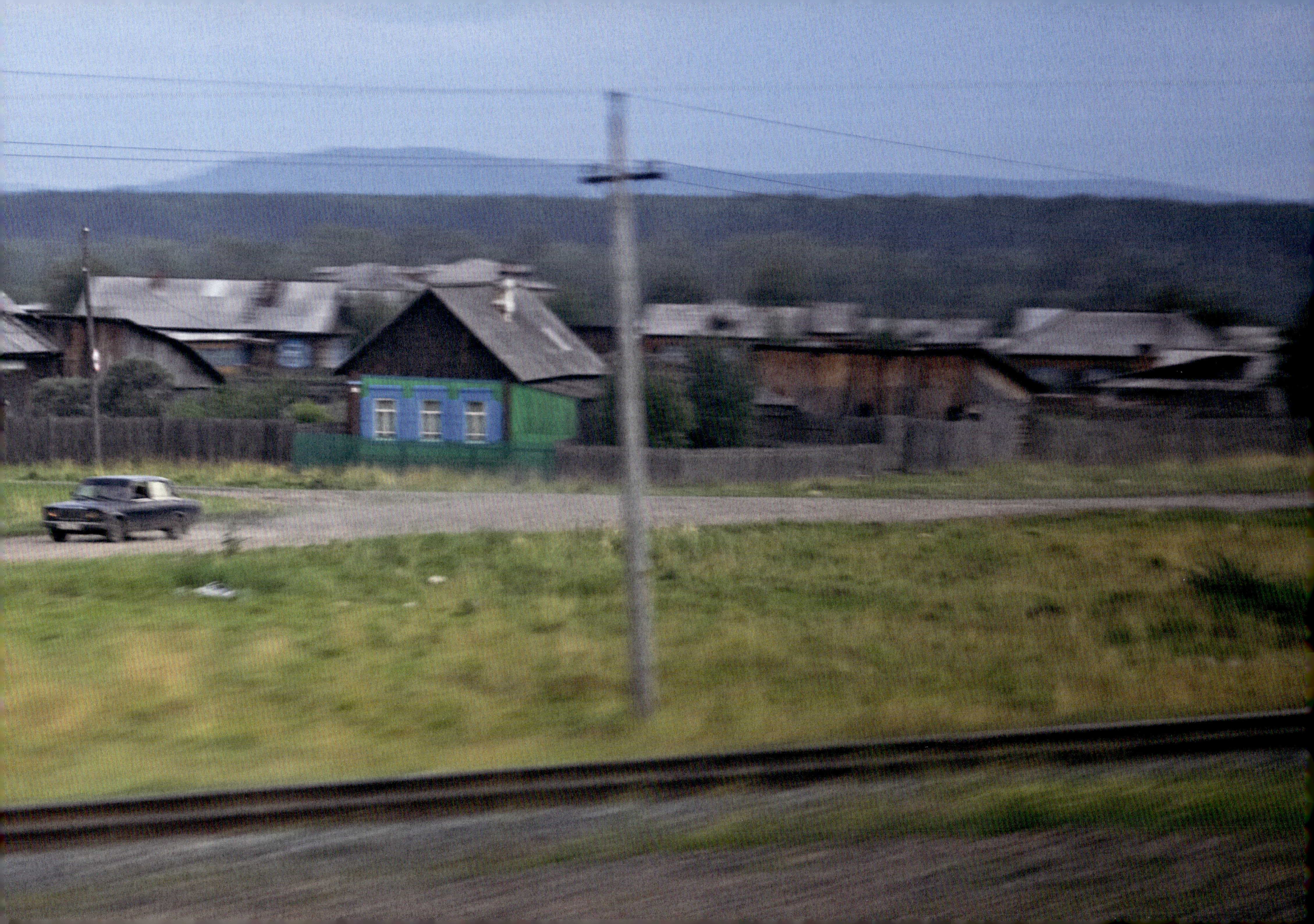

In South Africa the increasing coverage provided by the nation's highway system has lead to a decline in long distance rail travel. While many commuters still use rail daily, only half of the nation's 20,000 km / 12,000 miles of track is being fully utilised, and some 35% of the nation's track has no or very low activity.

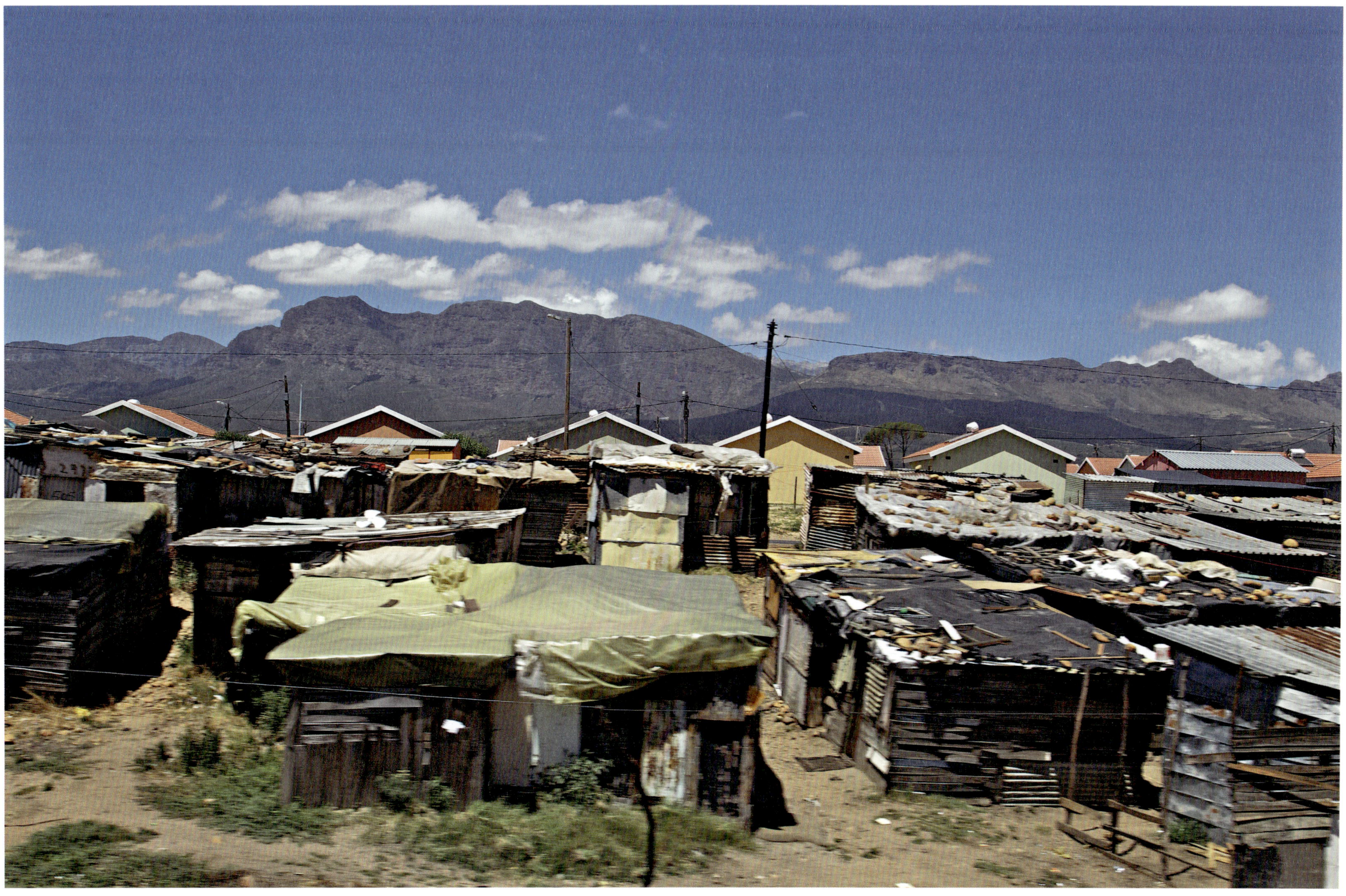
South Africa

Paris, France

Johannesburg, South Africa

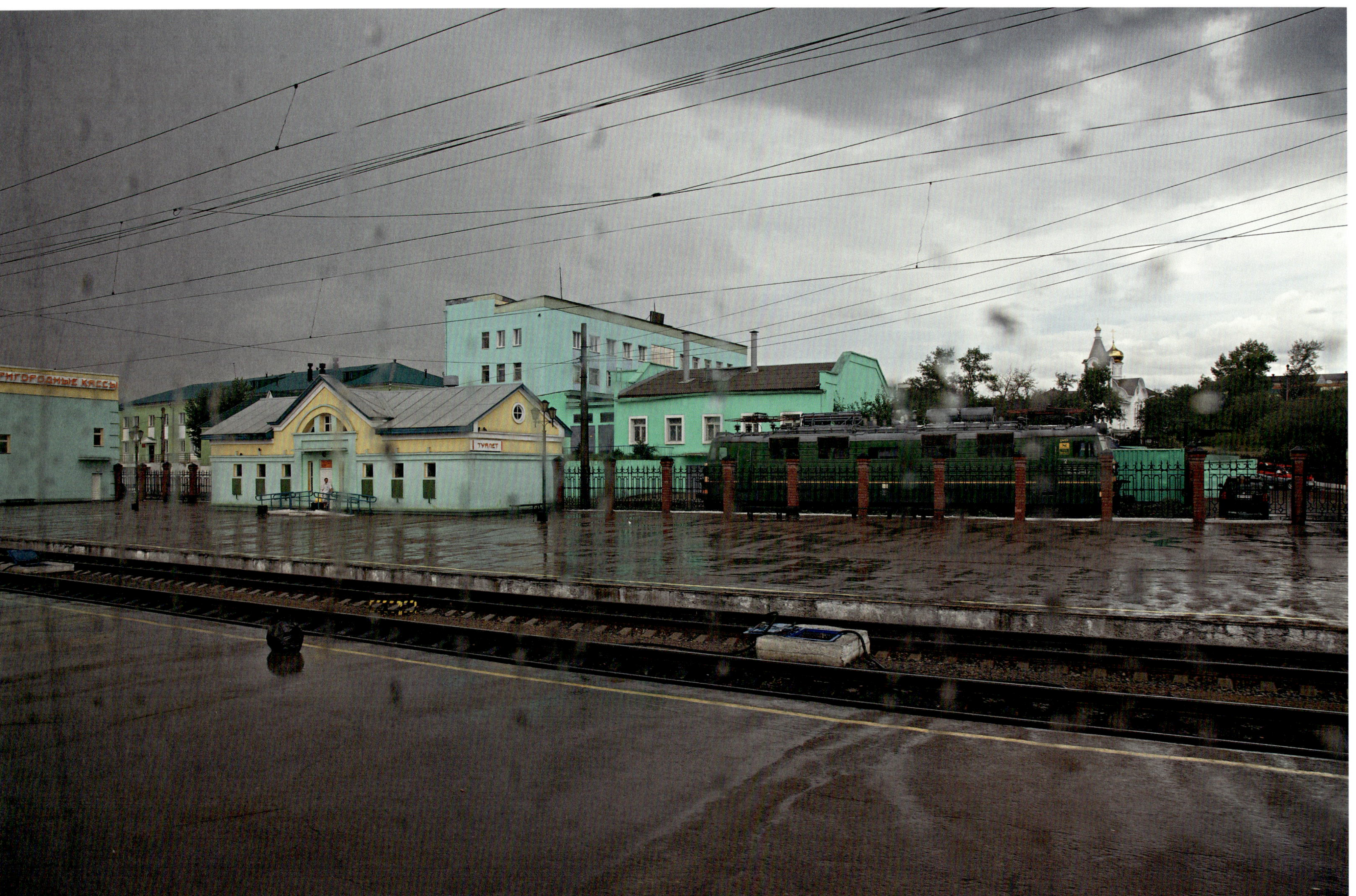
ТУАЛЕТ

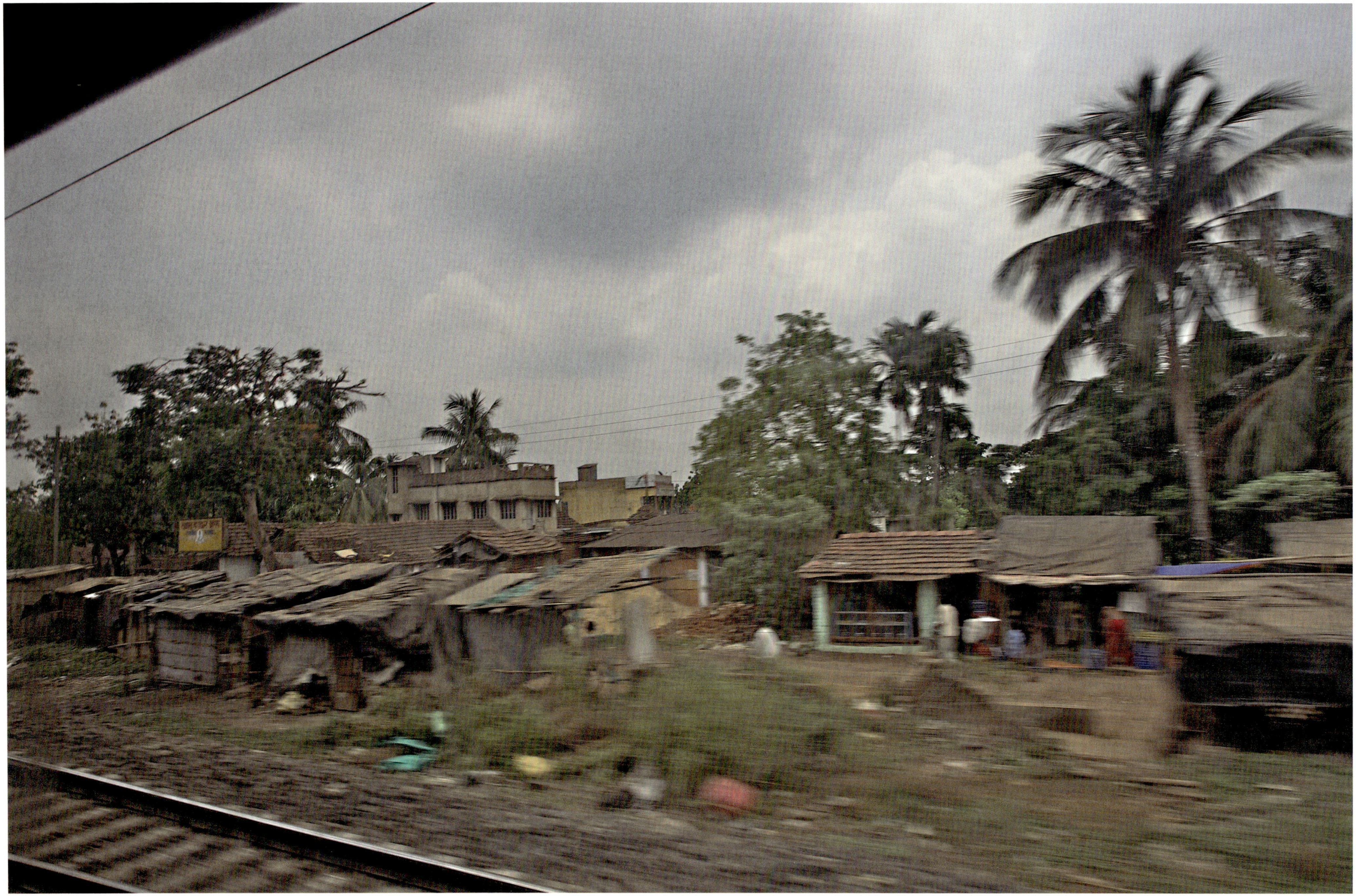

Near Calcutta, India

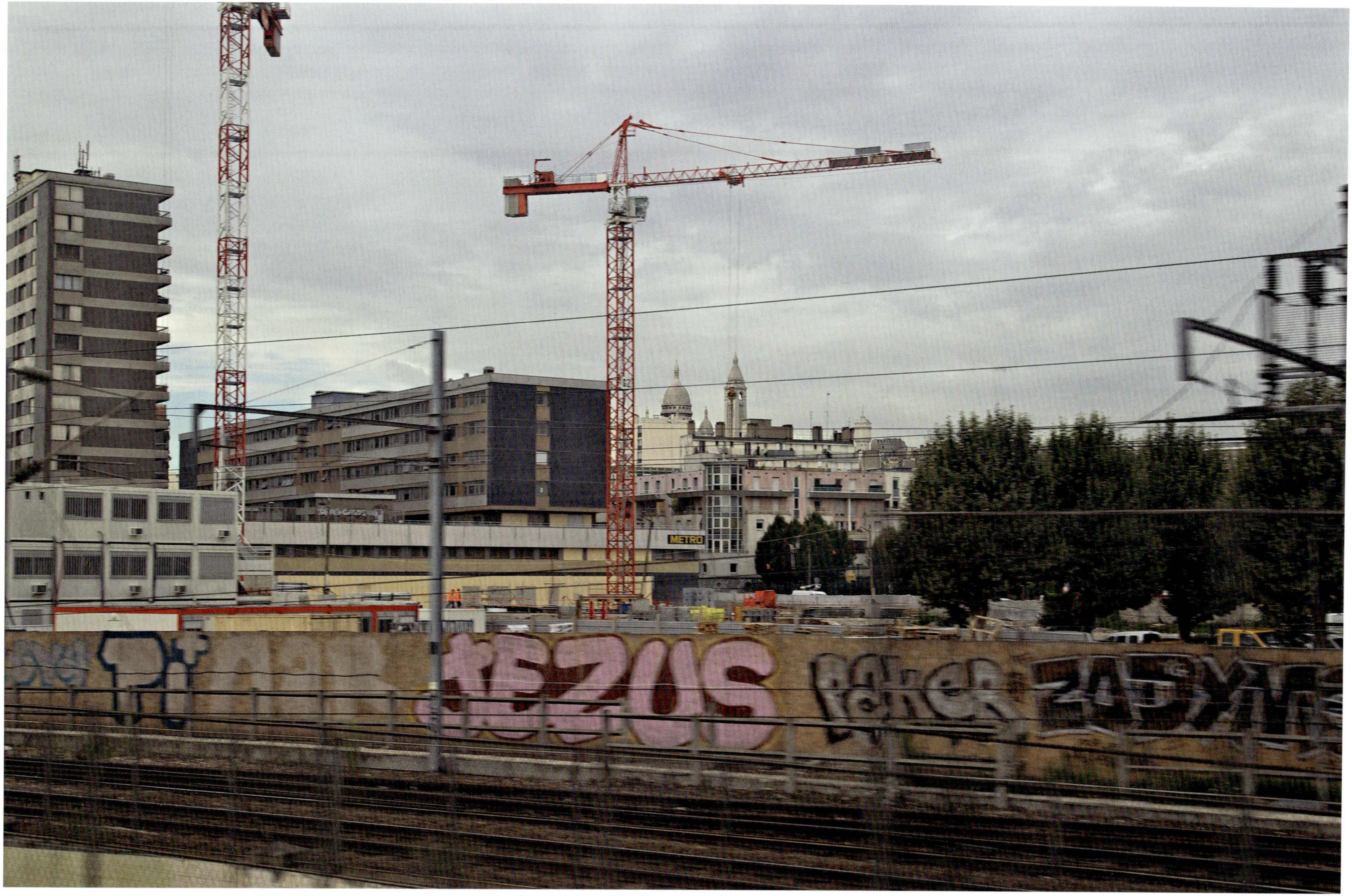

METRO
JEZUS

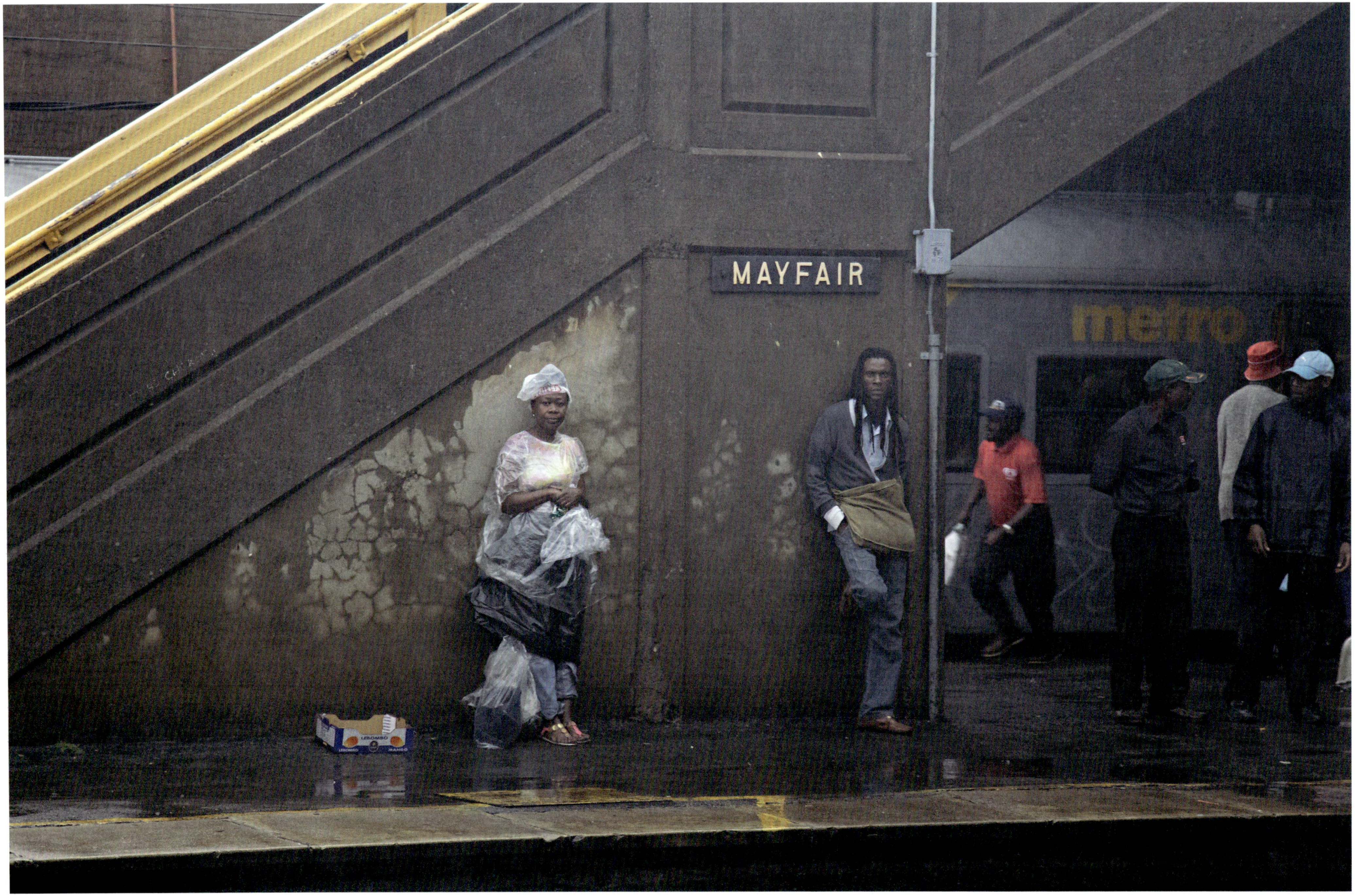

MAYFAIR
metro

Shosholoza Meyl is a division of the Passenger Rail Agency of South Africa (PRASA), that operates long-distance passenger rail services and carries approximately 4 million passengers annually. 'Shosholoza' is the name of a popular South African song about workers on a train and means 'moving forward'. 'Meyl' is related to a South African word that means 'long distance train'.

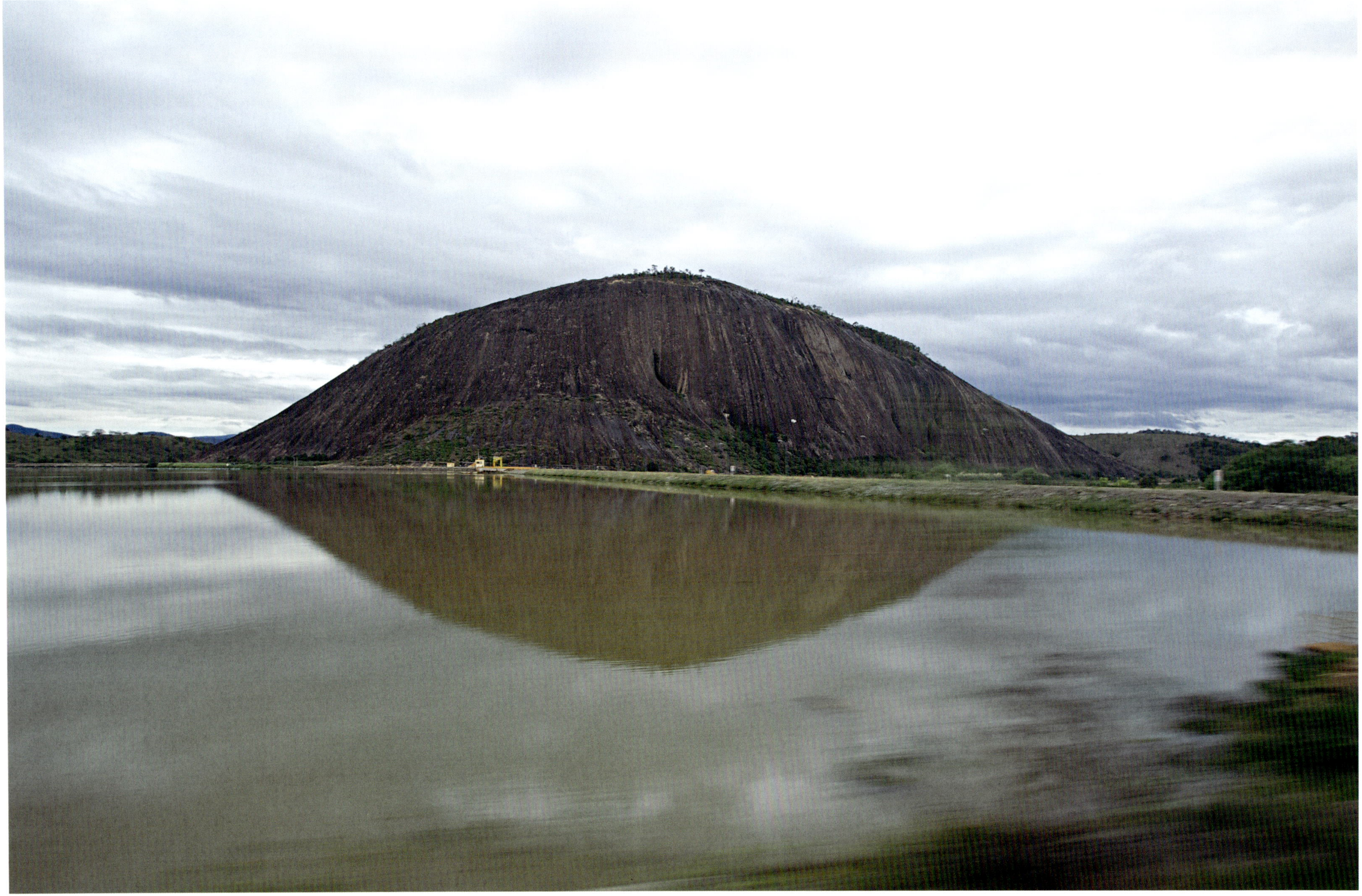

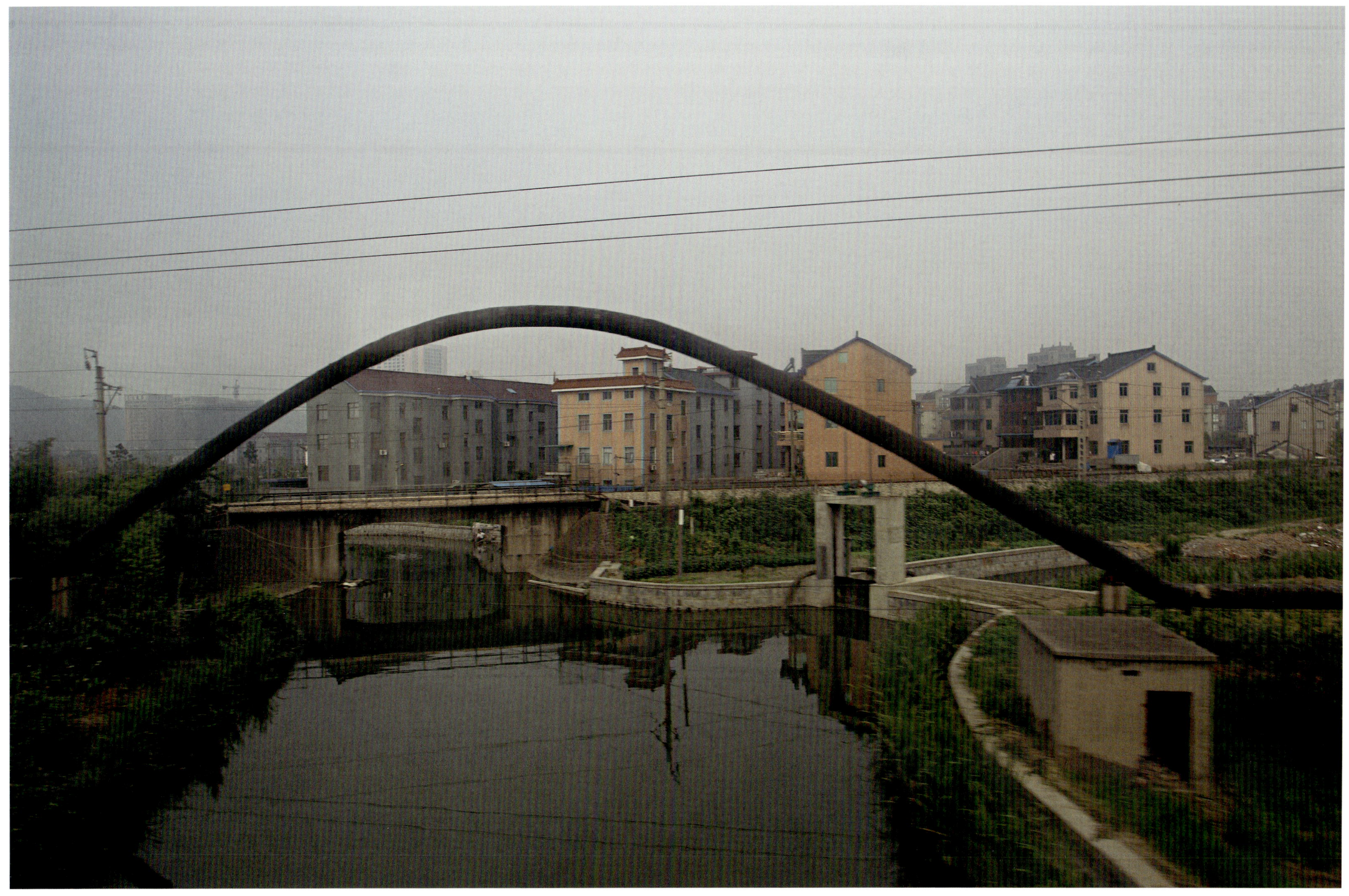

Although the palatial Neo-Baroque station was criticised for its extravagance when it was first completed in 1905, Antwerp Central Station in Belgium is today considered one of the most beautiful train stations in the world.

Brussels, Belgium

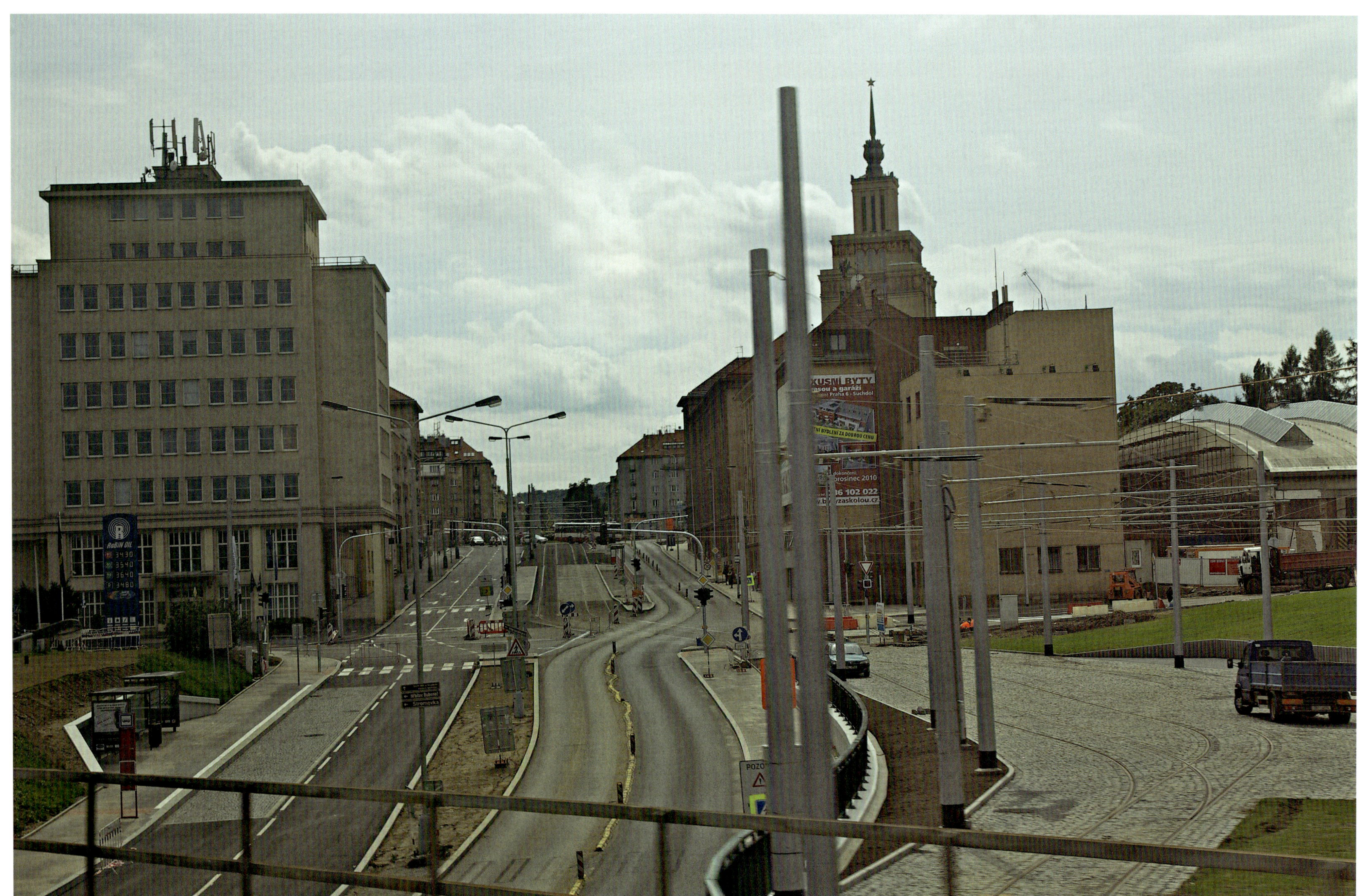

RoBiN OIL
LUXUSNÍ BYTY
102 022
zaskolou.cz
POZO

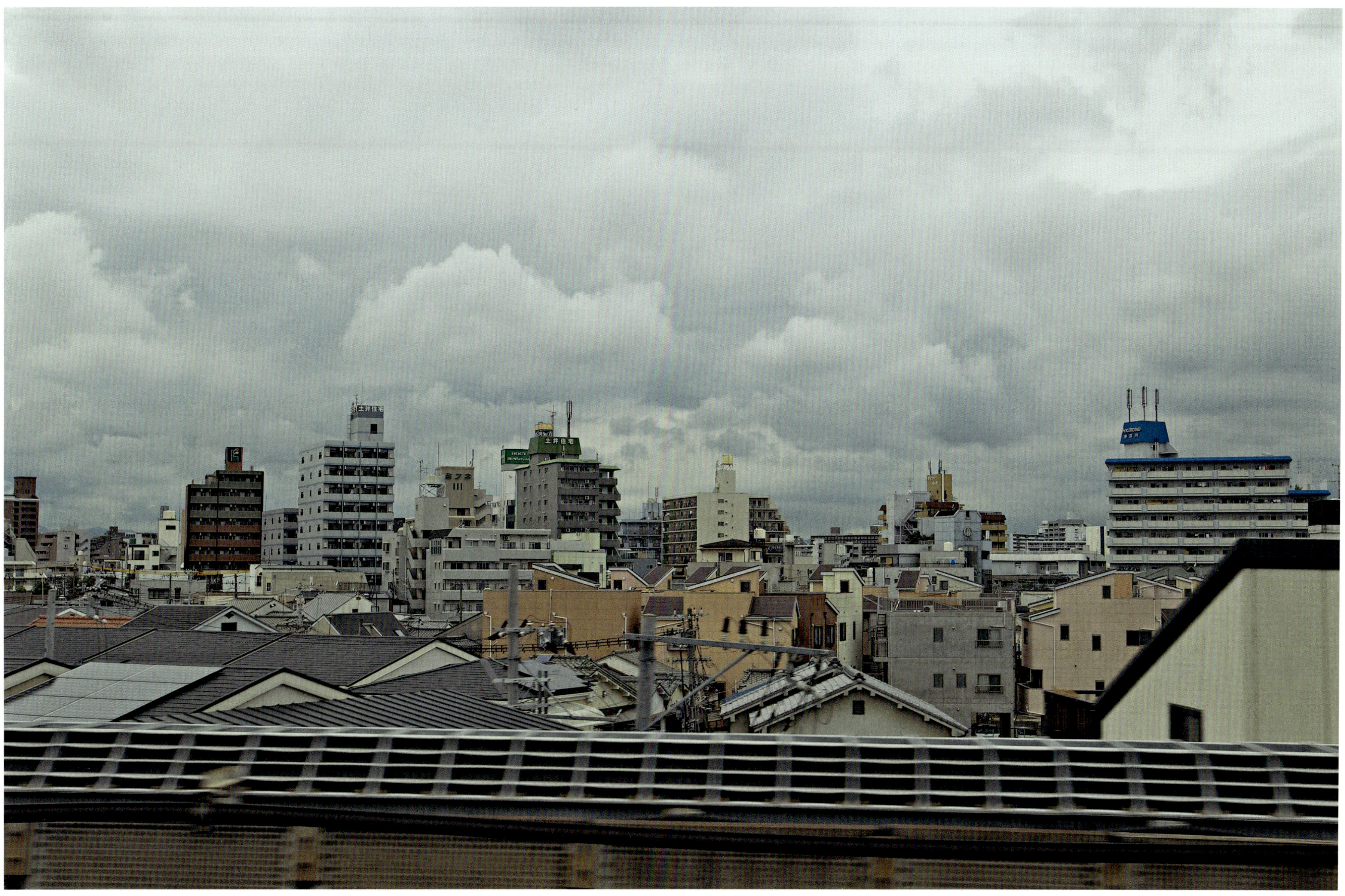

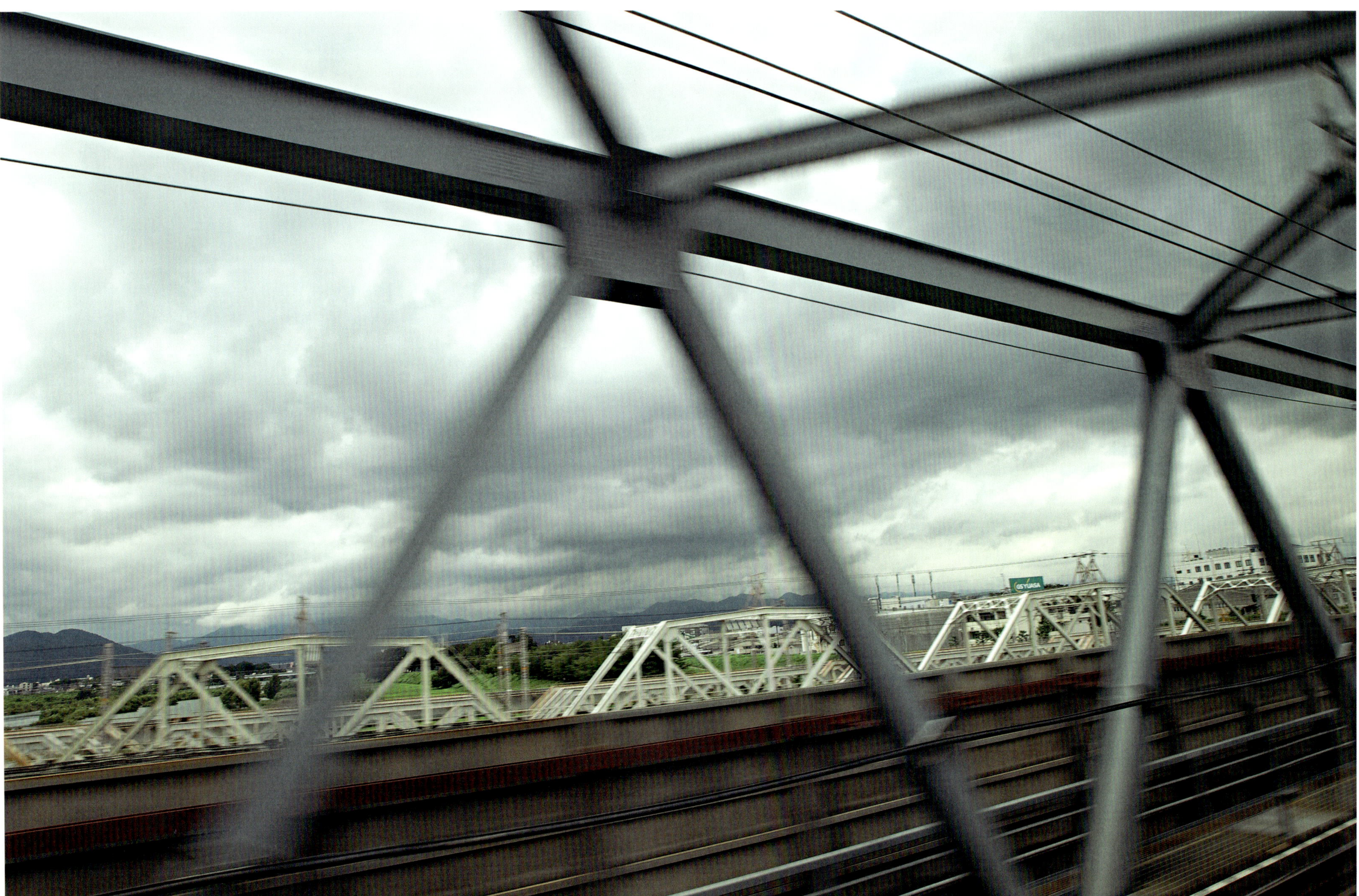

Japan

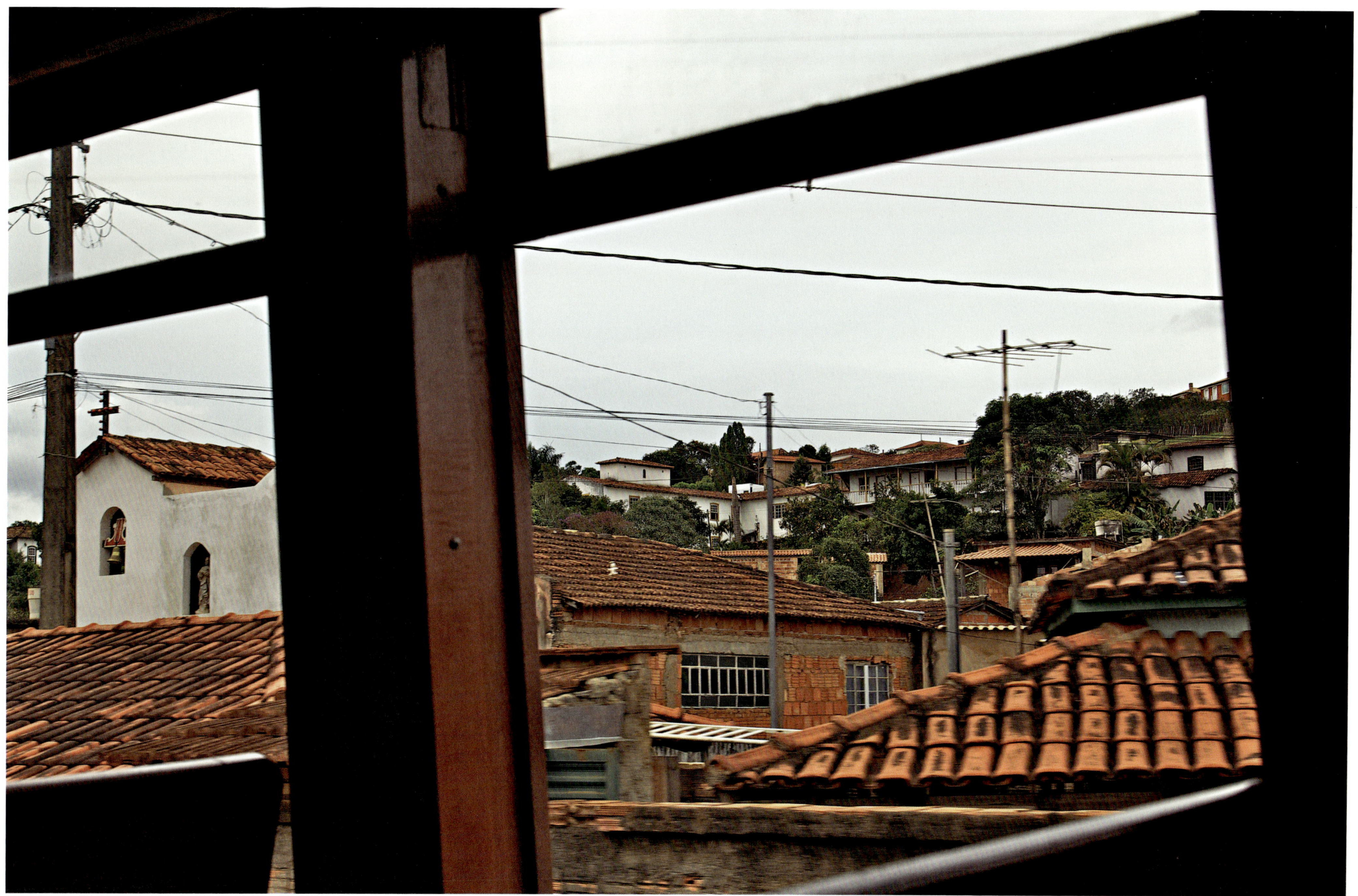

Brazil

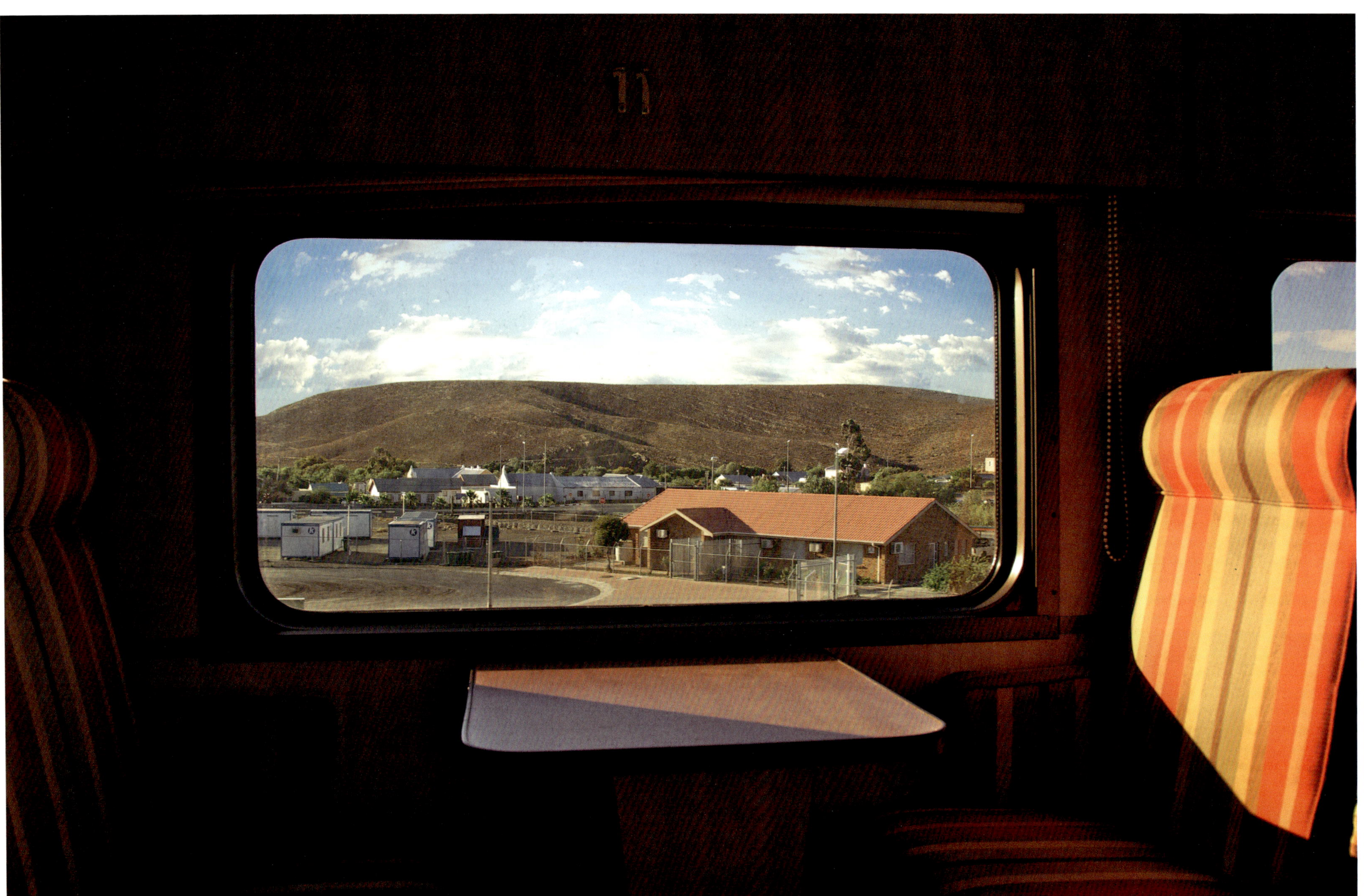

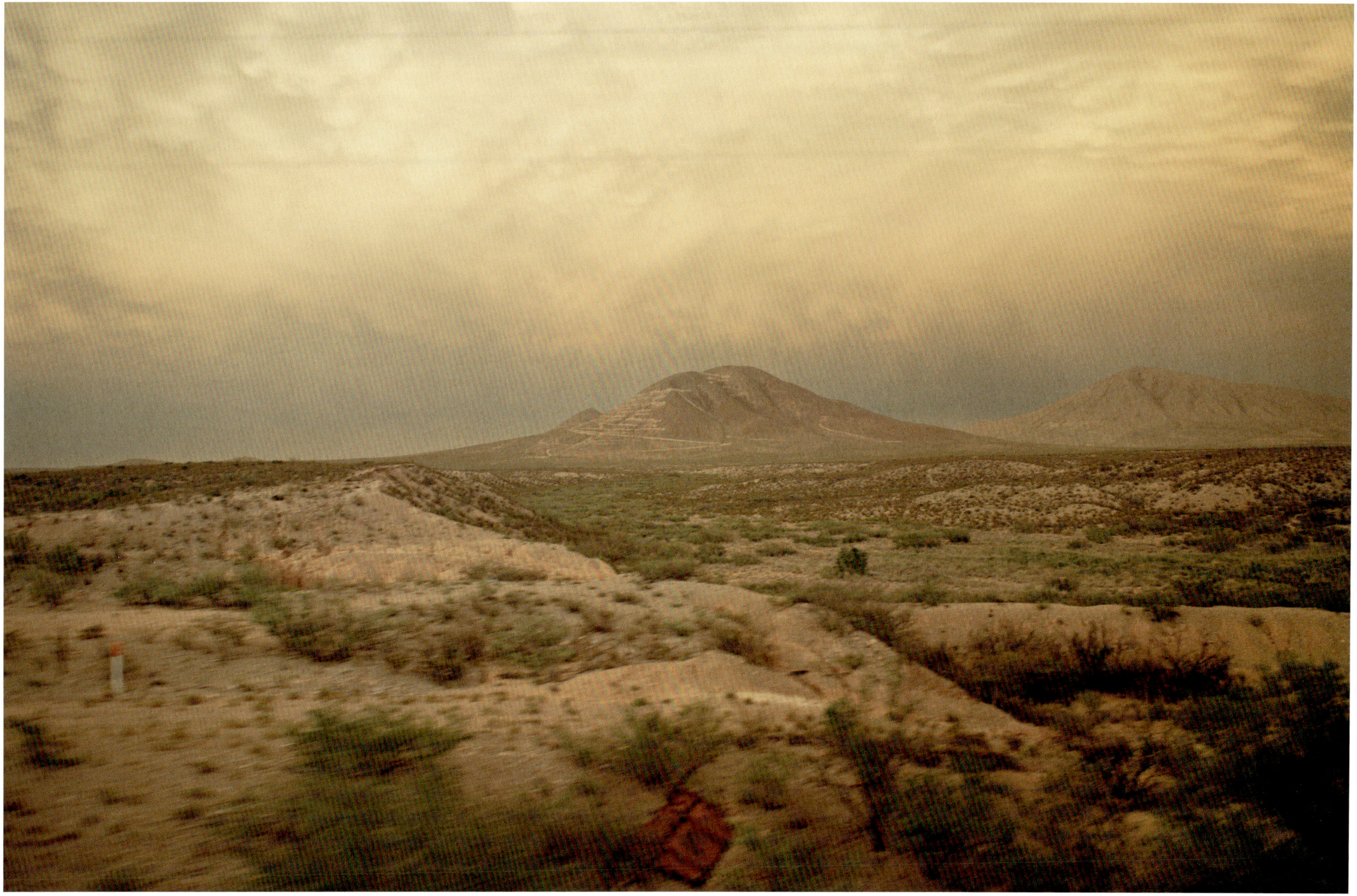

Texas, USA

The Trans-Siberian Railway remains the most important transportation link within Russia, with around 30% of Russian exports travelling on the line. In terms of passengers, while it attracts many foreign tourists, it gets most of its use from the domestic population.

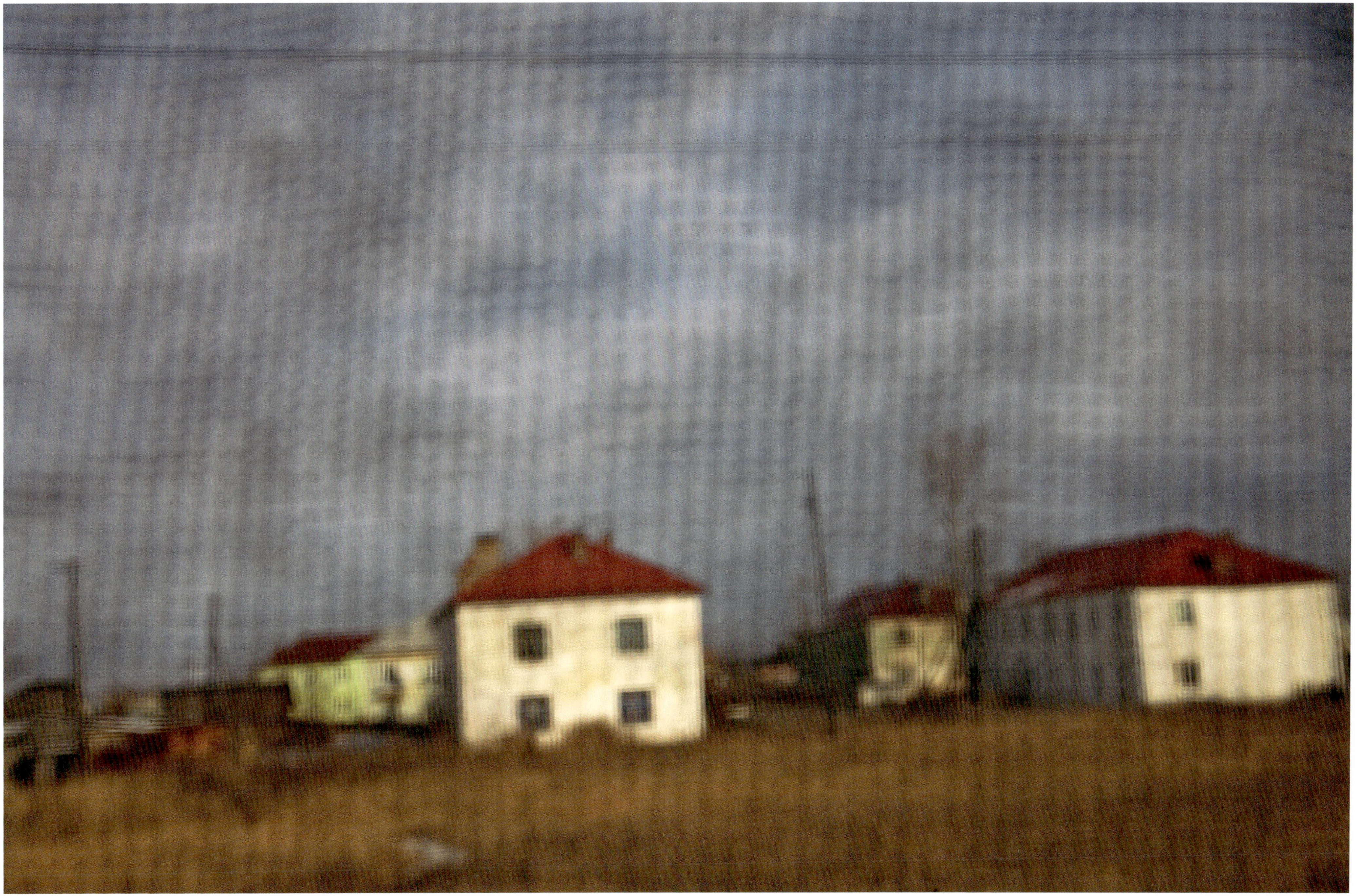

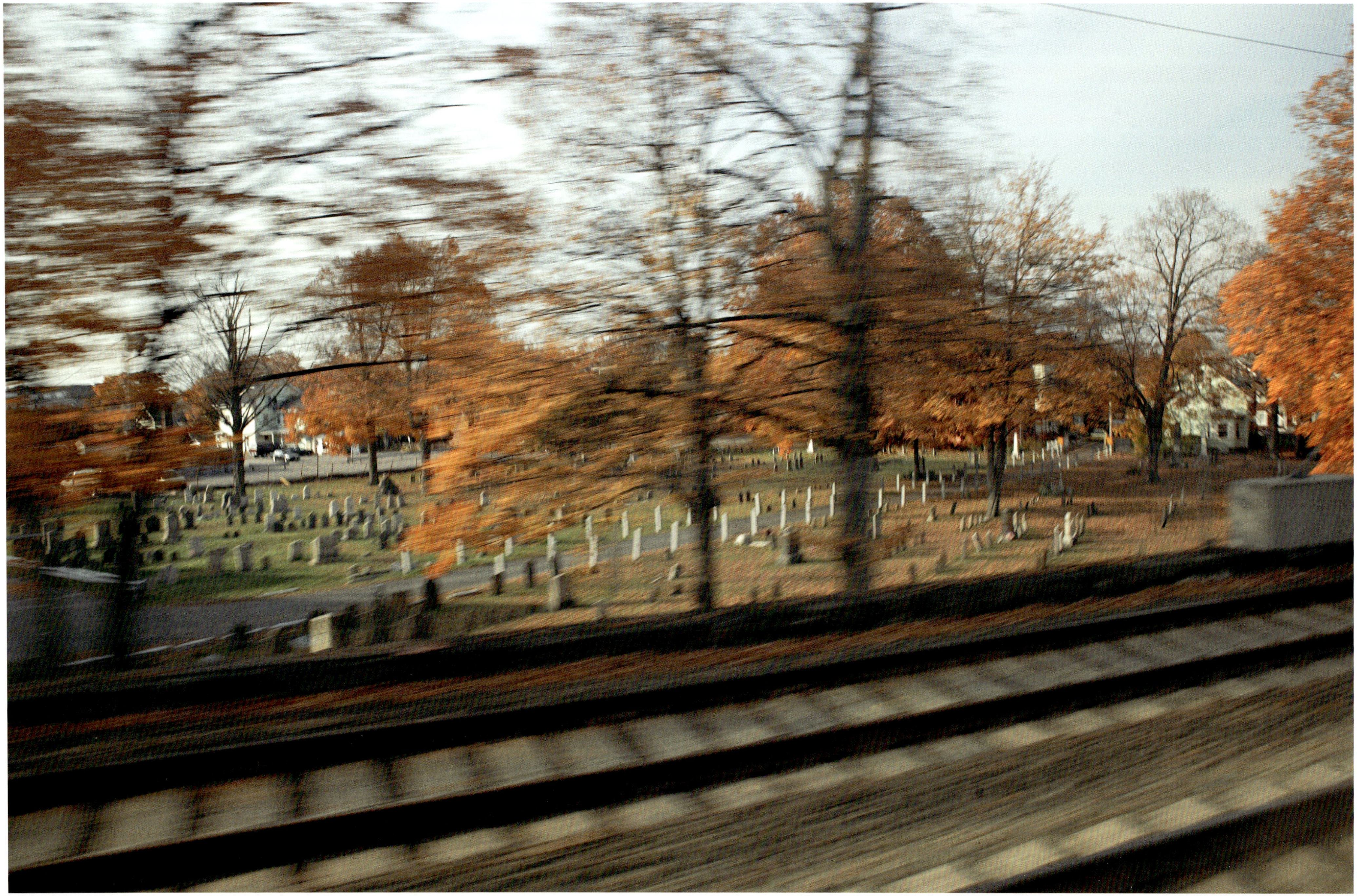

Connecticut, USA

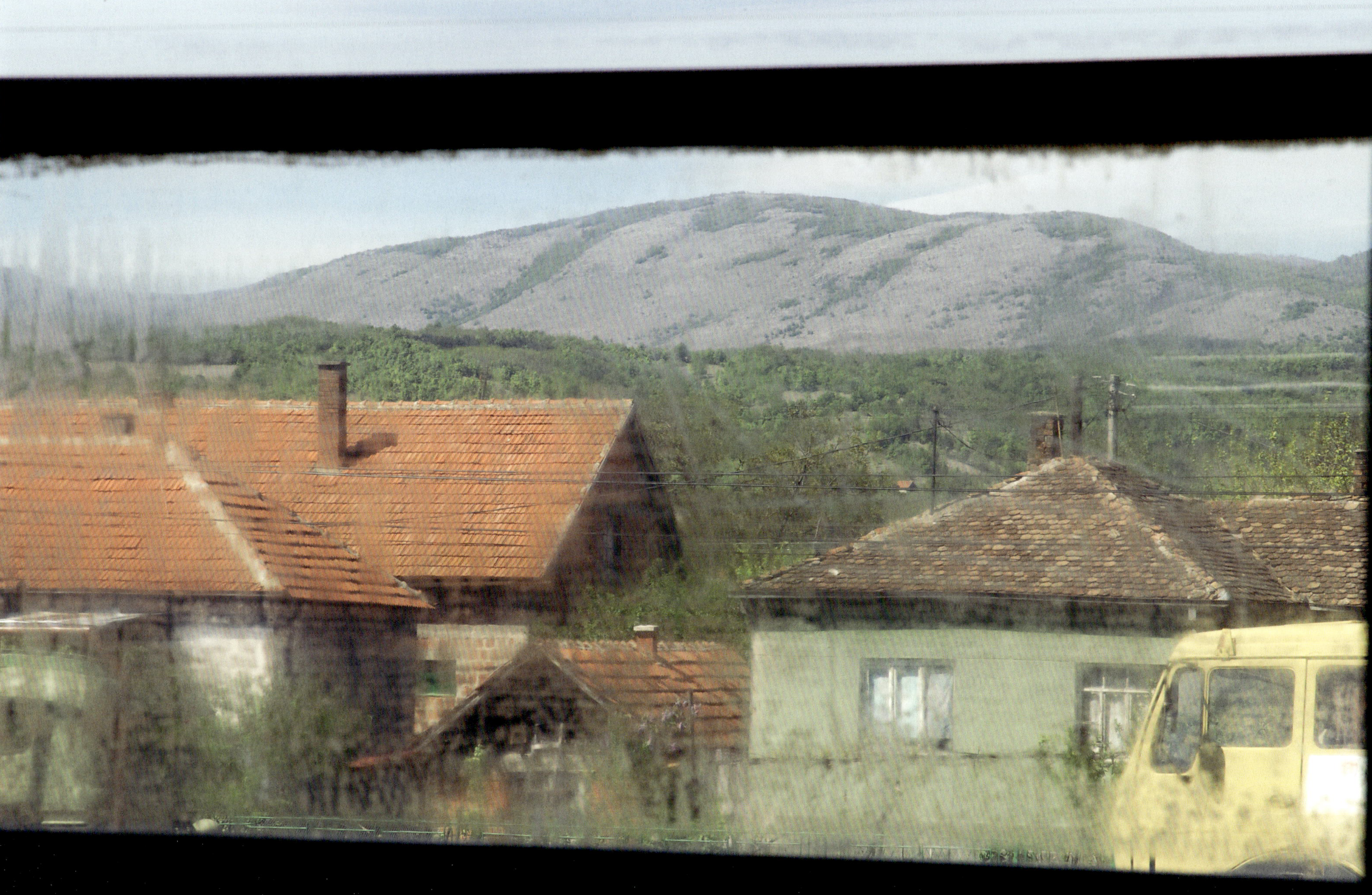
Serbia

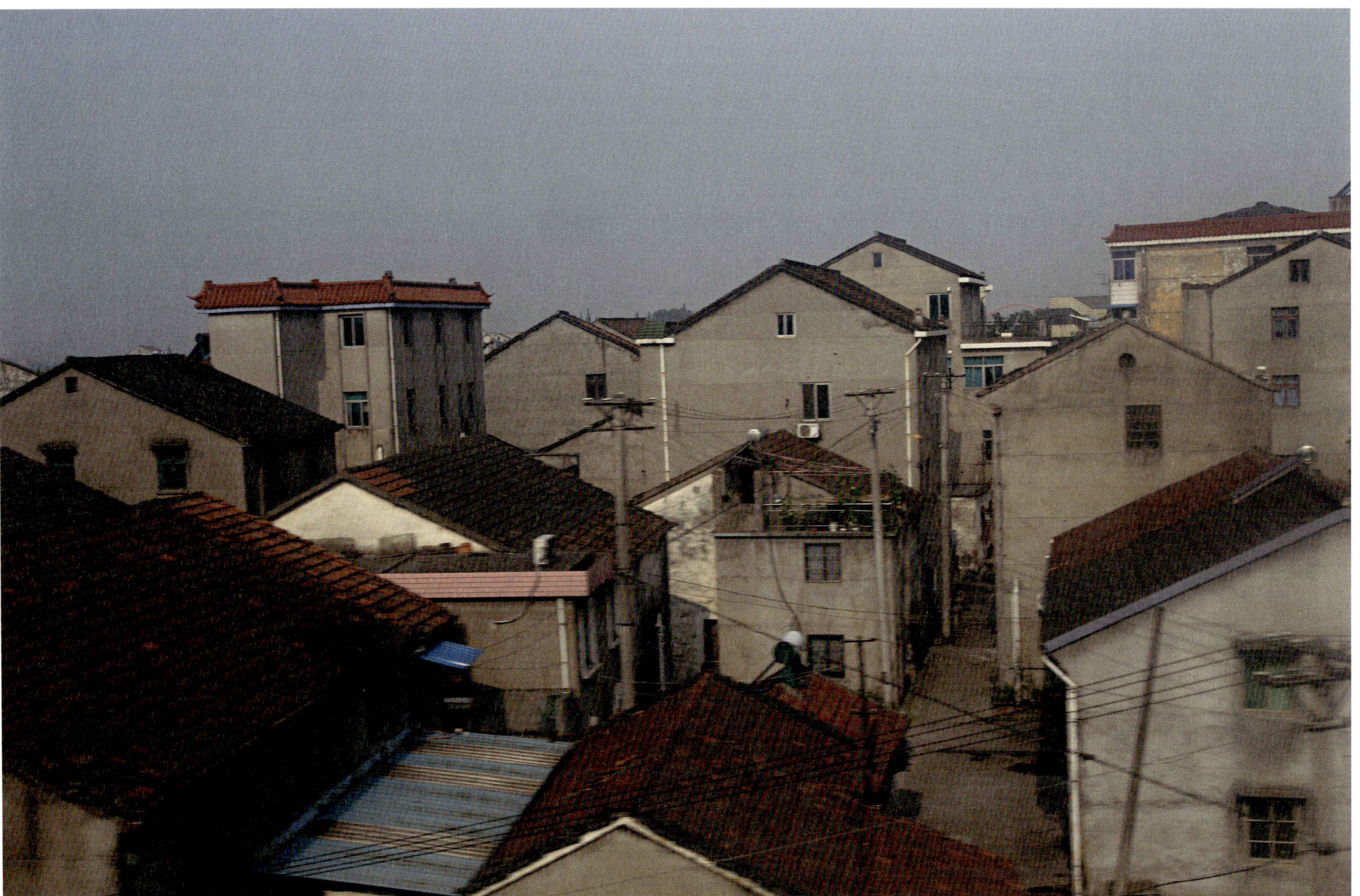
China

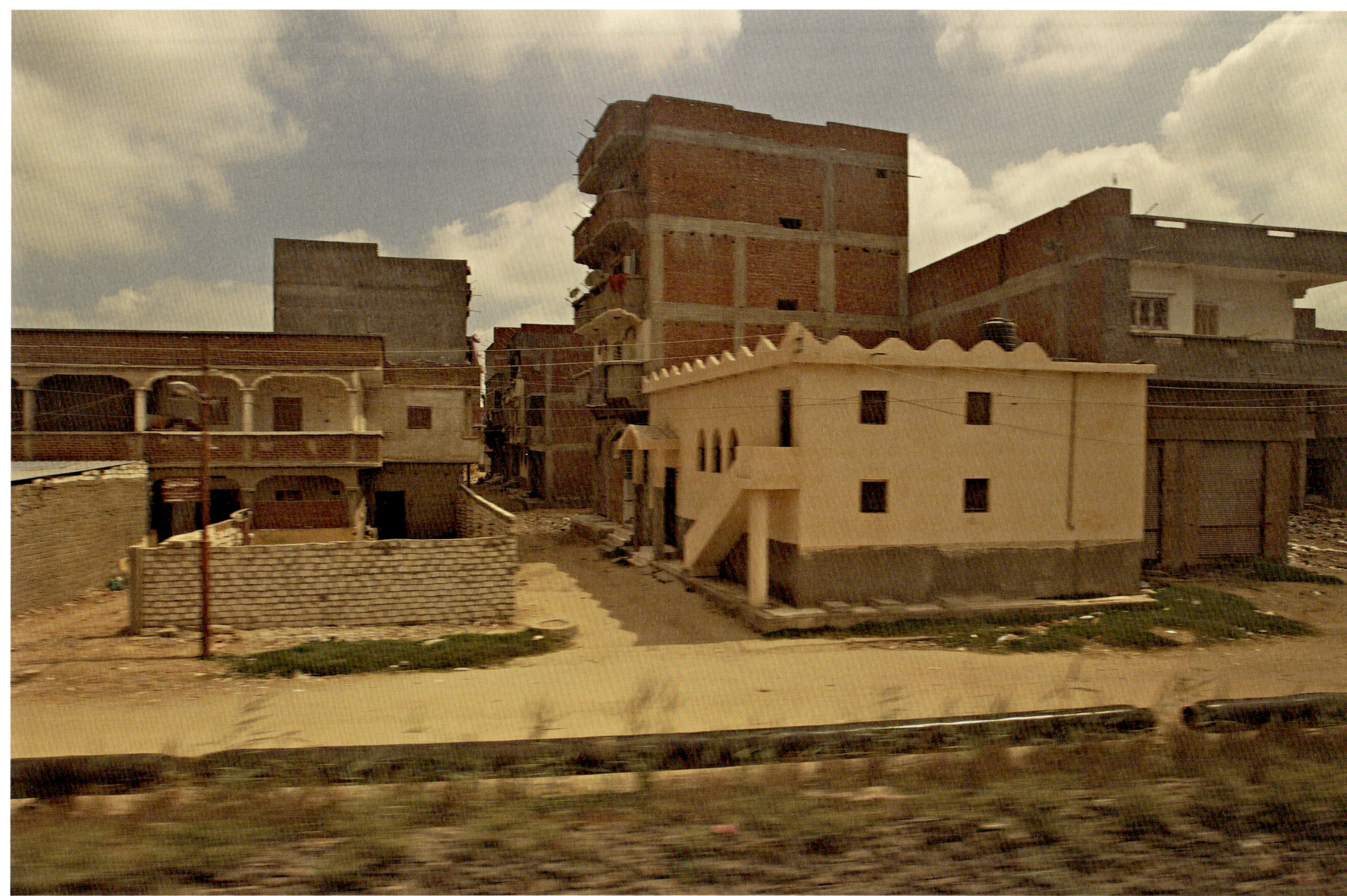

Egypt

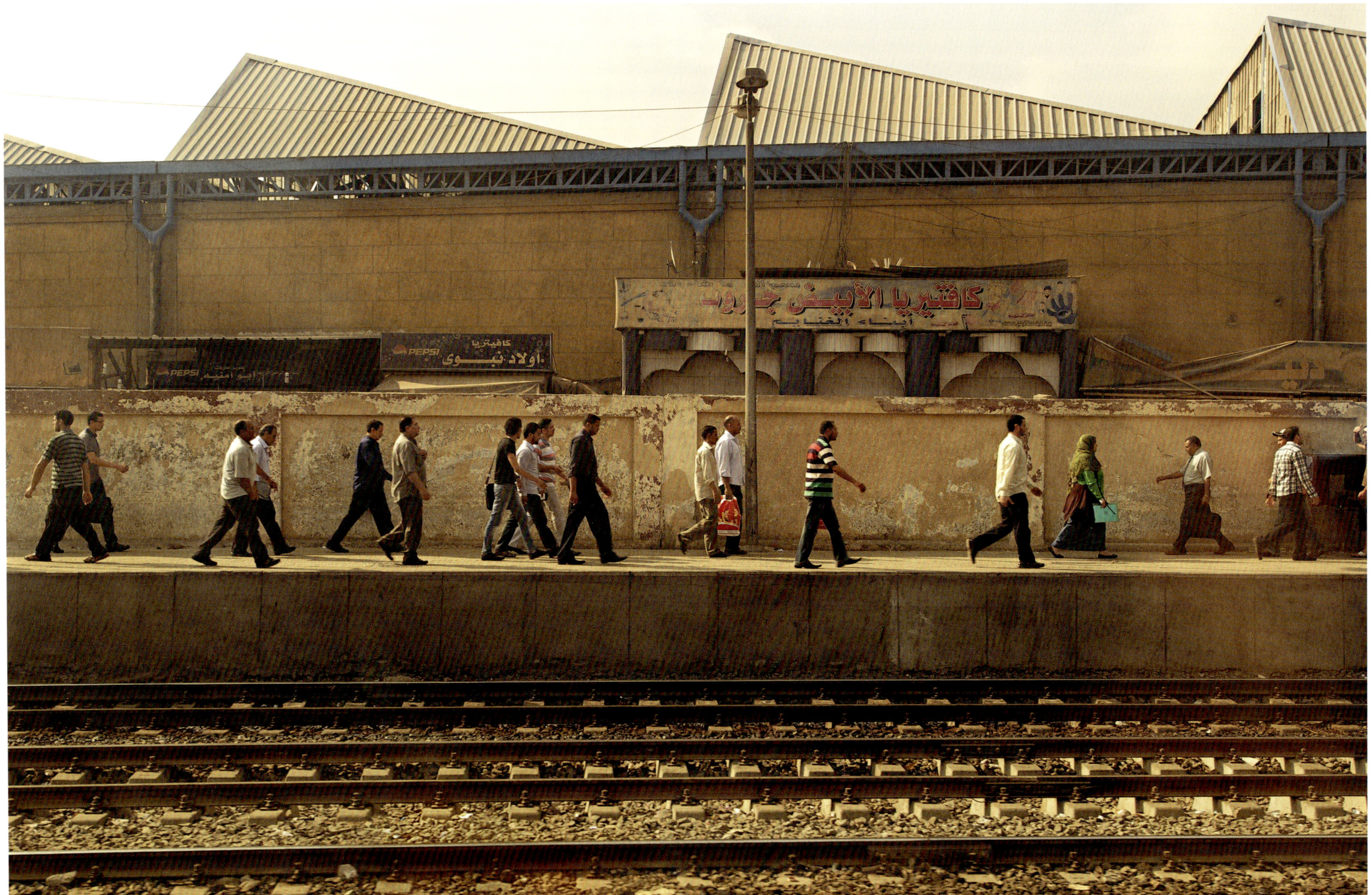
كافتيريا الأبيض جروب
أبناء الغنايم
كافيتريا
اولاد نبوى
PEPSI

Egyptian National Railroads (ENR) is predominantly a passenger railway, with passenger traffic constituting more than 90% of the traffic volume and freight the remaining 10%.

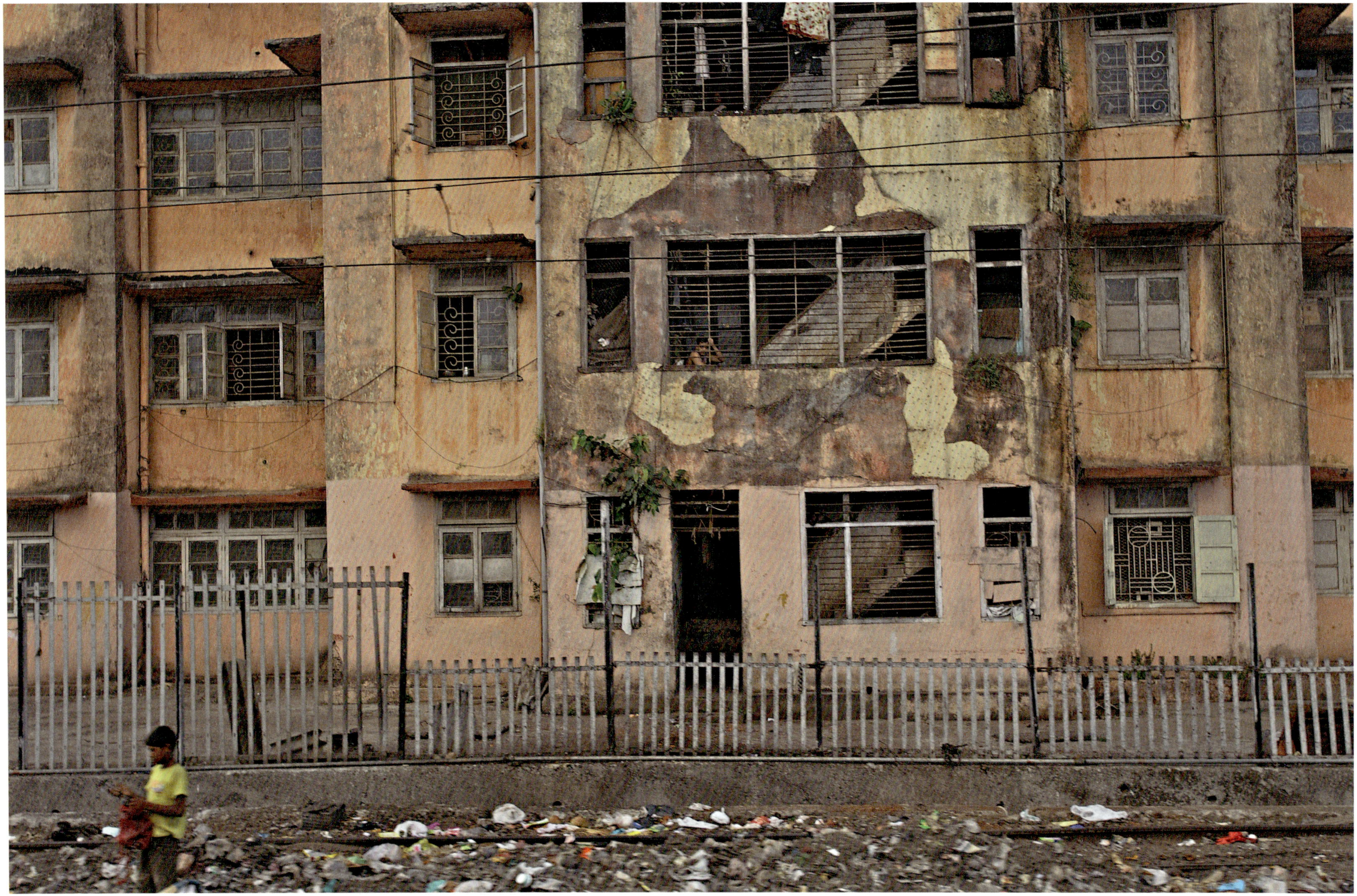

Mumbai, India

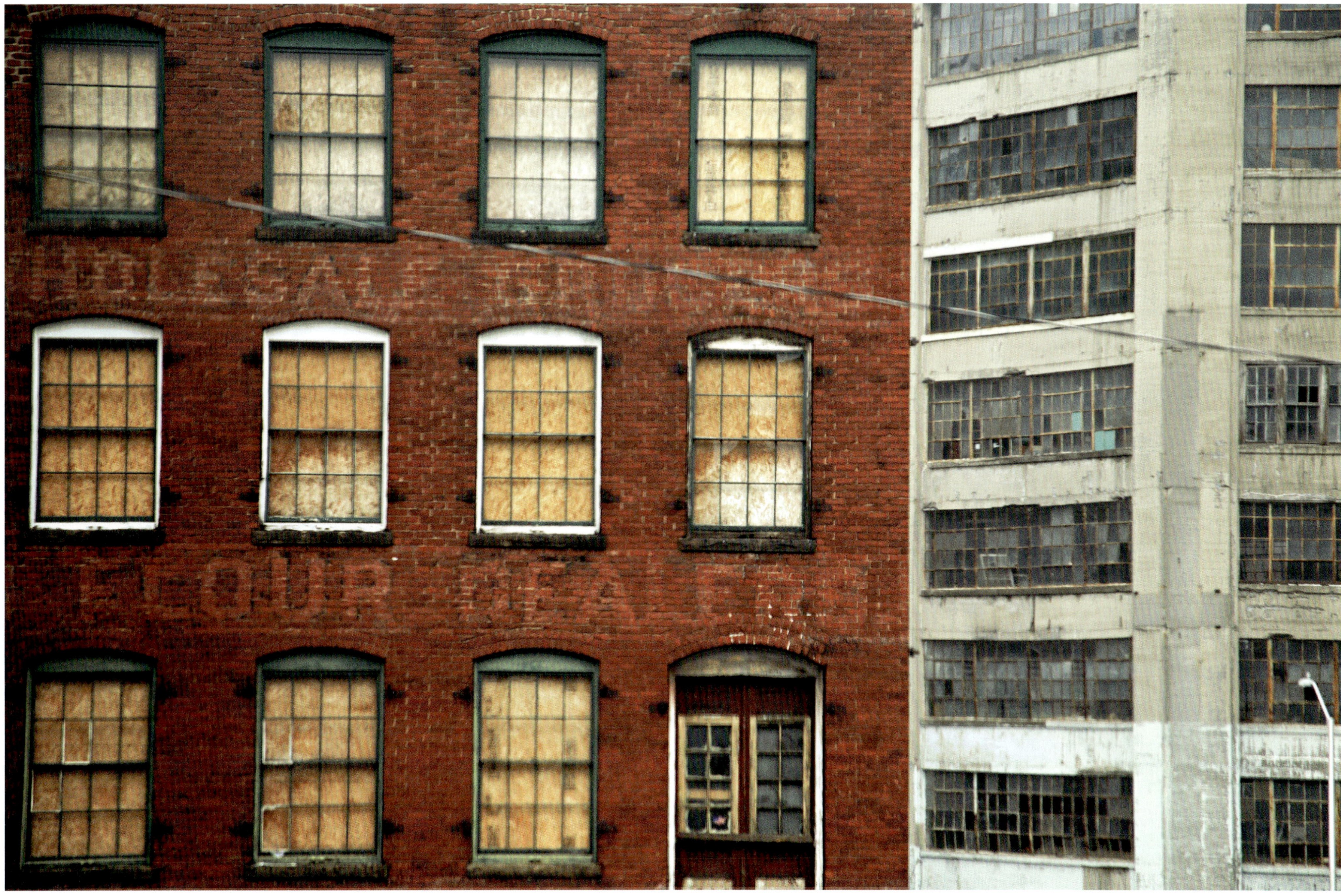
Massachusetts, USA

San Antonio, Texas, USA

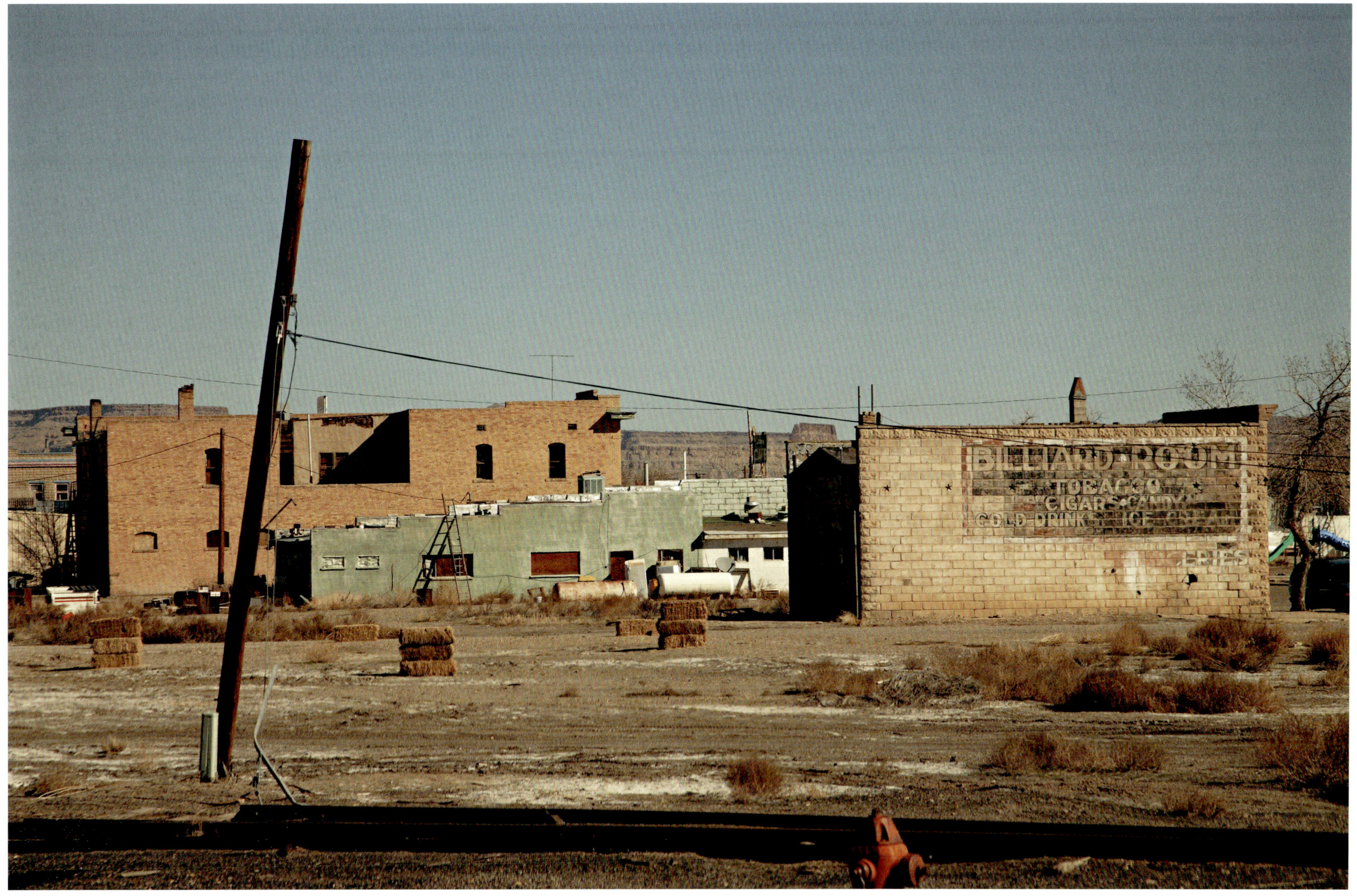
BILLIARD ROOM
TOBACCO
CIGARS CANDY
COLD DRINKS ICE CREAM
GROCERIES

The Cape to Cairo Railway was begun in the nineteenth century and covers 9,656 km / 6000 miles from one end of Africa to the other, however it remains uncompleted, with around 804 km / 500 miles missing between northern Sudan and Uganda.

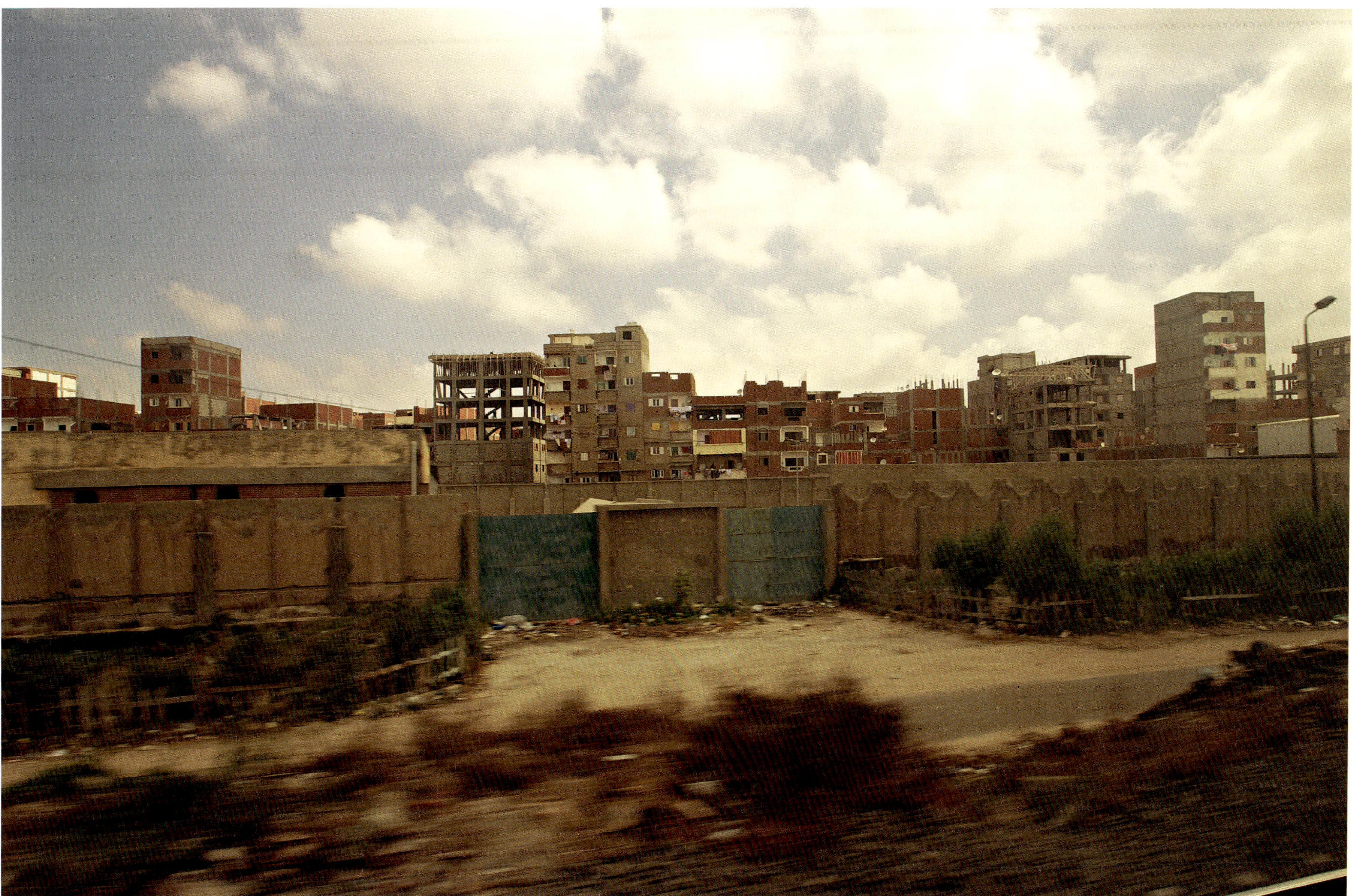

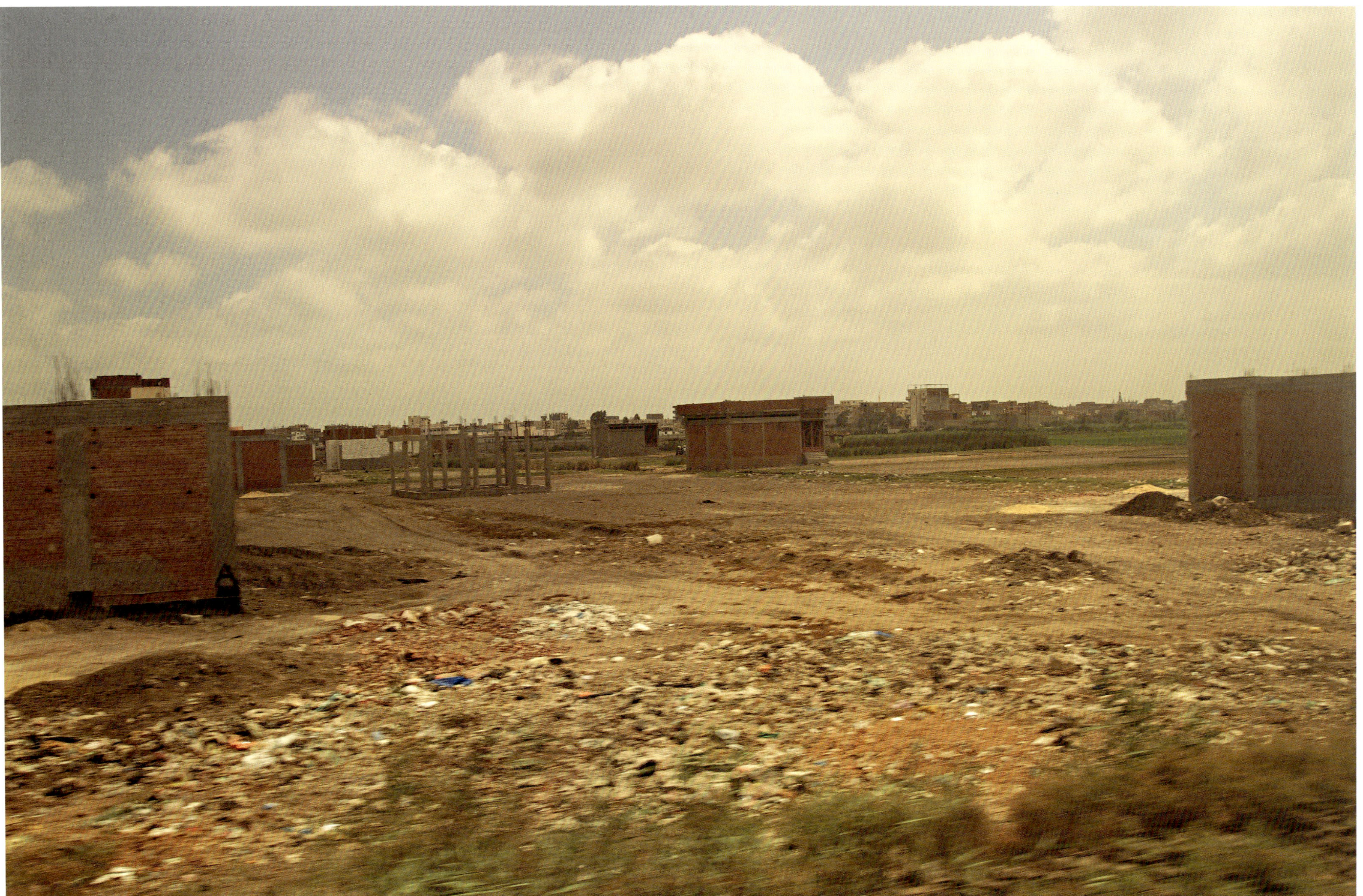
Egypt

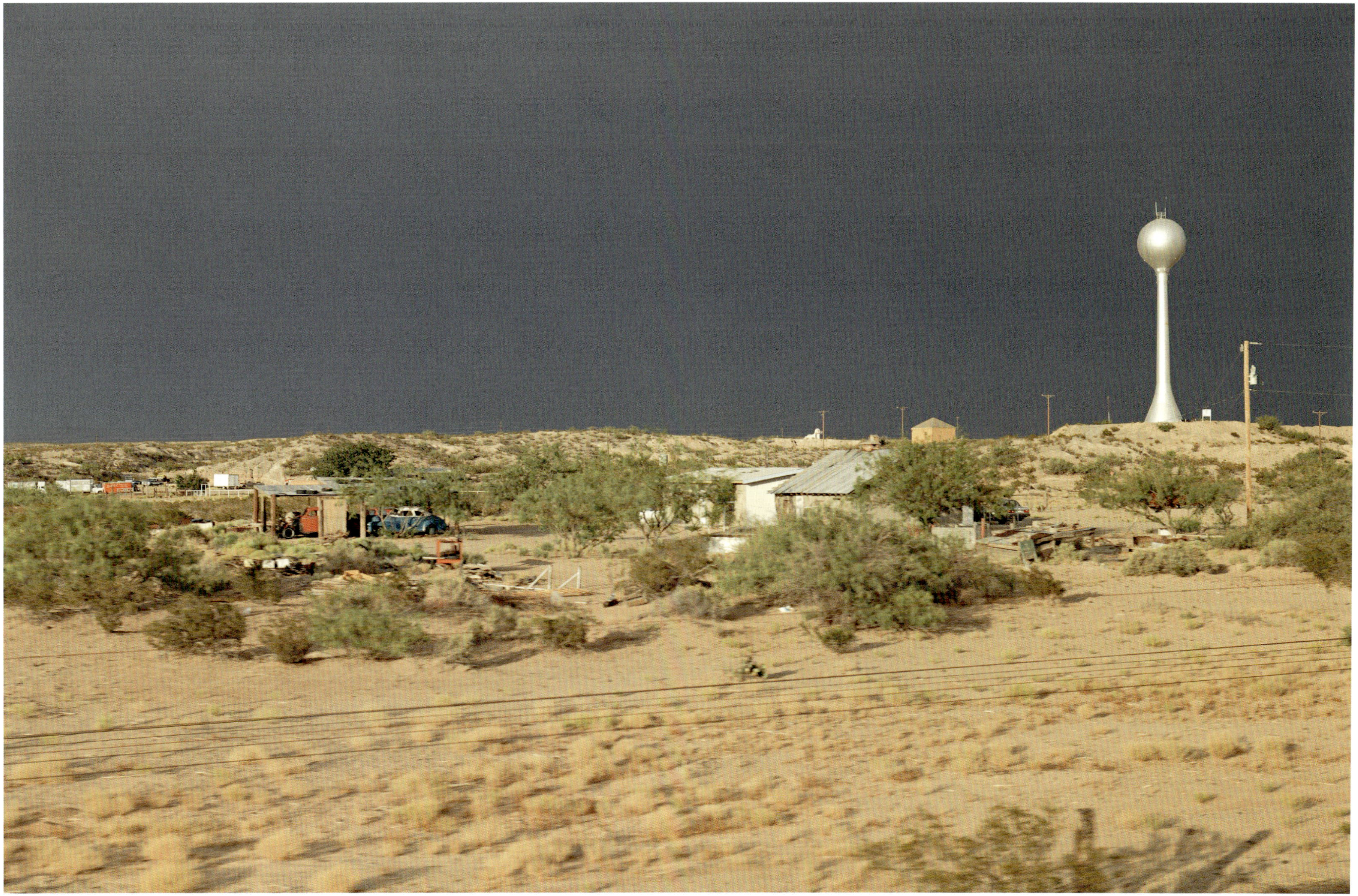

Texas, USA

Following spread: South Africa

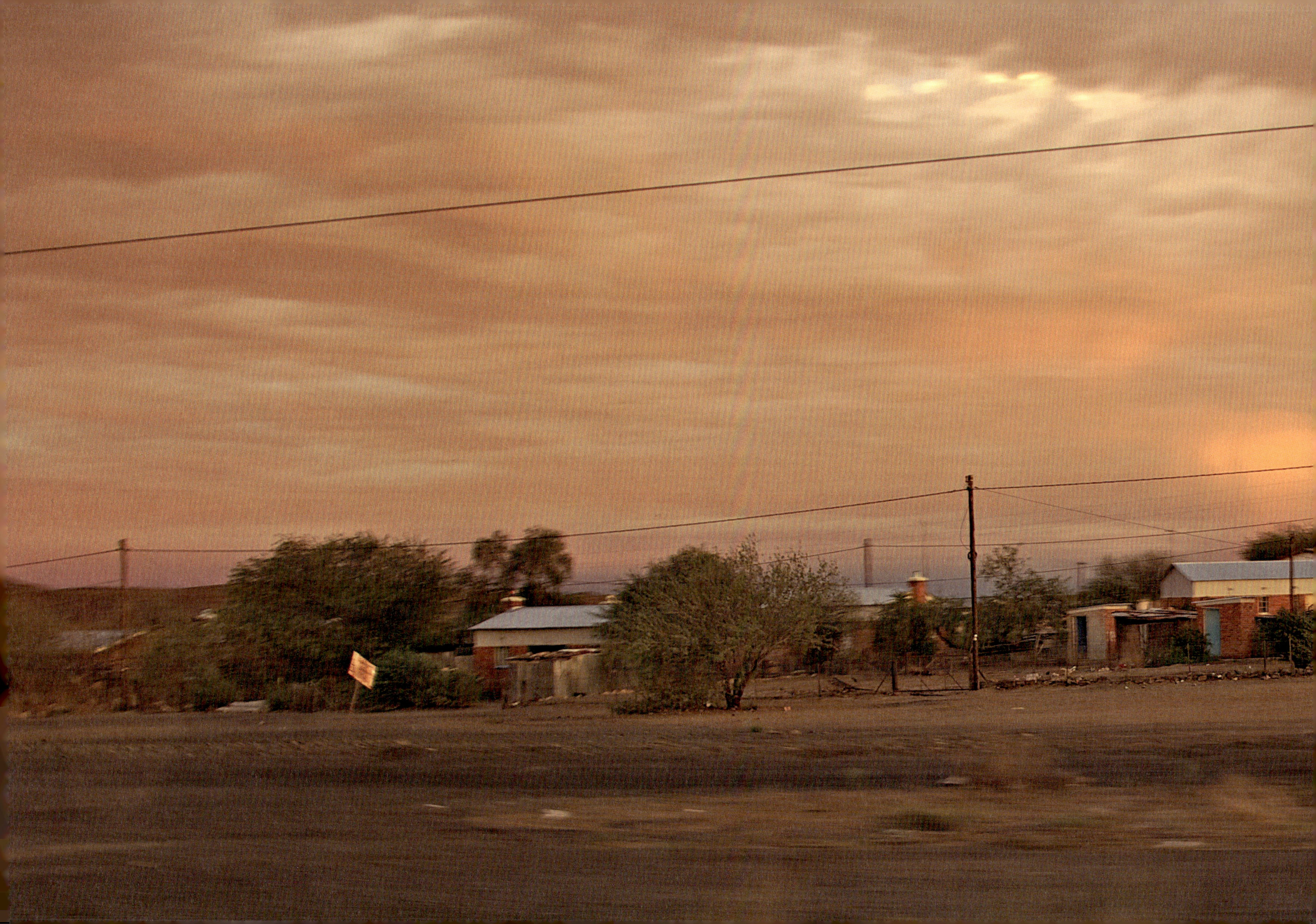

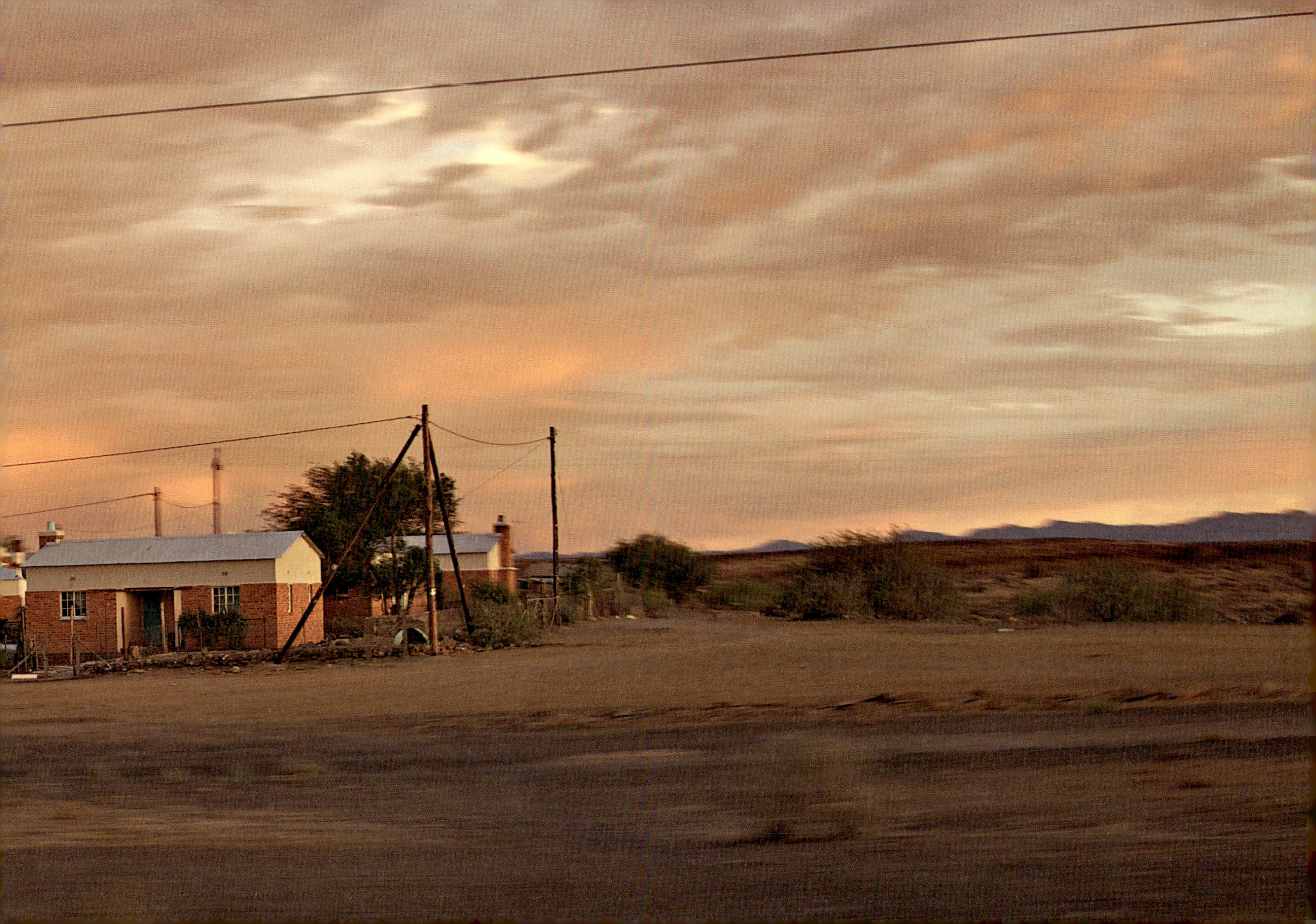

Egypt

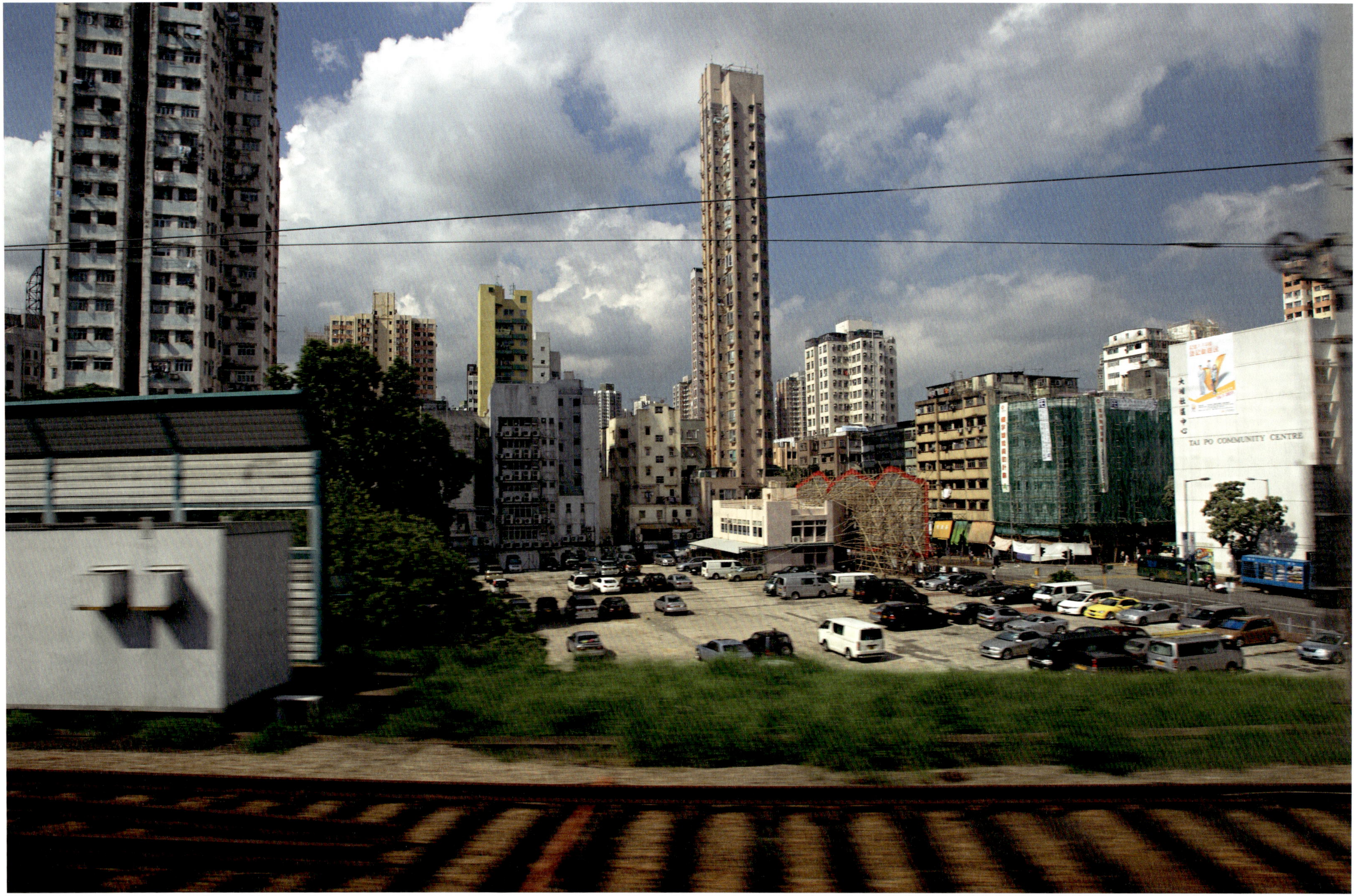

TAI PO COMMUNITY CENTRE

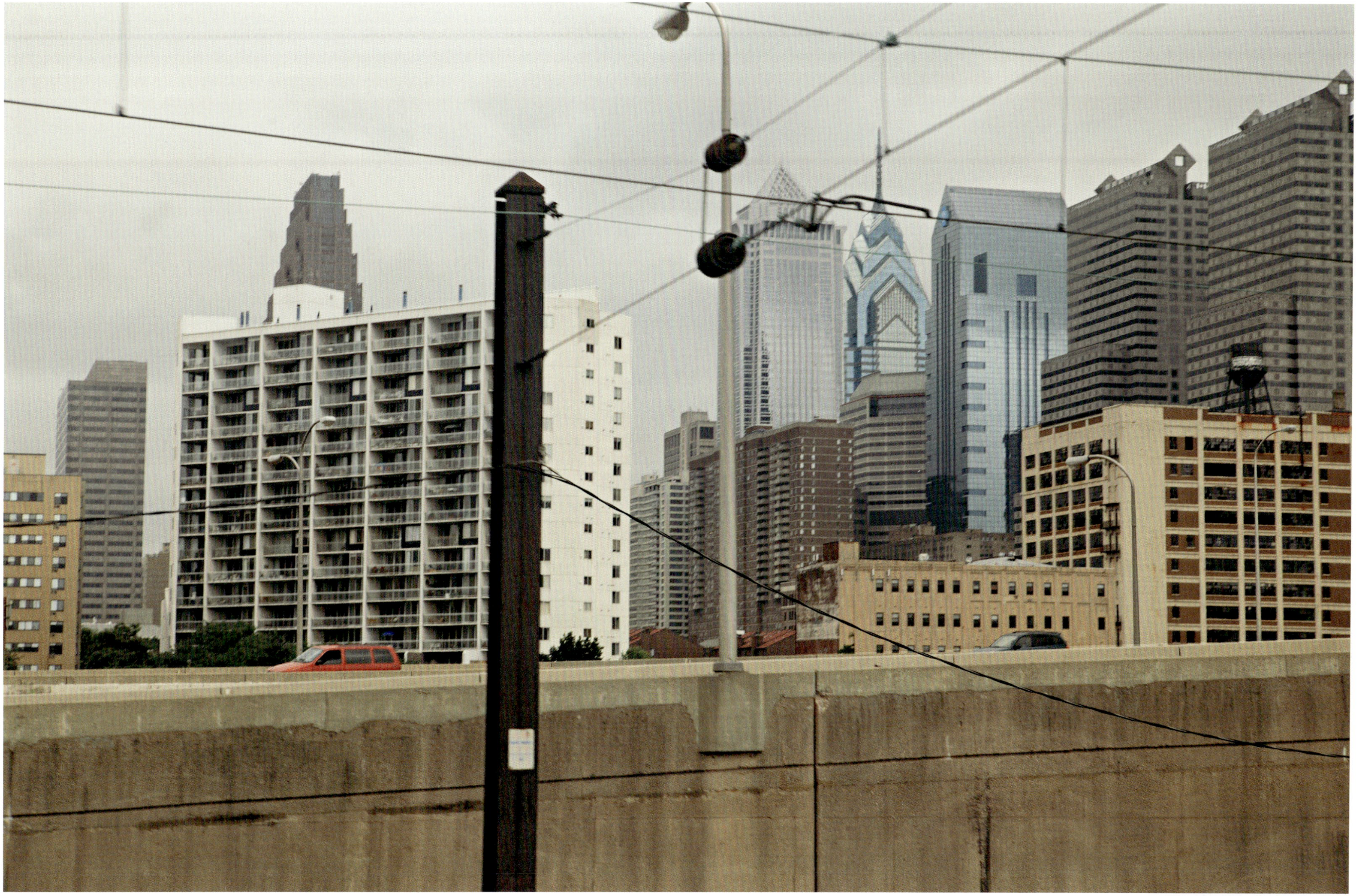

Philadelphia, Pennsylvania, USA

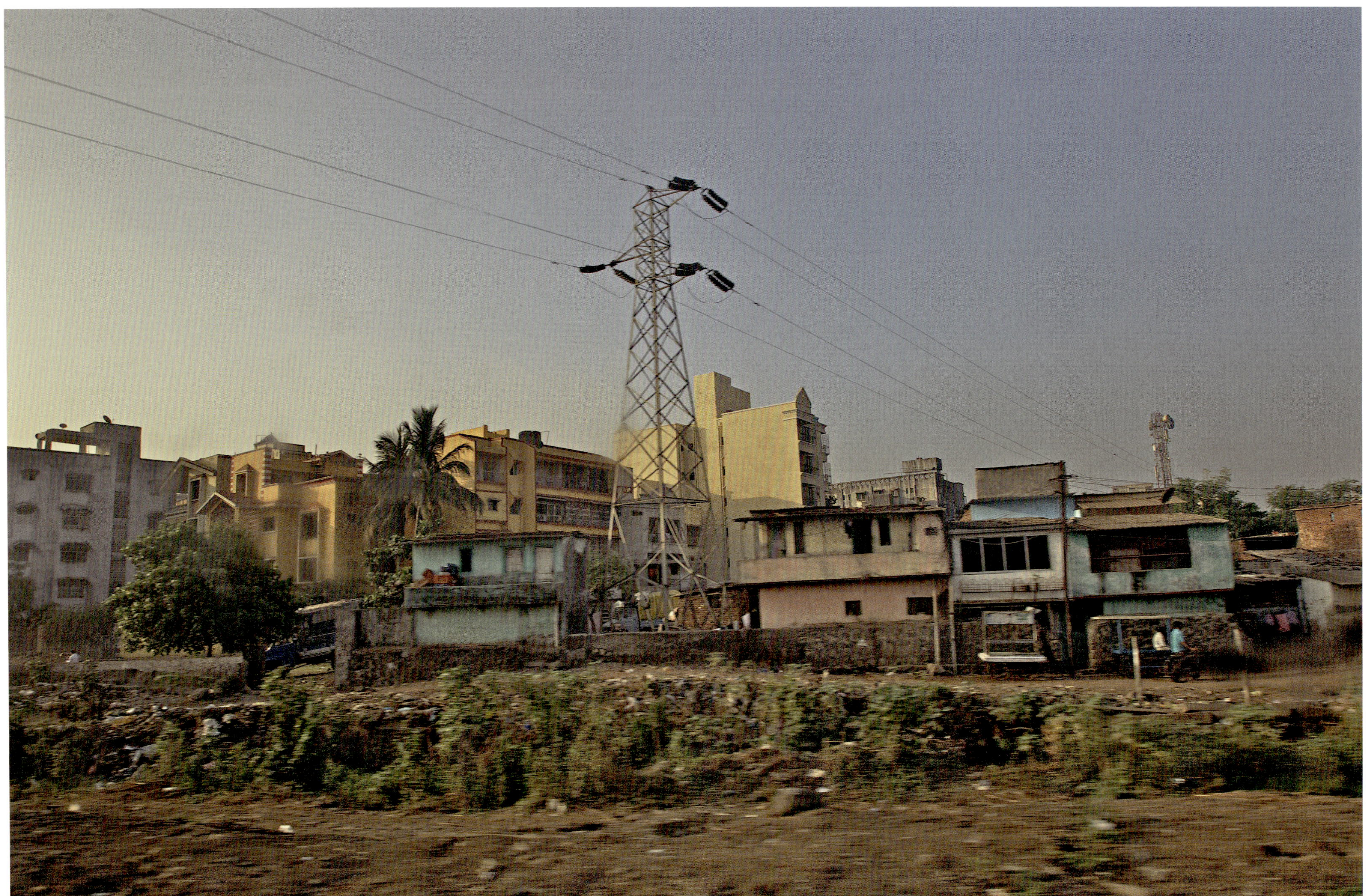

Egypt

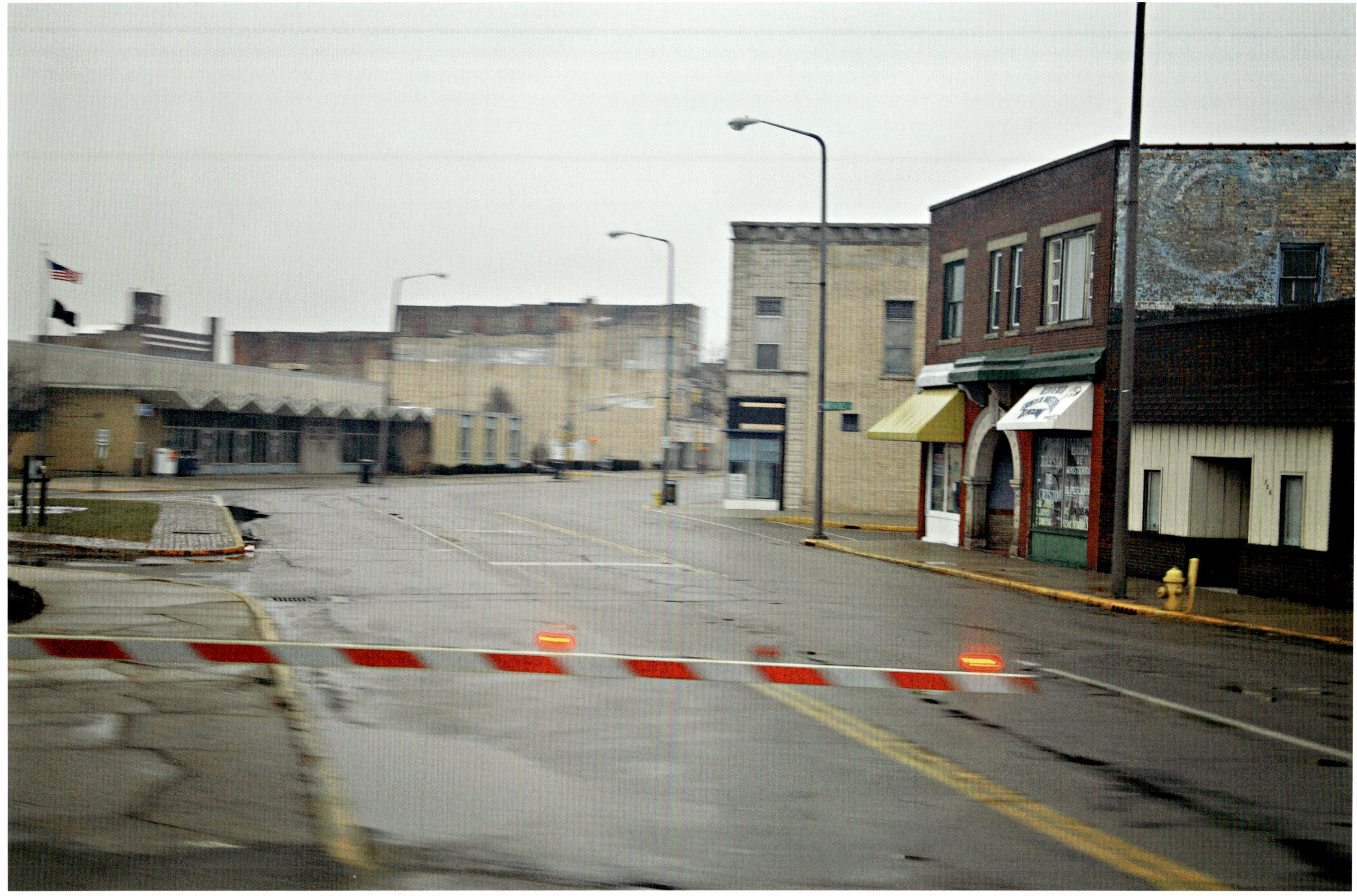

Indiana, USA

In terms of area, Brazil is more closely aligned with the USA, China, India and Russia. In terms of train travel it is a long way off, with virtually no rail links between even the major cities.

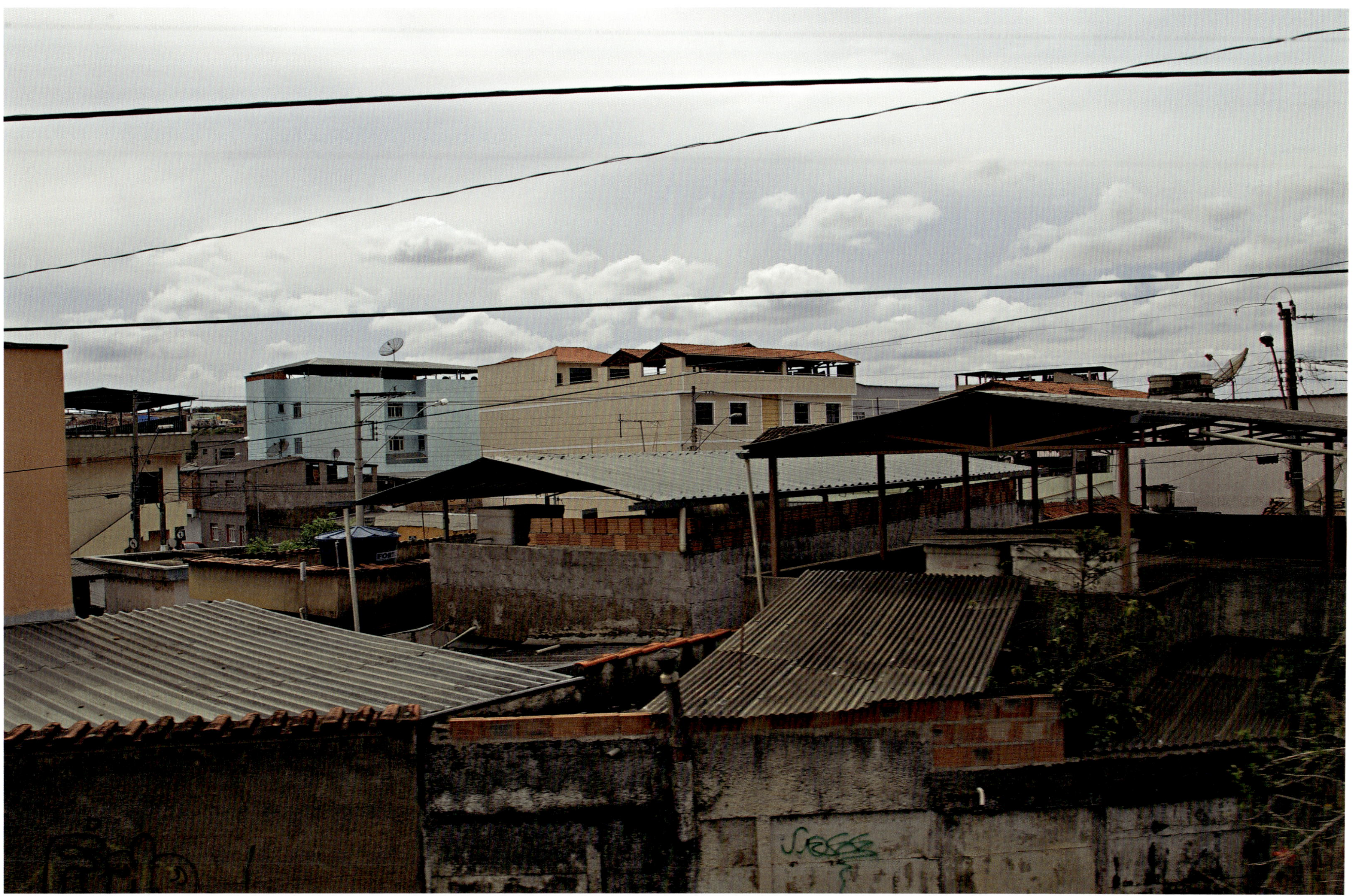

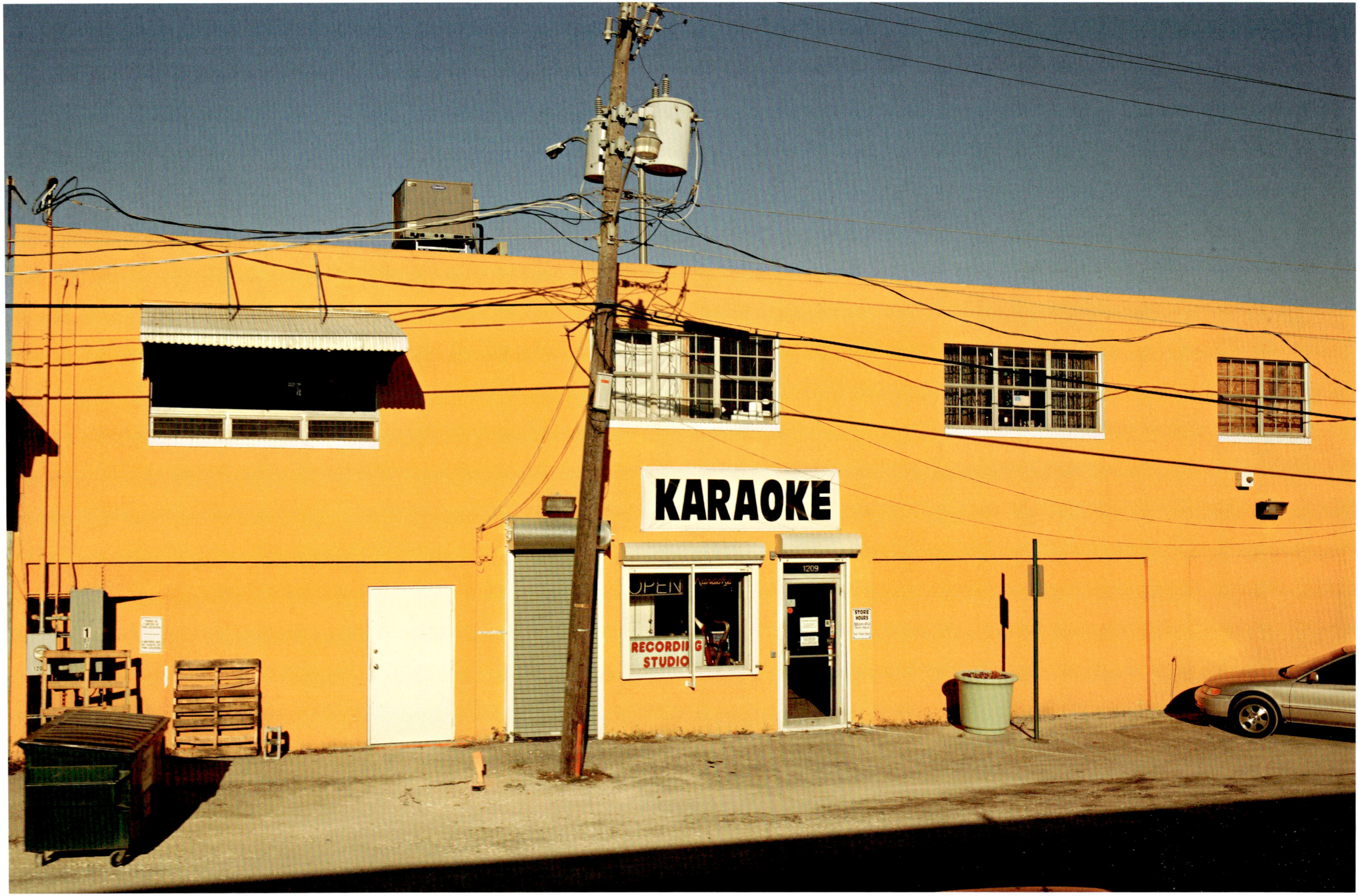

KARAOKE
OPEN
Karaoke
RECORDING STUDIO
1209
STORE HOURS
Mon–Fri

Miami, Florida, USA

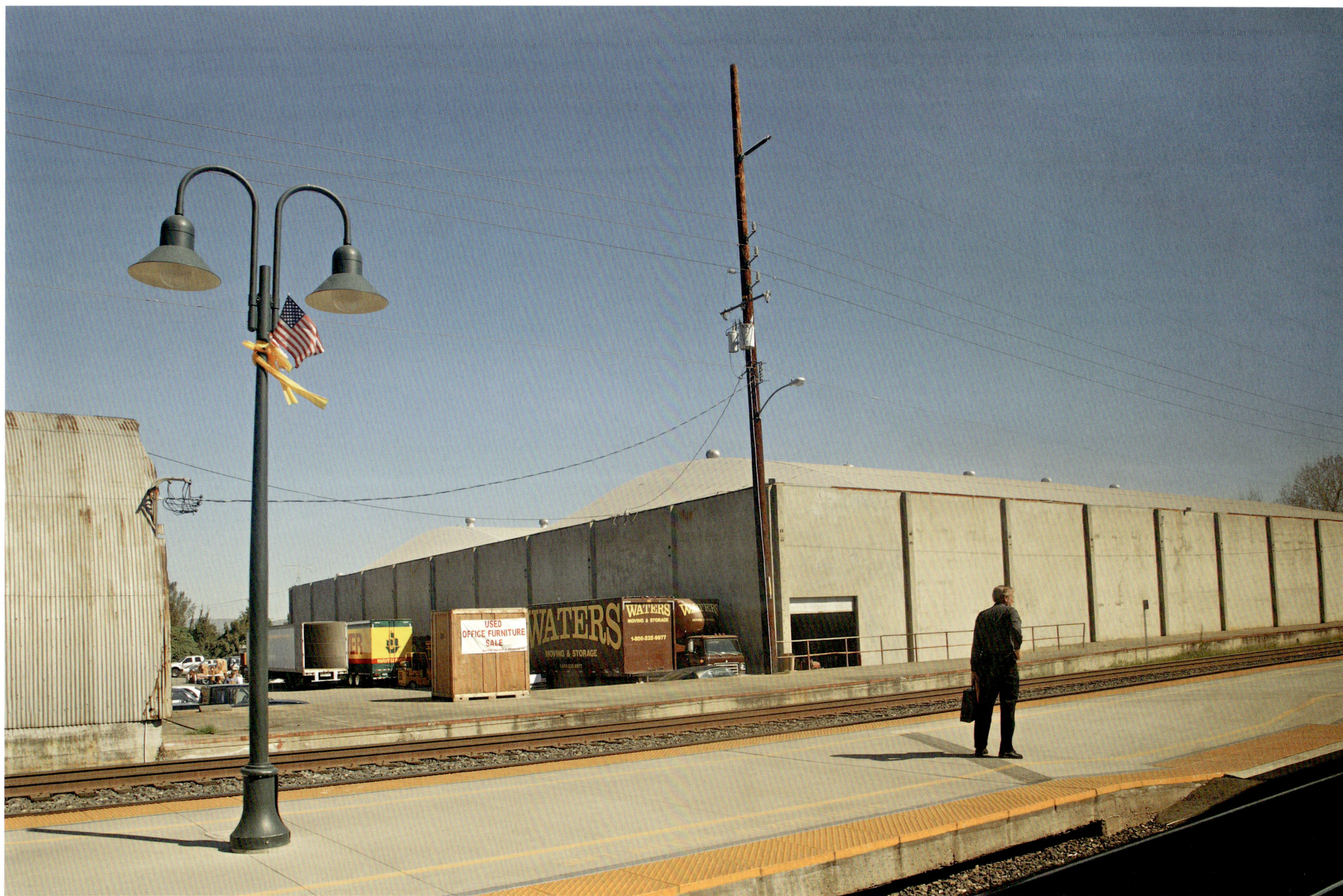

USED
OFFICE FURNITURE
SALE
WATERS
MOVING & STORAGE
WATERS
MOVING & STORAGE
1-800-232-9977

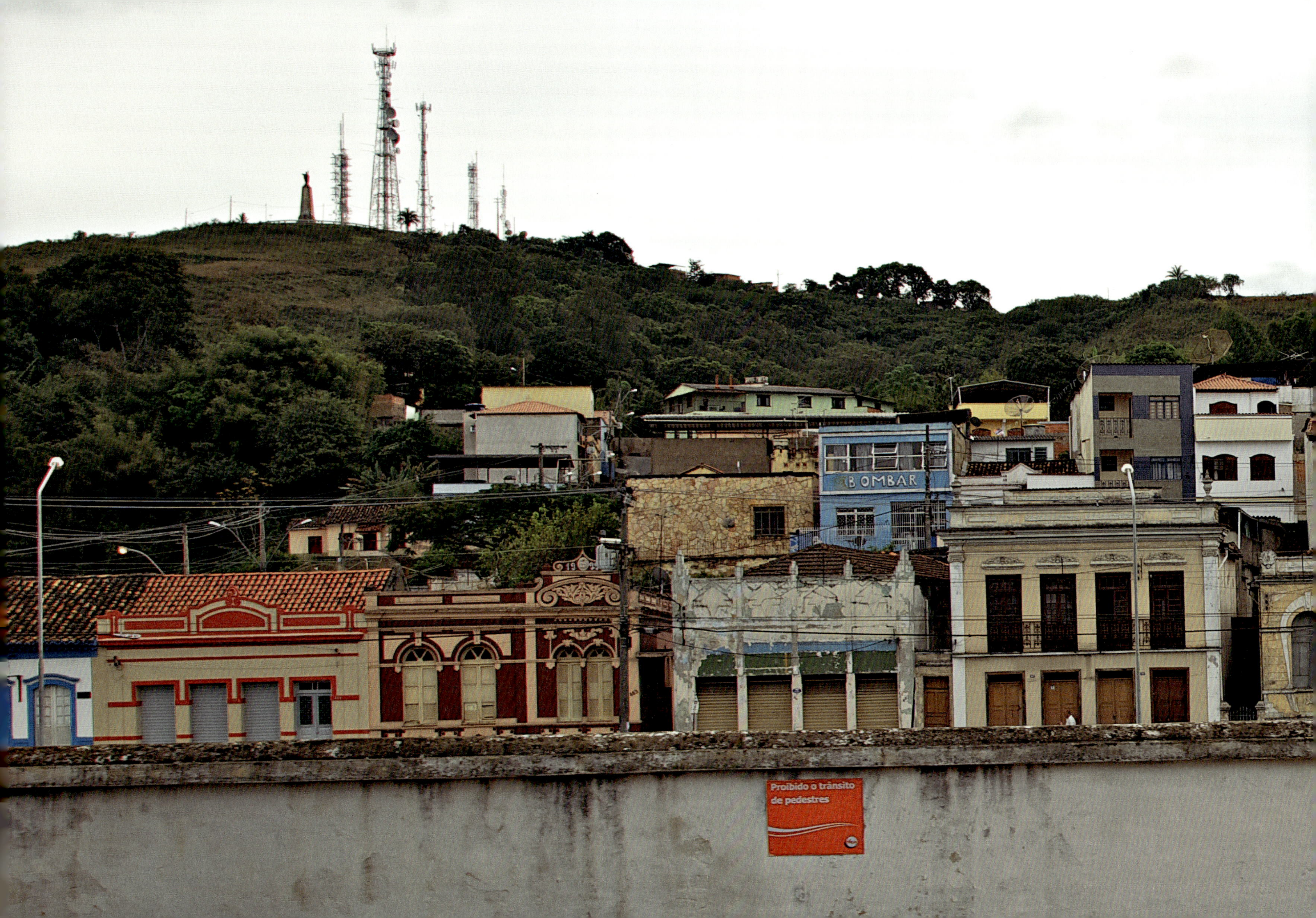
BOMBAR
Proibido o trânsito
de pedestres

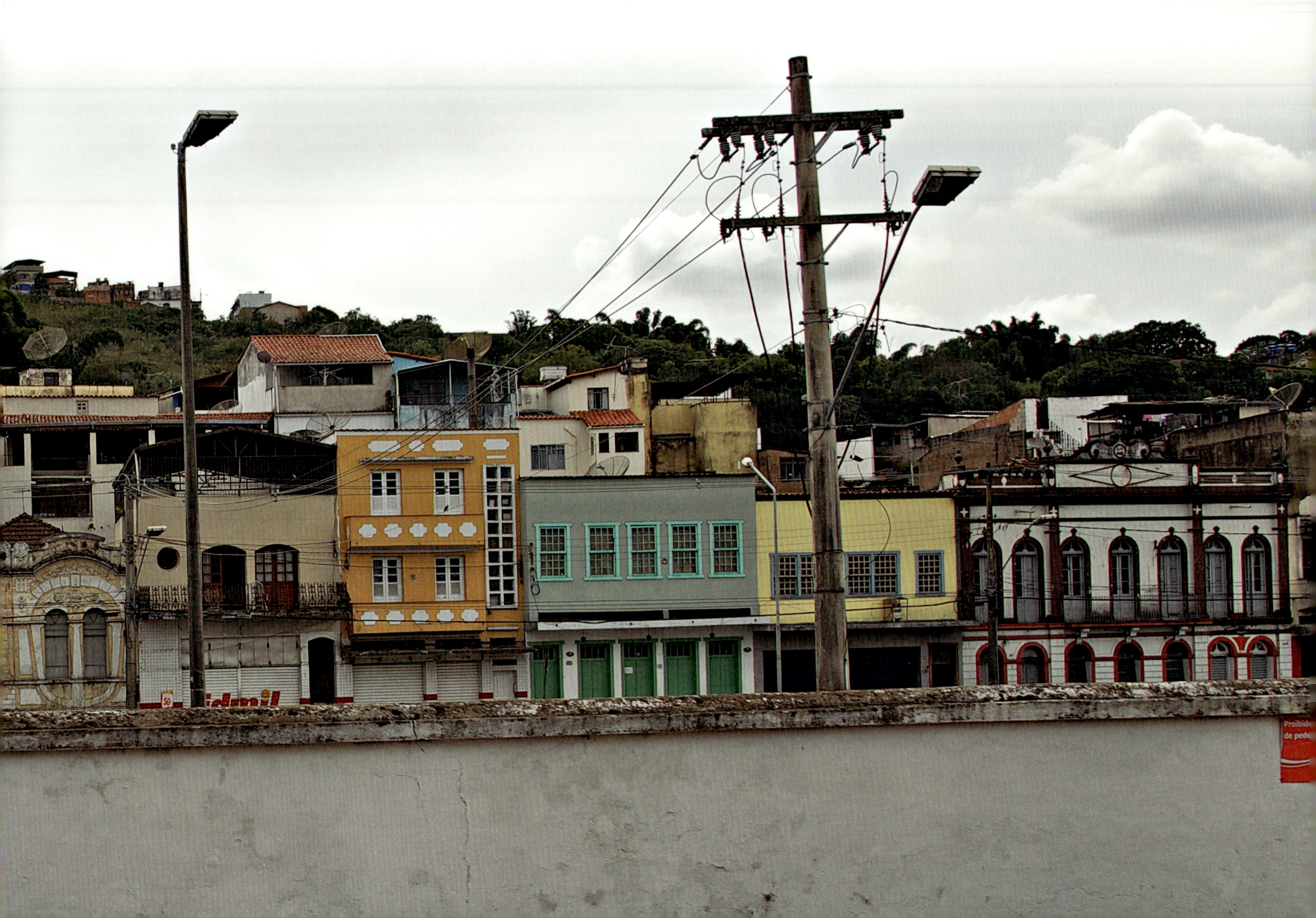

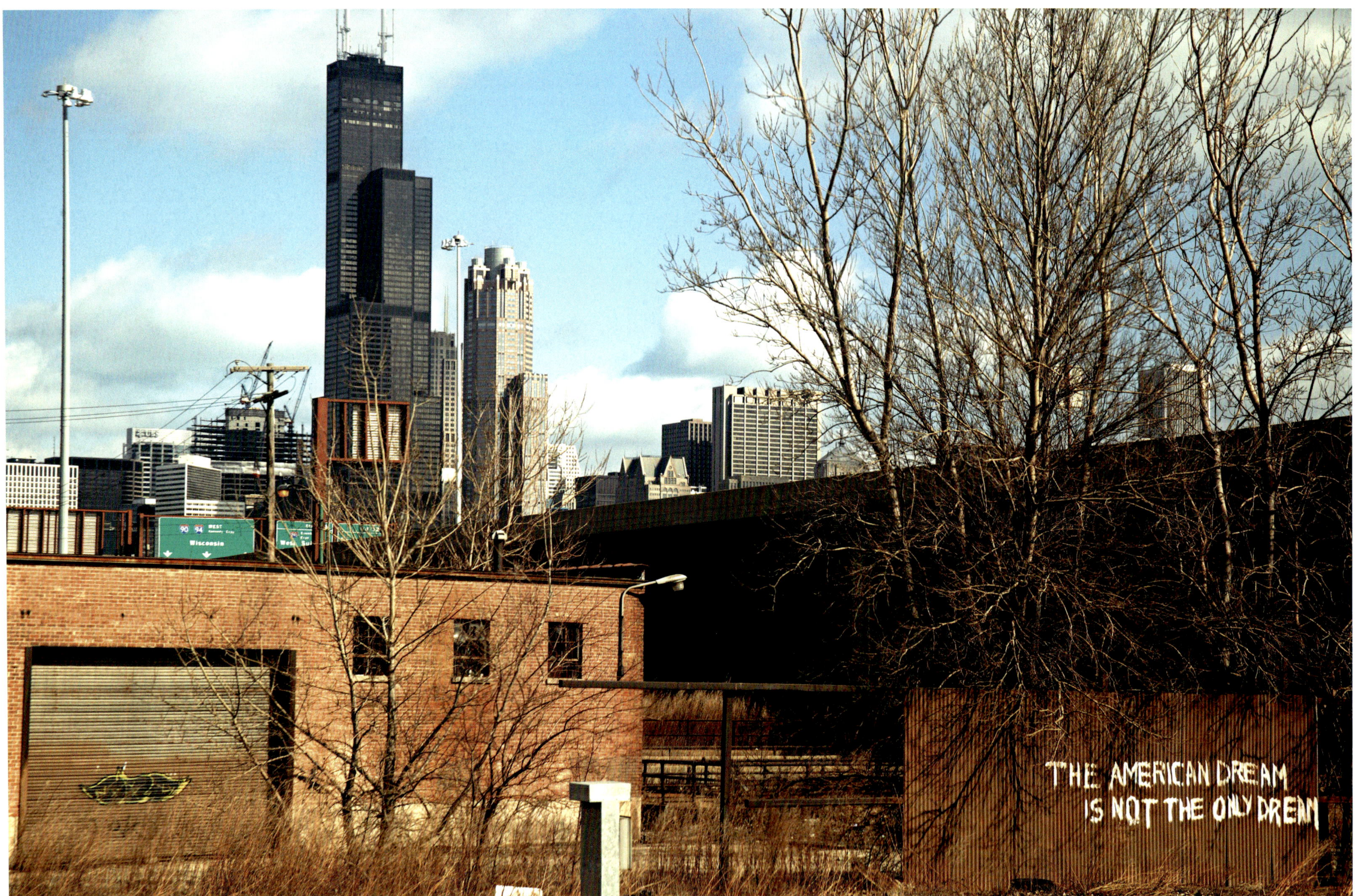

90 94 WEST
Wisconsin
THE AMERICAN DREAM
IS NOT THE ONLY DREAM

Considering it has 5% of the world's population and over 25% of the world's energy usage, the USA has a very under-utilised and underdeveloped train system in Amtrak. Rail, as a more extensive, efficient and economic alternative to air and road travel, would reduce the USA's insatiable energy hunger and relieve pressure on its oil acquisition abroad.

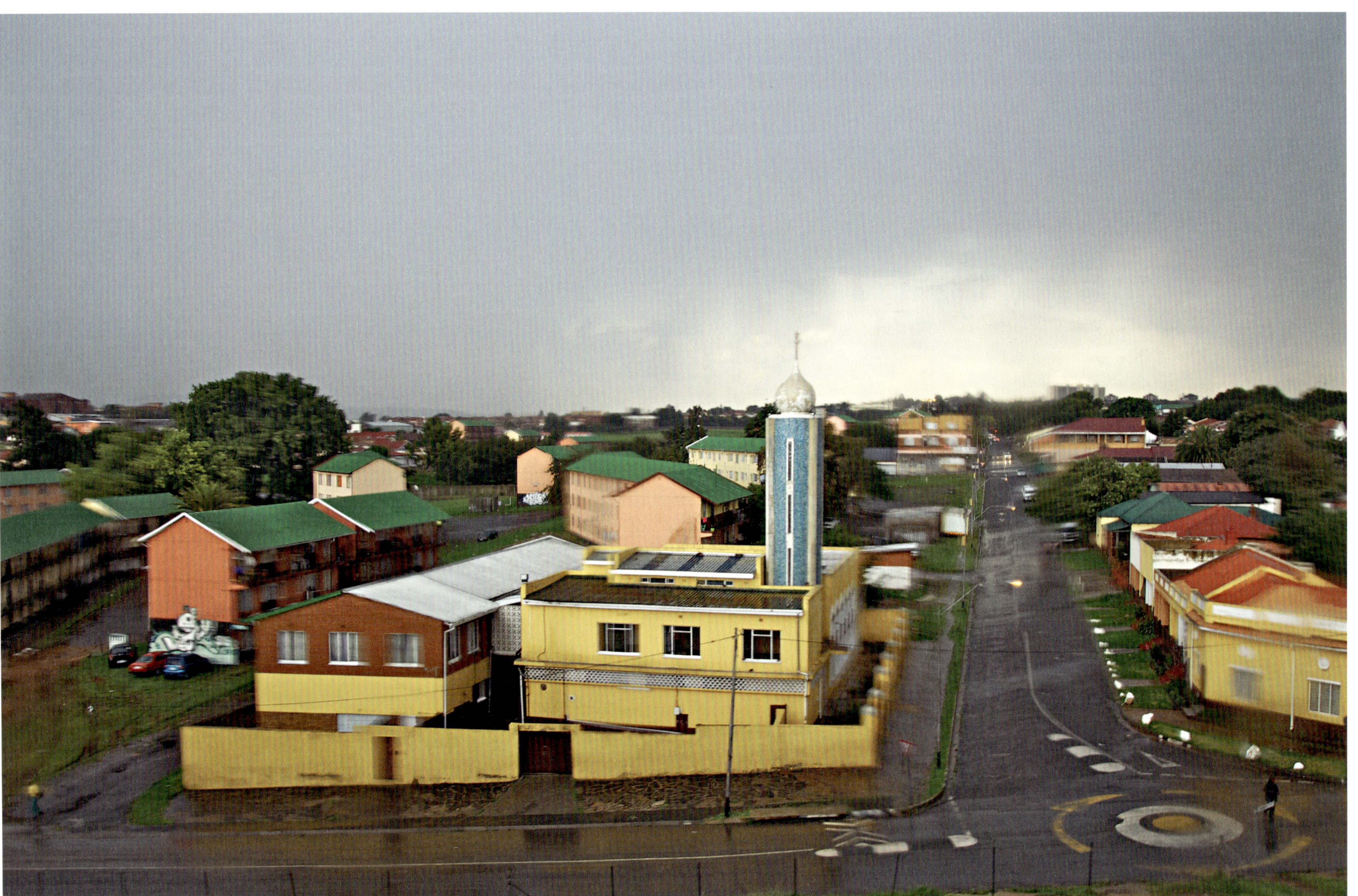

Johannesburg, South Africa

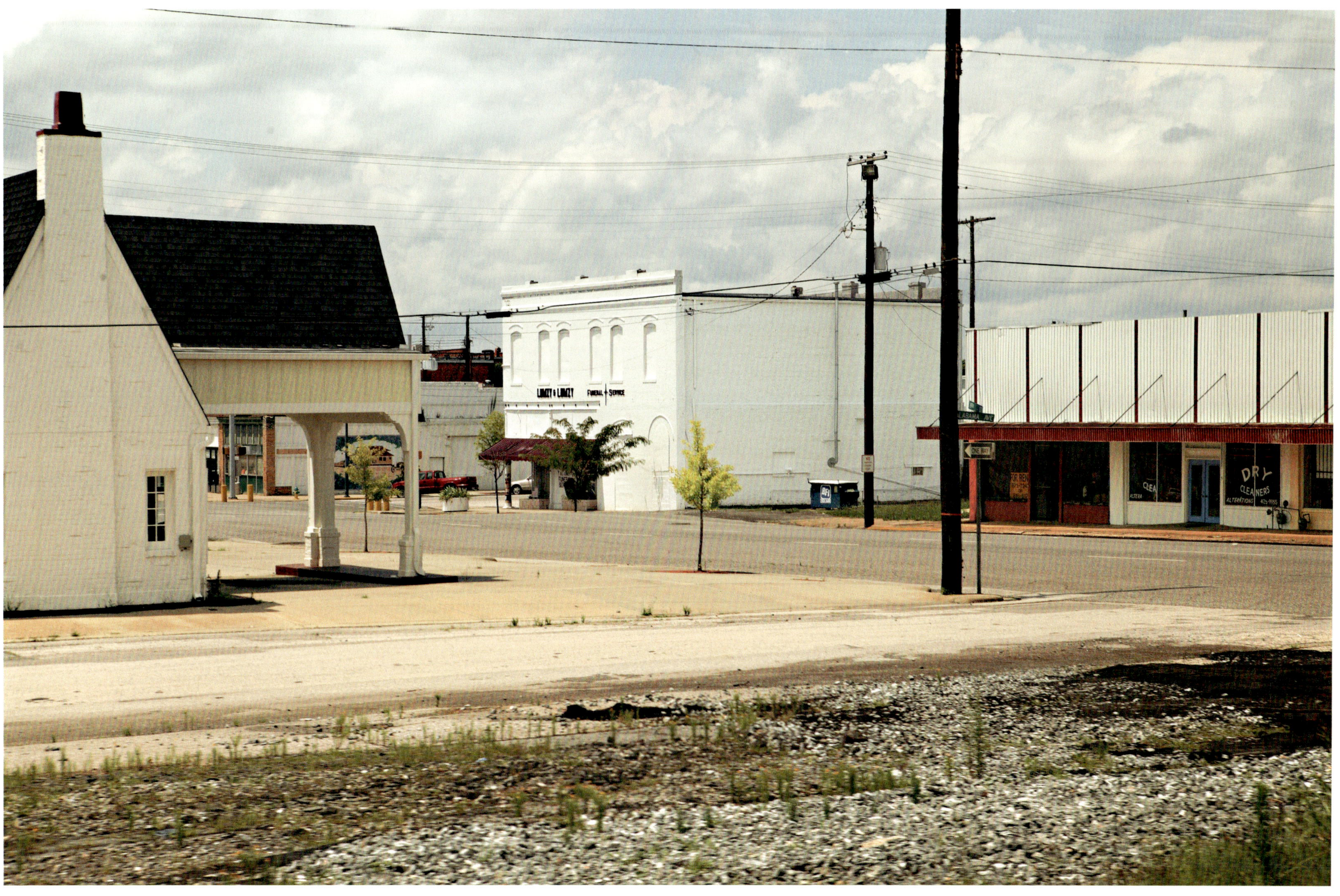

LUMZY & LUMZY   FUNERAL + SERVICE
DRY CLEANERS
ALTERATIONS
426-9955
ONE WAY
ALABAMA AV

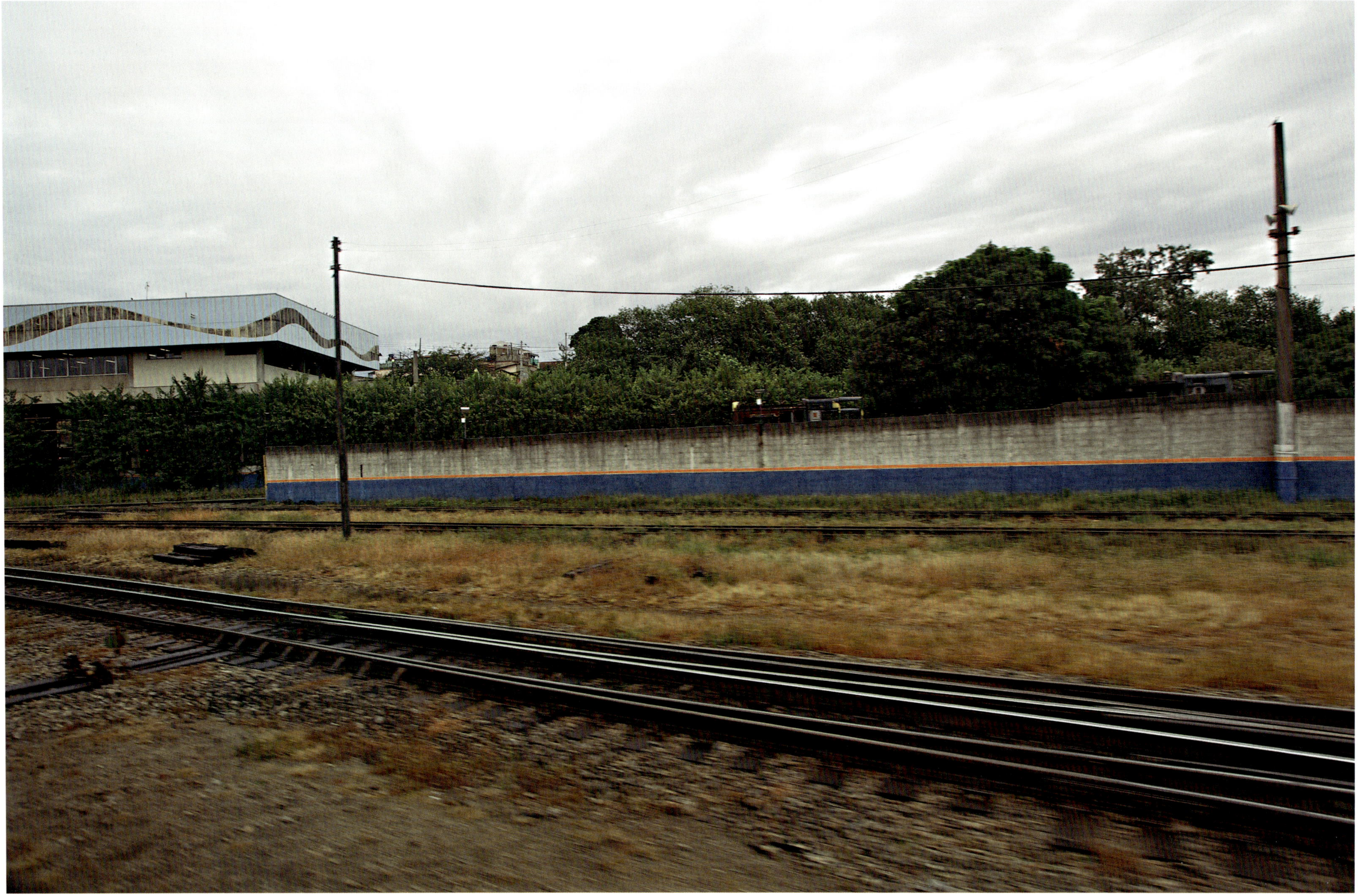

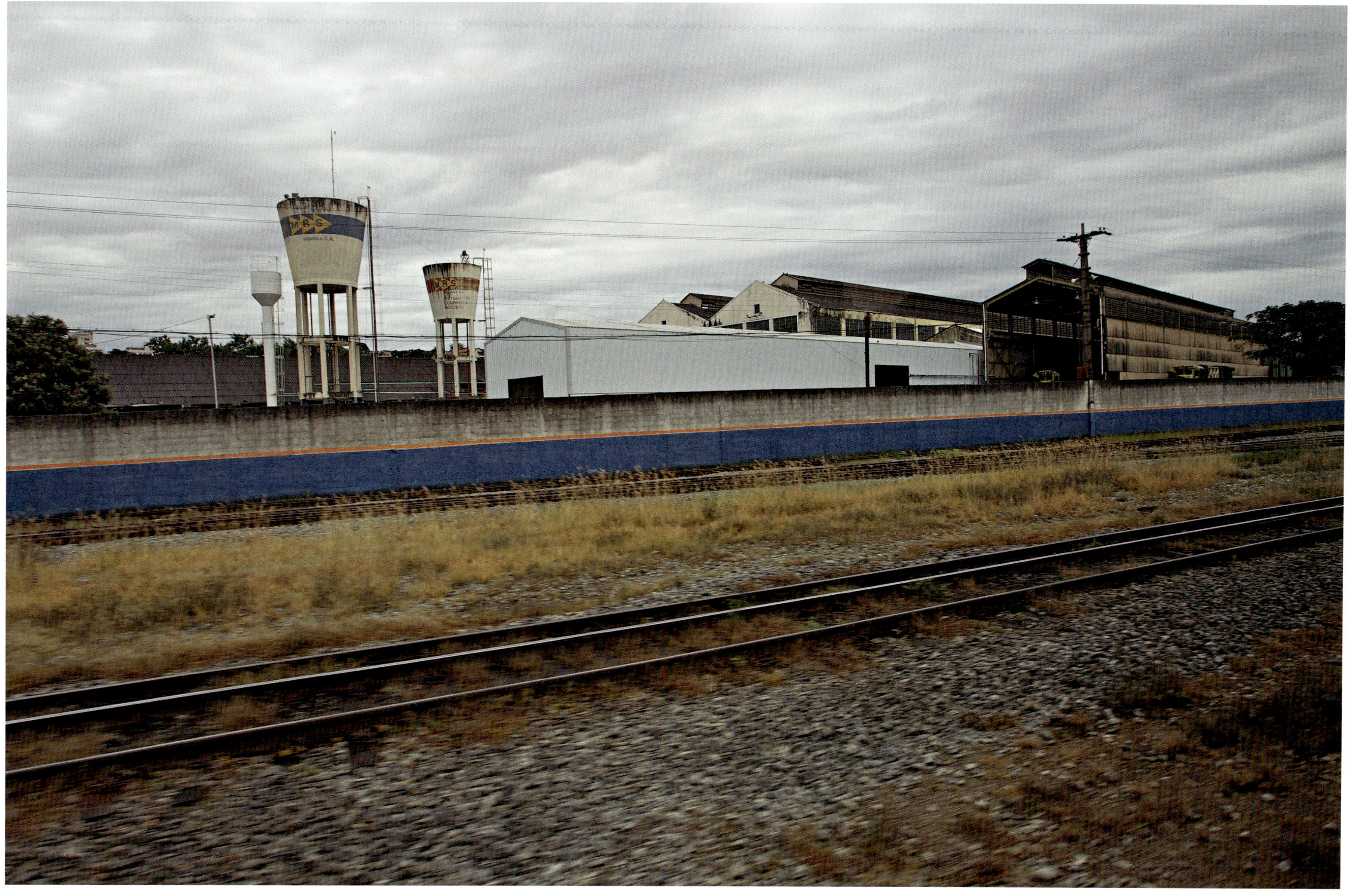

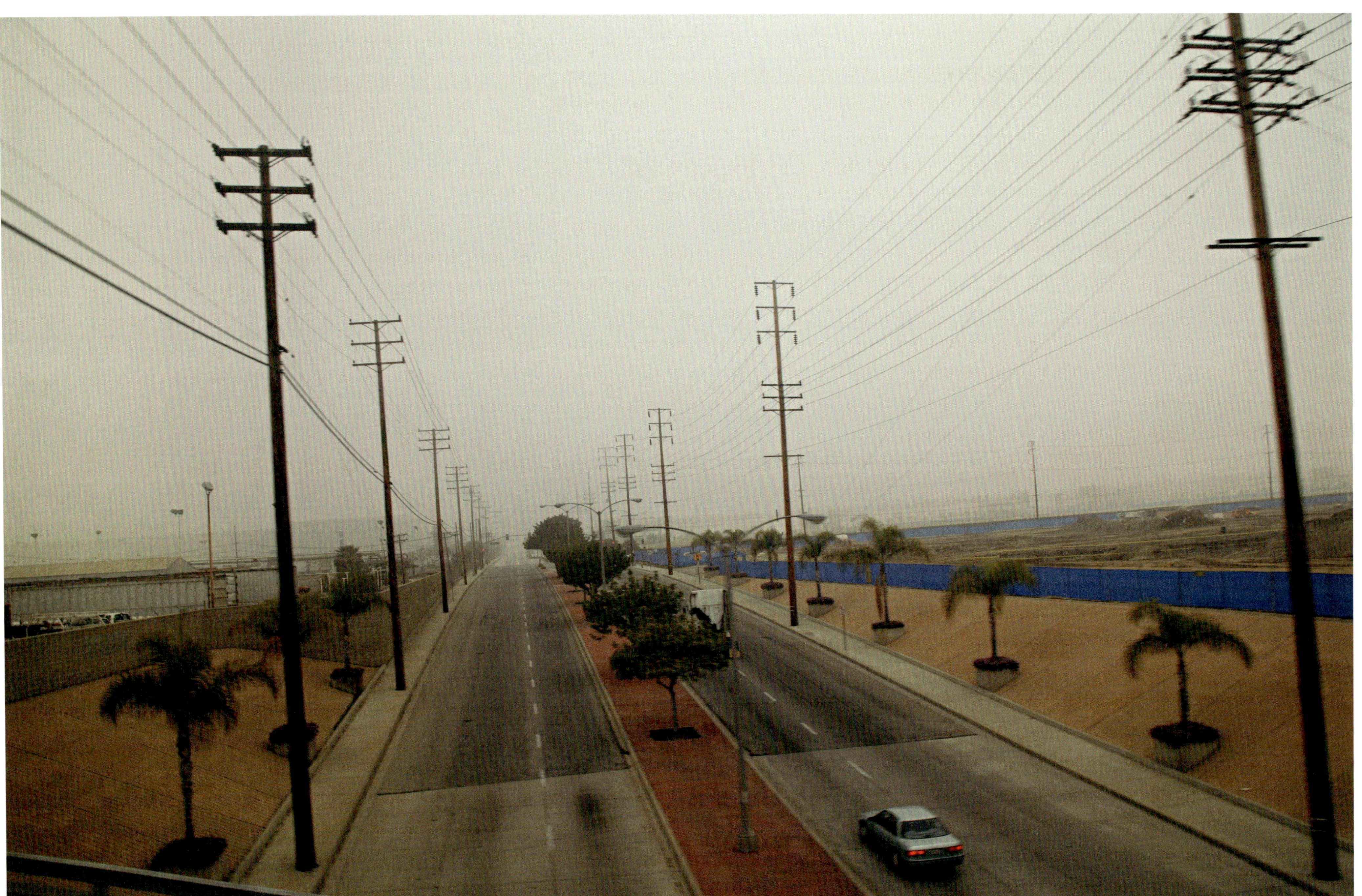
California, USA

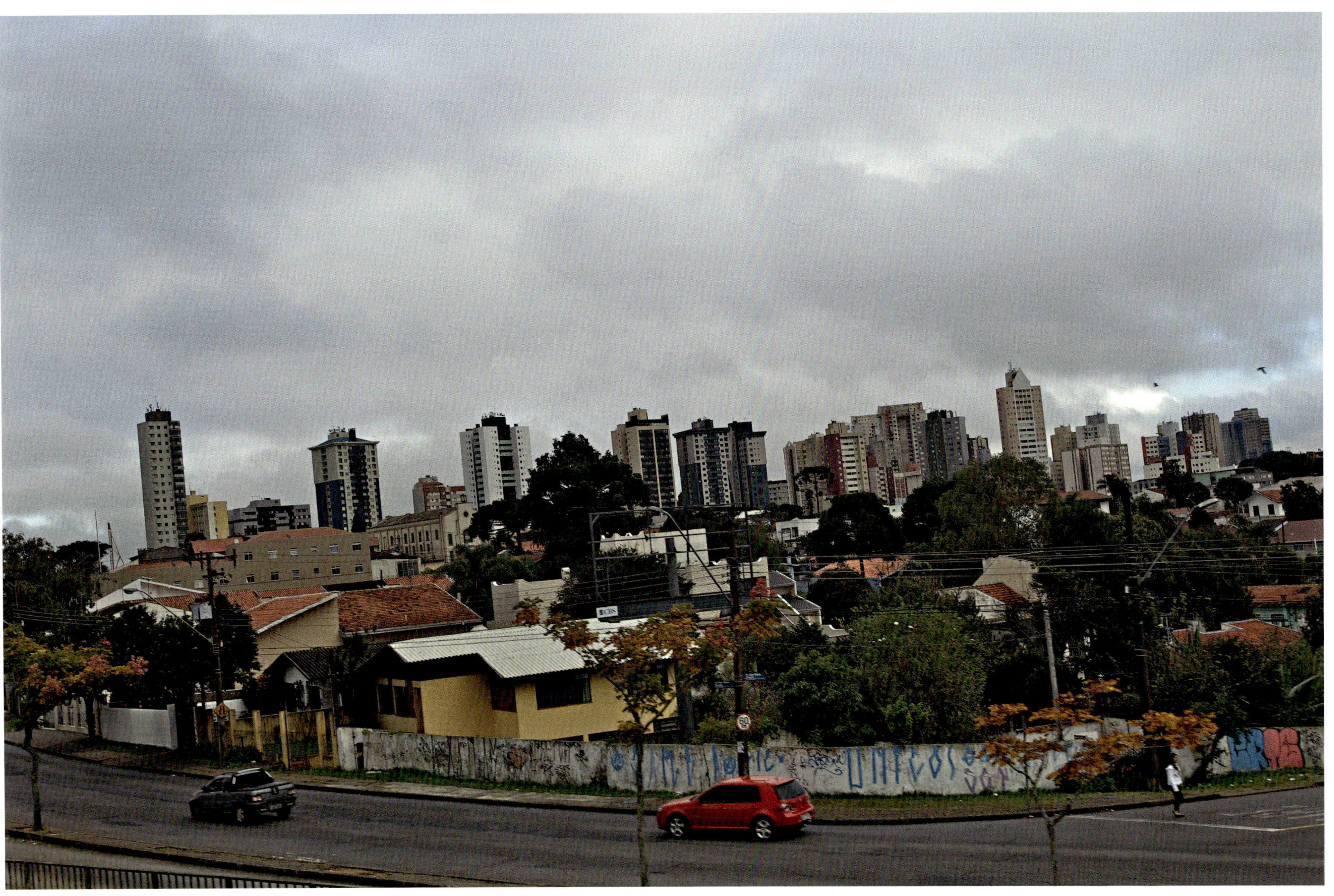

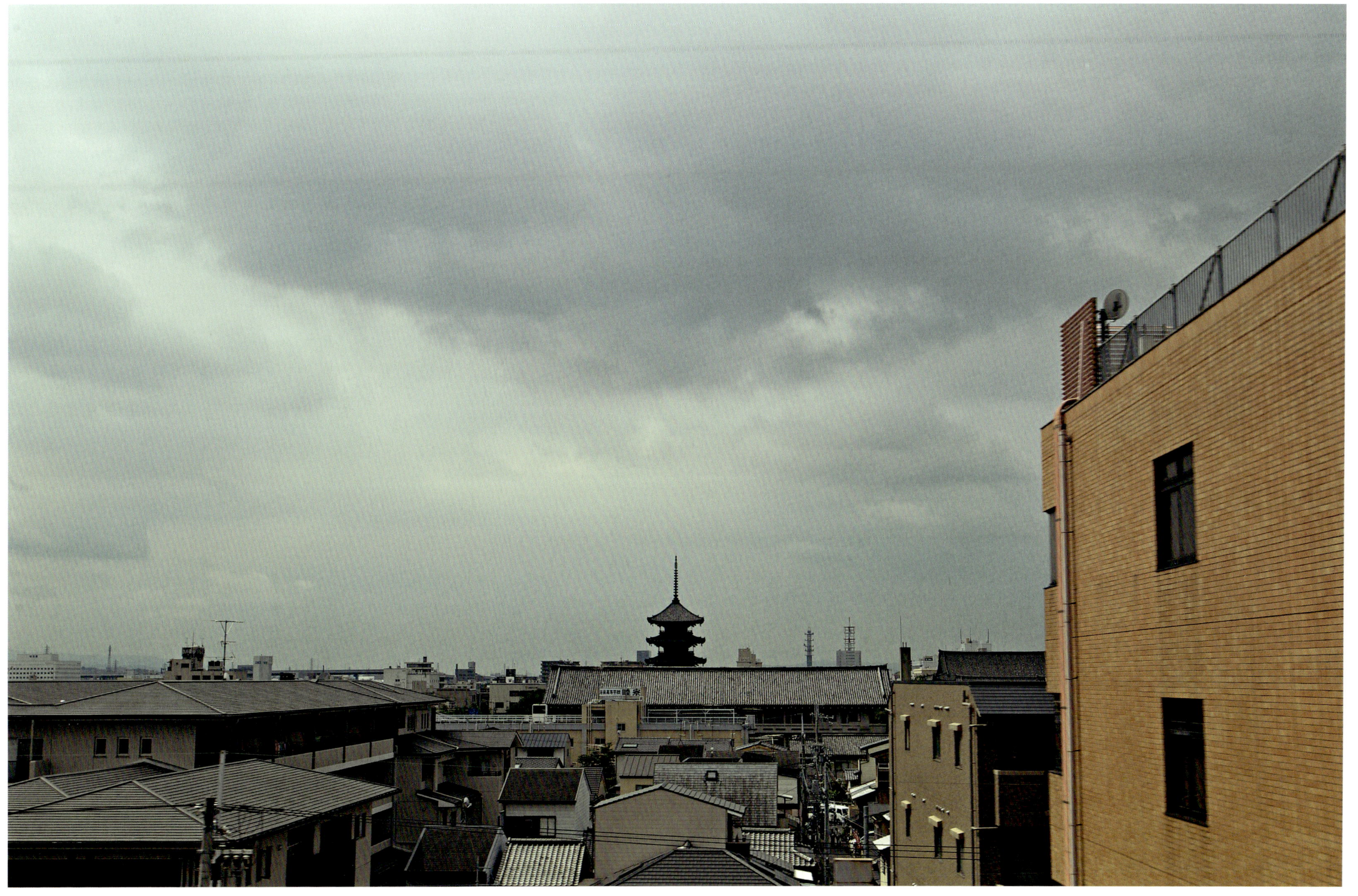
Japan

The first railroad in Japan opened in 1872 between Tokyo and Yokohama and was built by British engineers. Shortly afterwards, Japanese engineers began building railroads at a rapid rate, and their railways' expansion was promoted as part of national policy.

Japan
Kiosk
NEWS
NEWS
長
Nagasaki
熊
本
Kumamoto
大
分
Oita
宮
崎
Miyazaki
鹿
児
島
Kagoshima
21

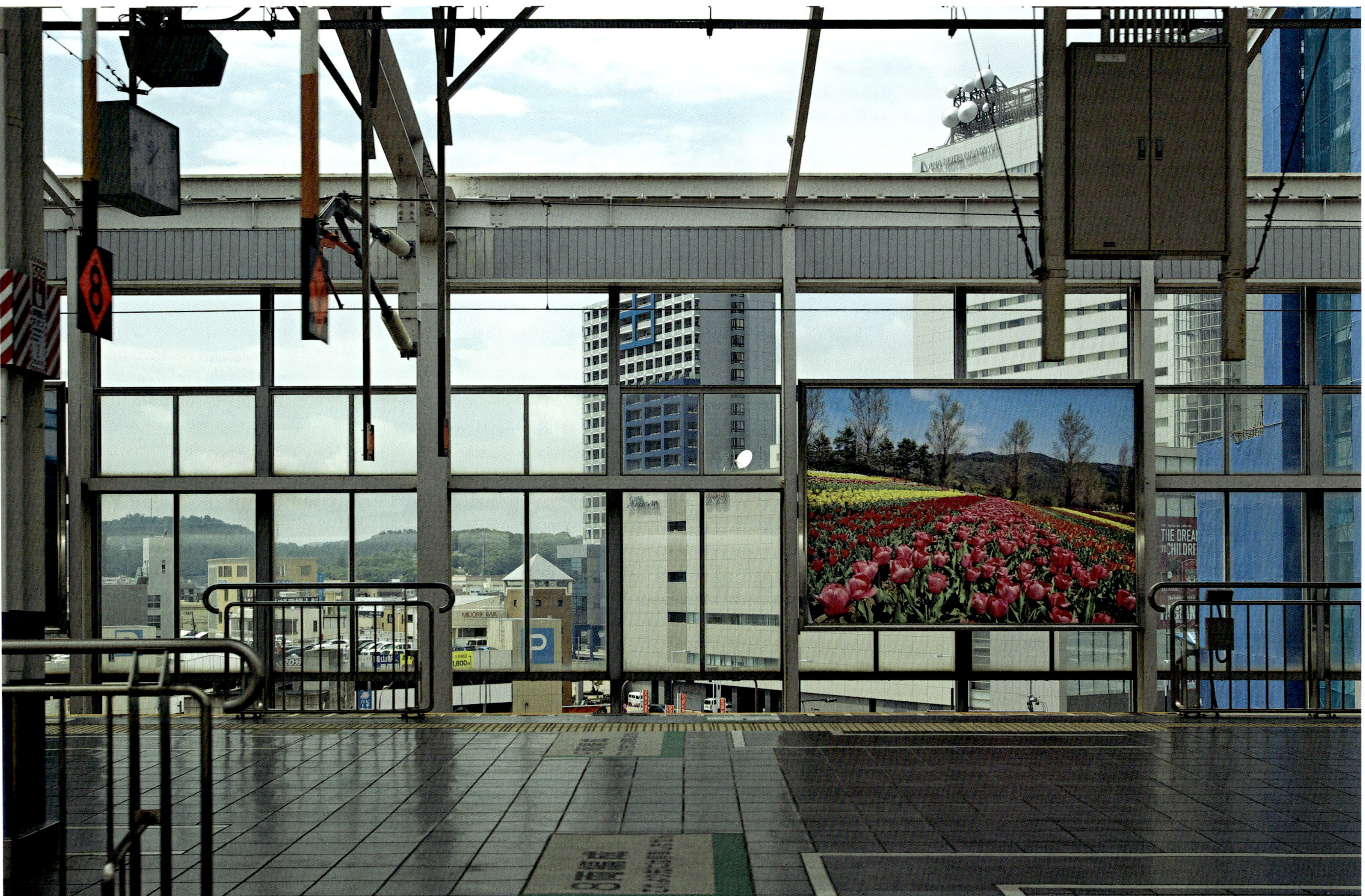
Japan

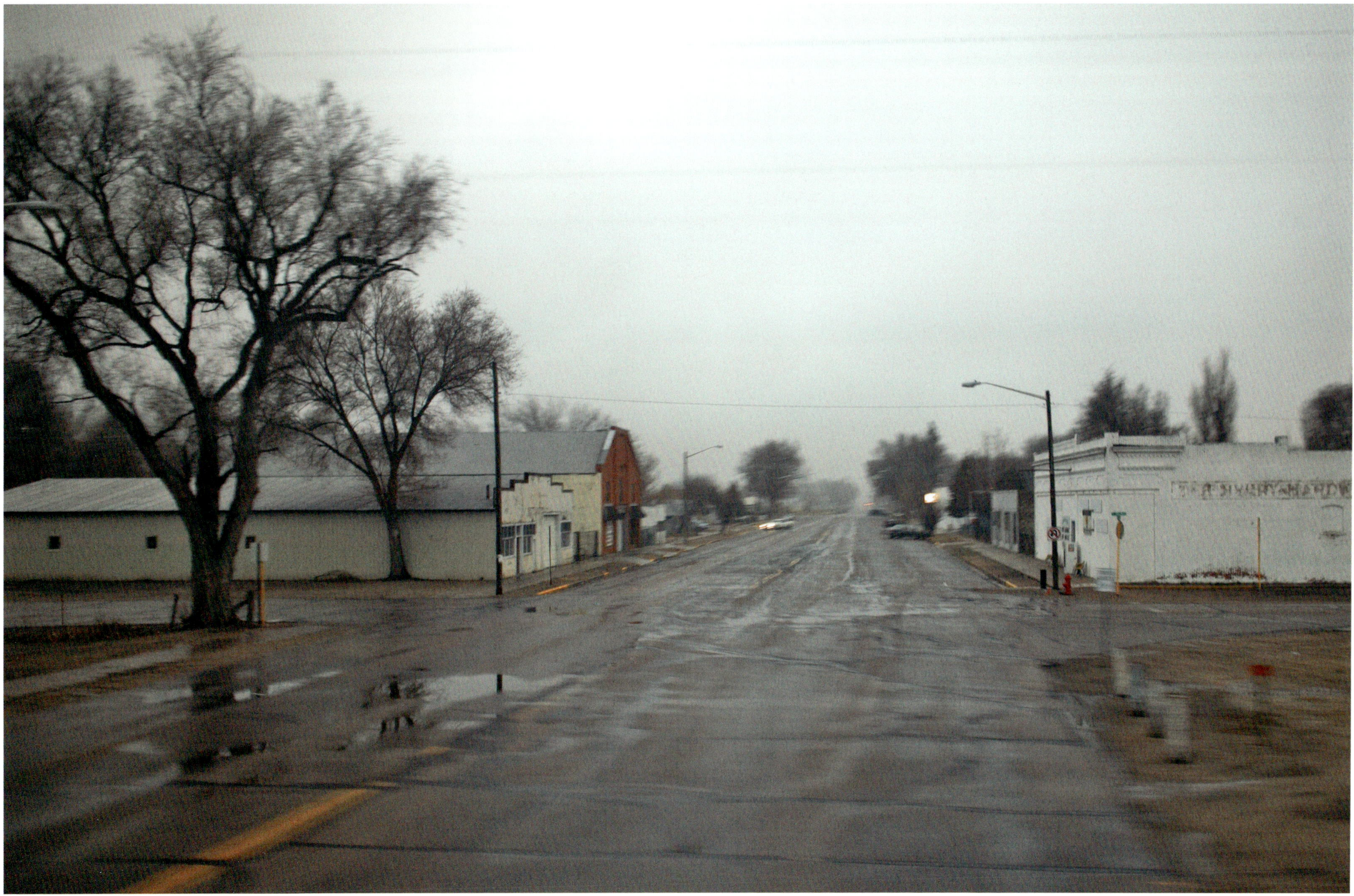
North Dakota, USA

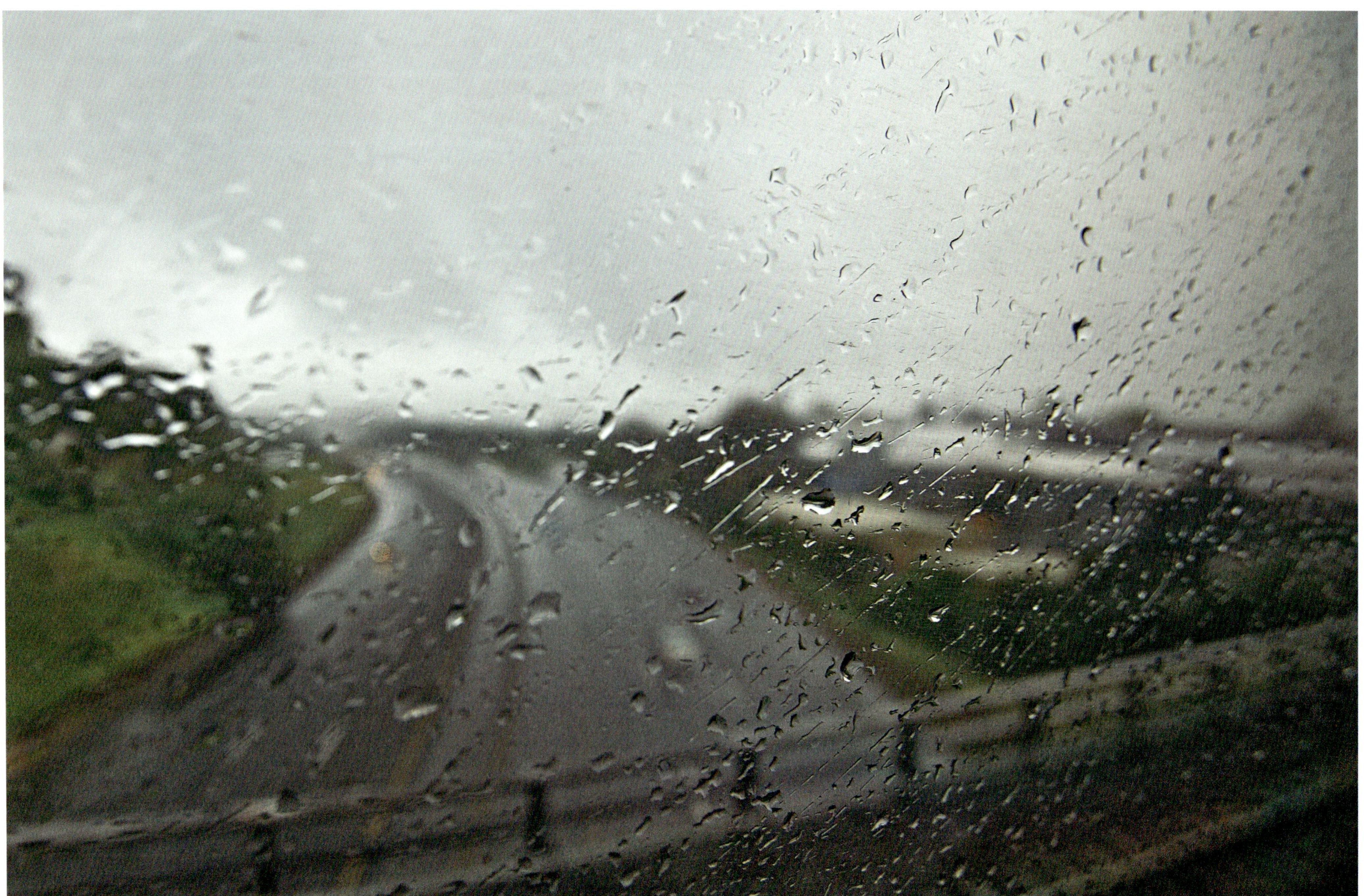
Maine, USA

Peak mileage for US railroads occurred in 1916, with 408,833 km / 254,037 miles of track in use. Today total mileage is under 274,000 km / 170,000 miles.

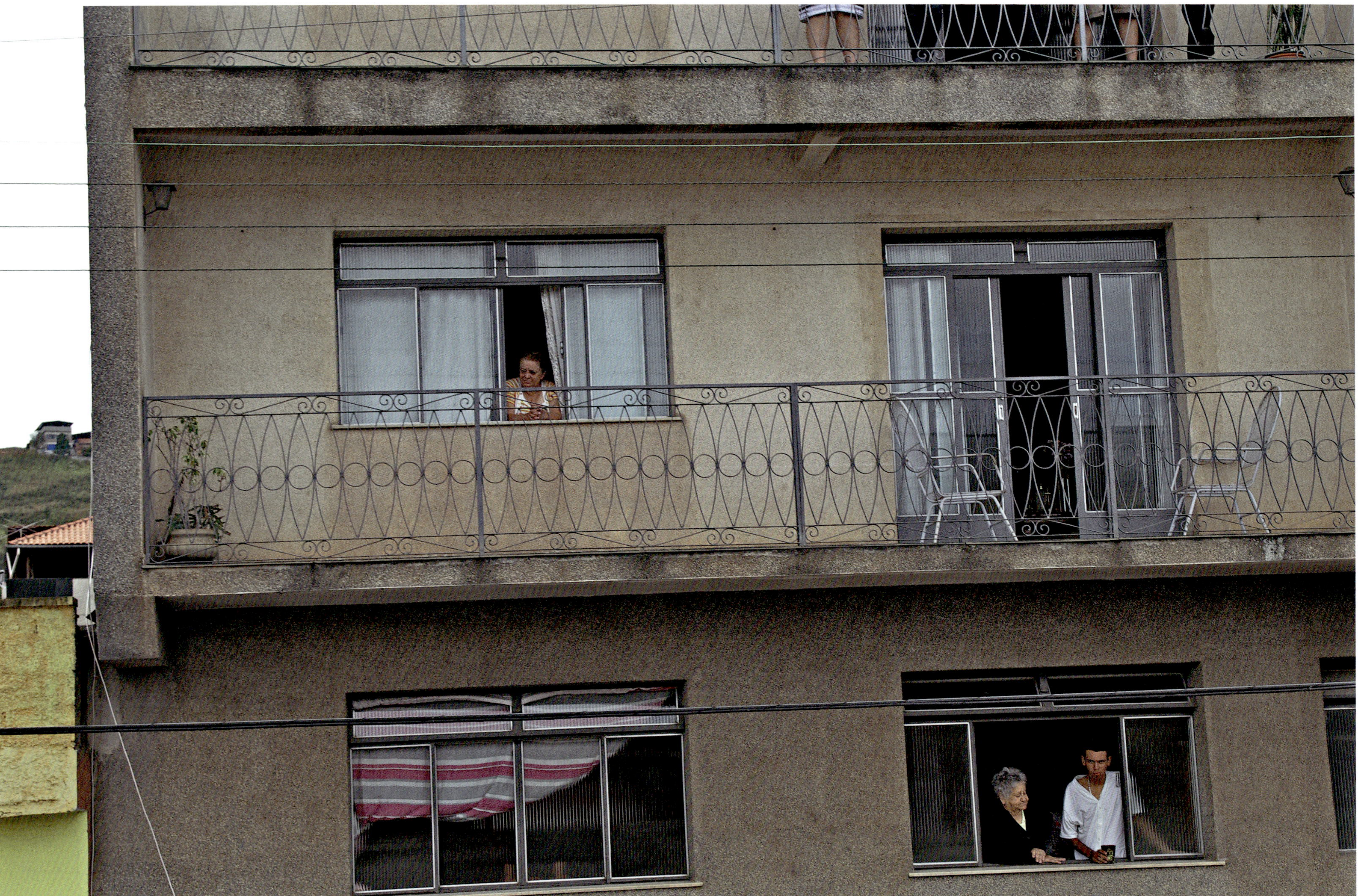

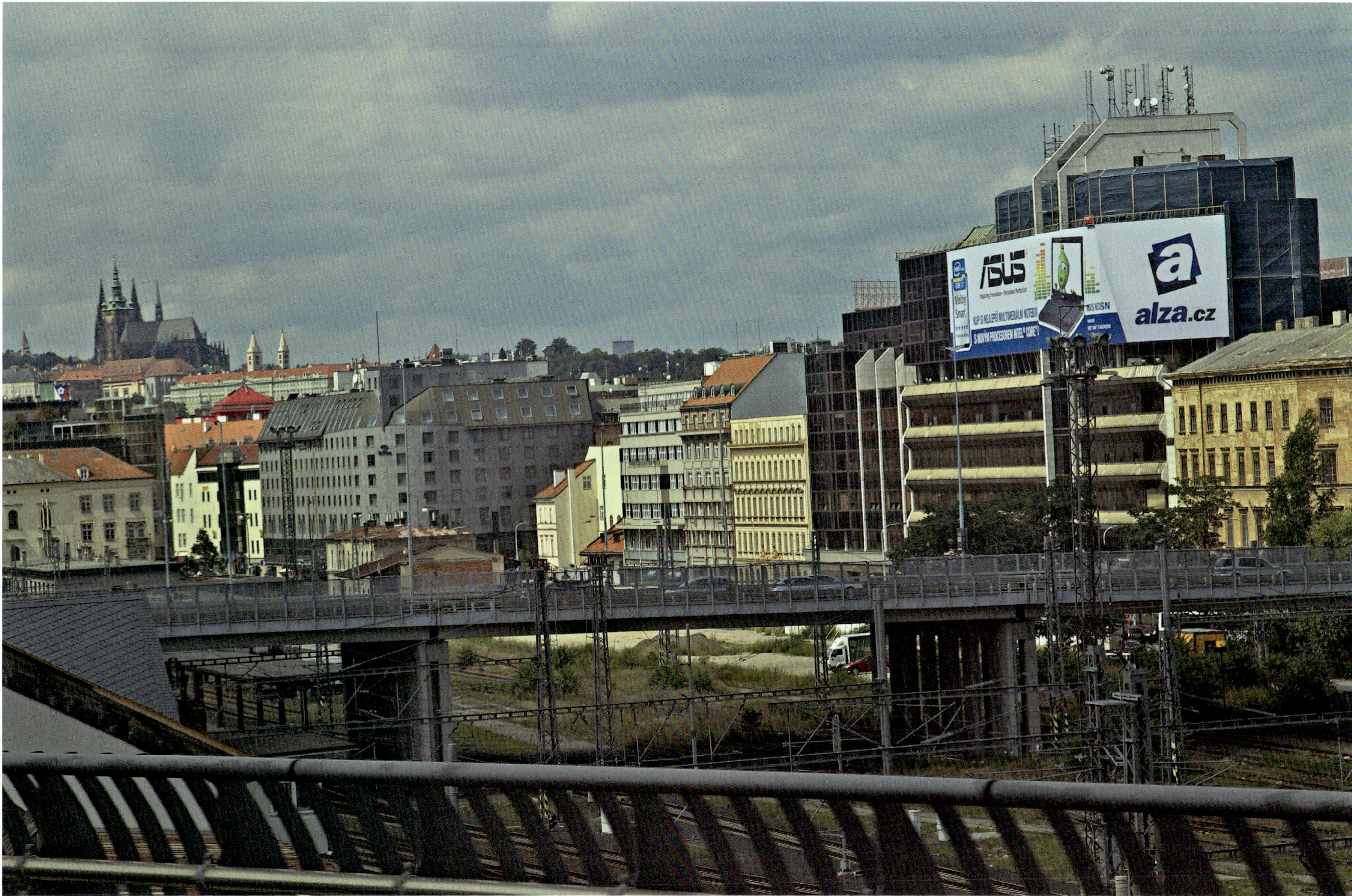

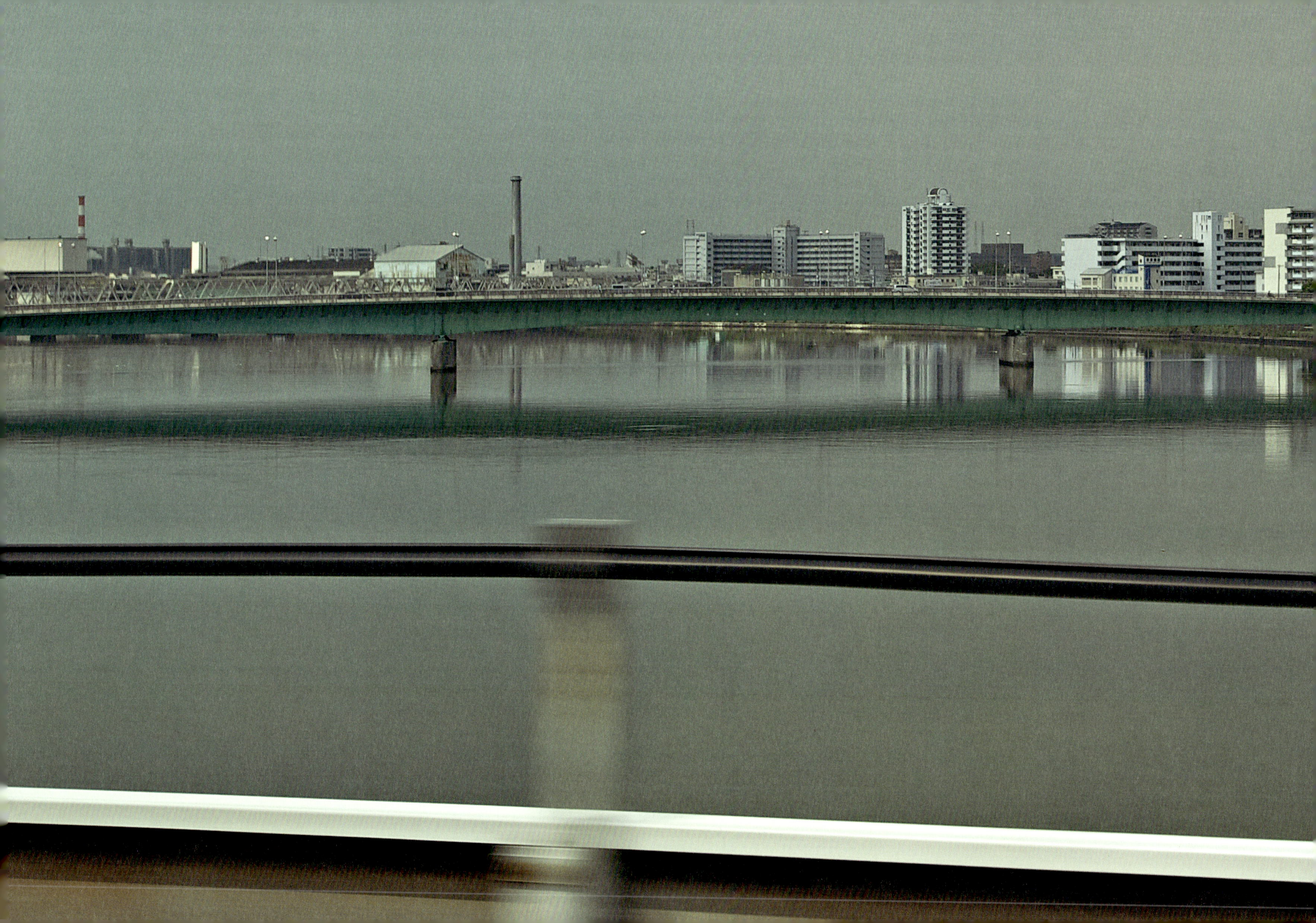

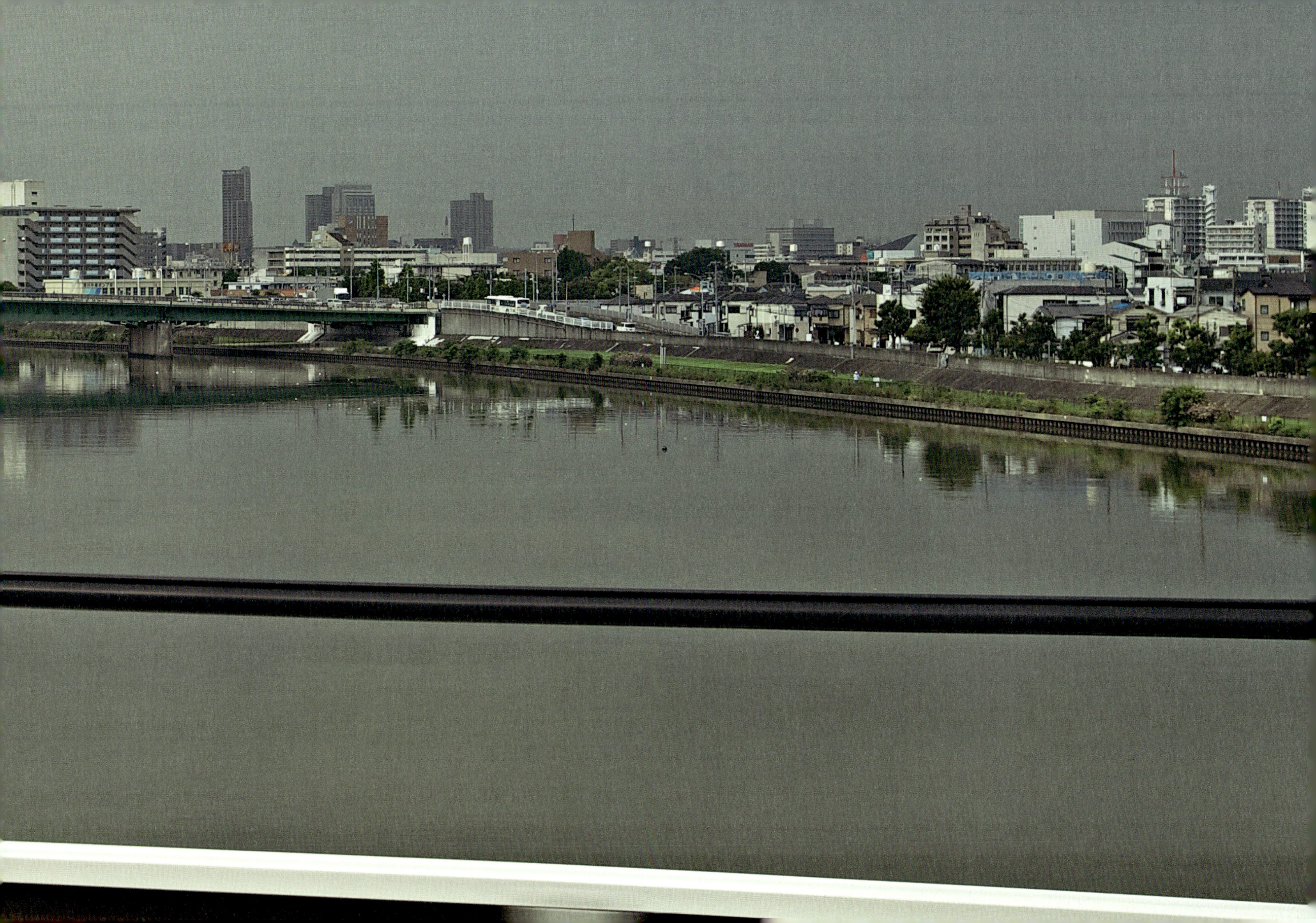

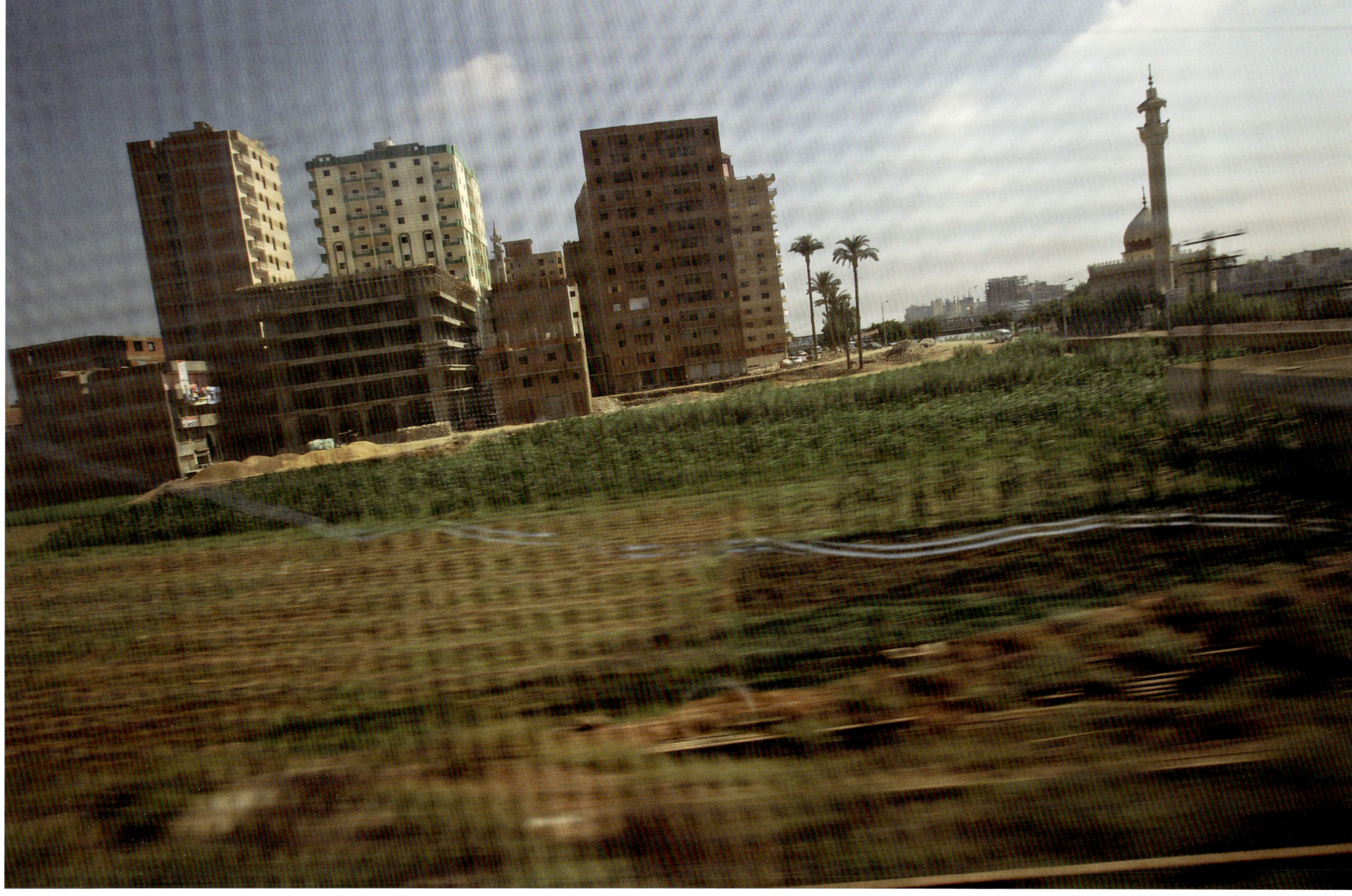

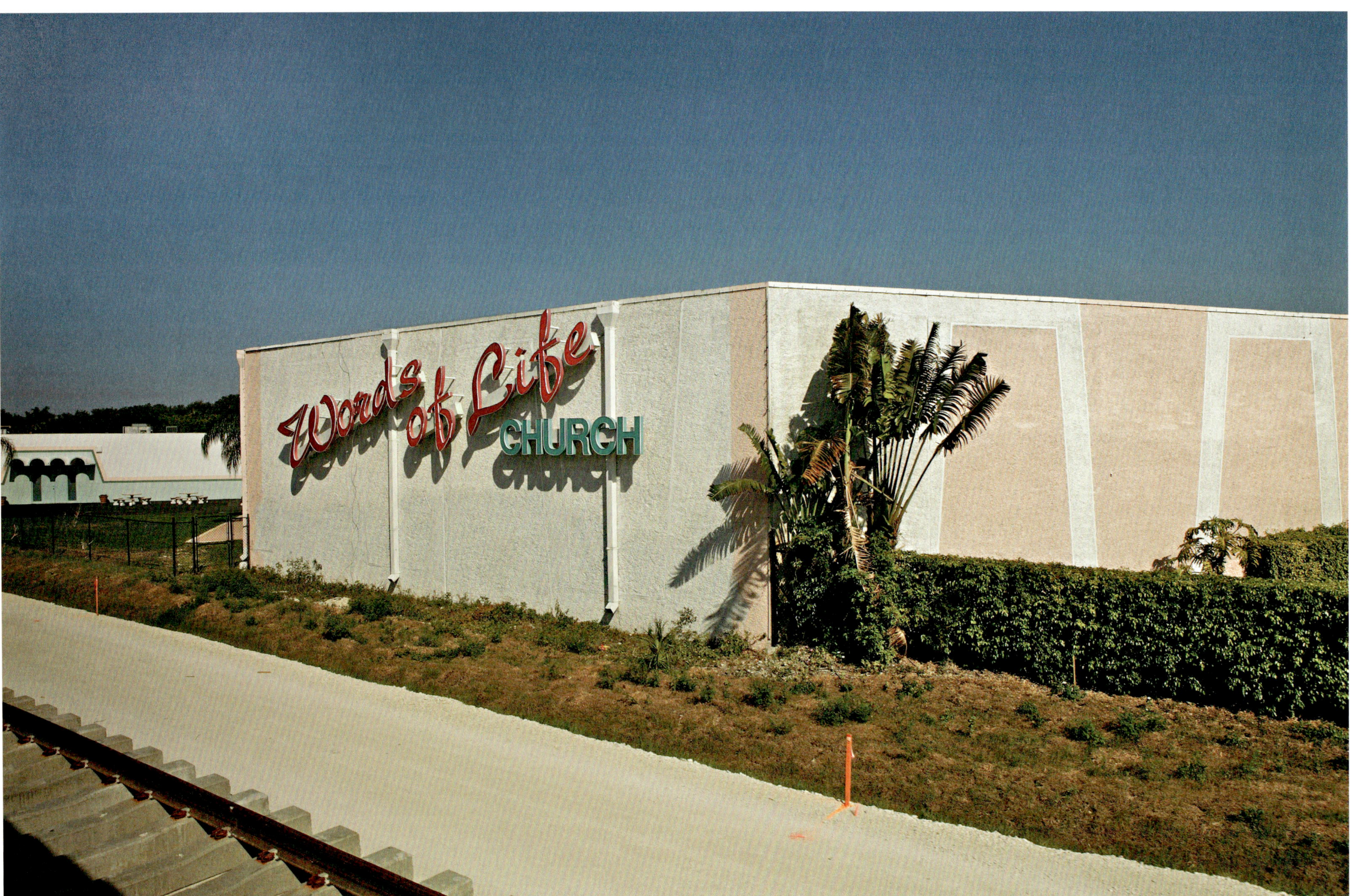

Words of Life
CHURCH

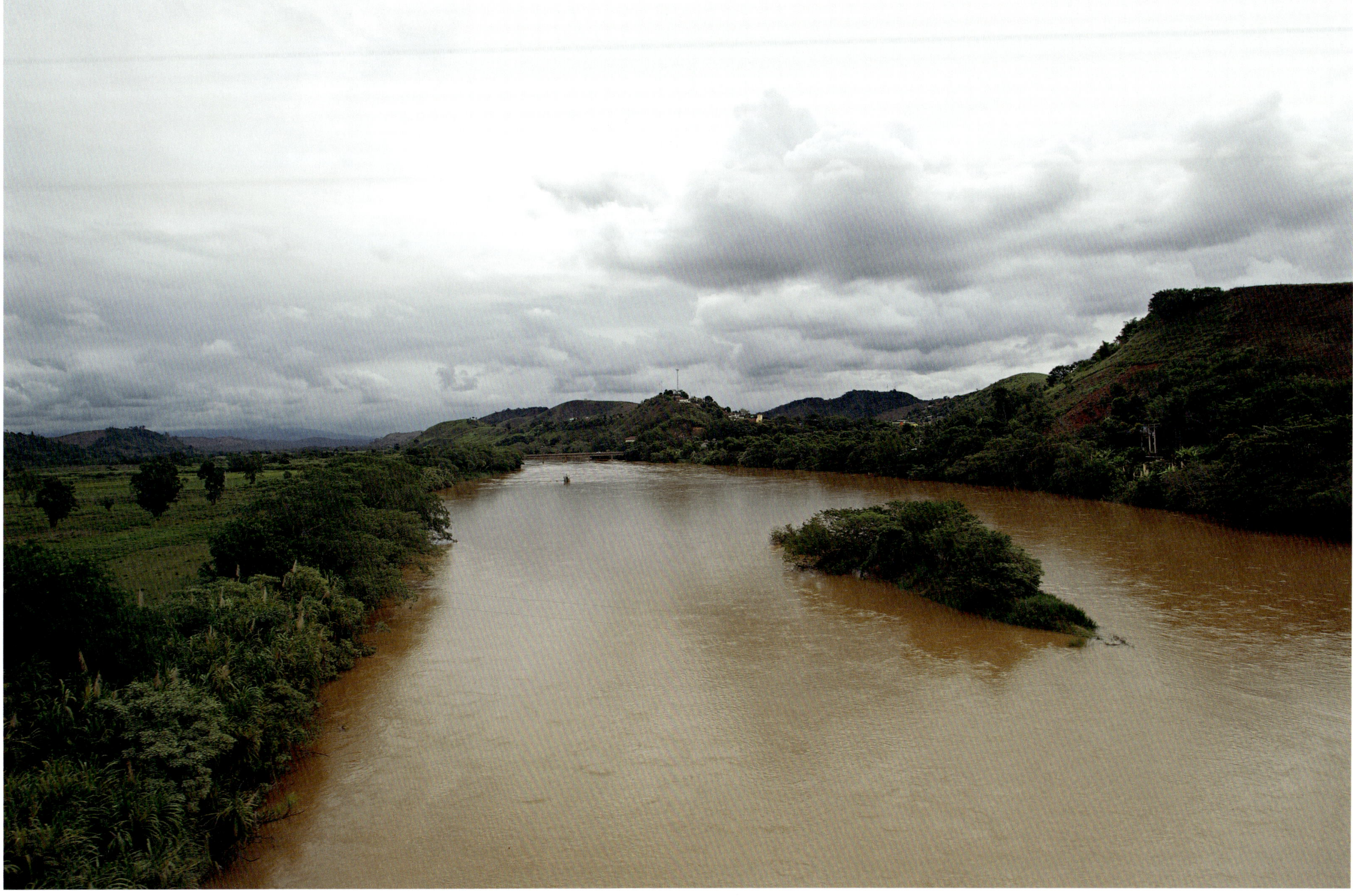

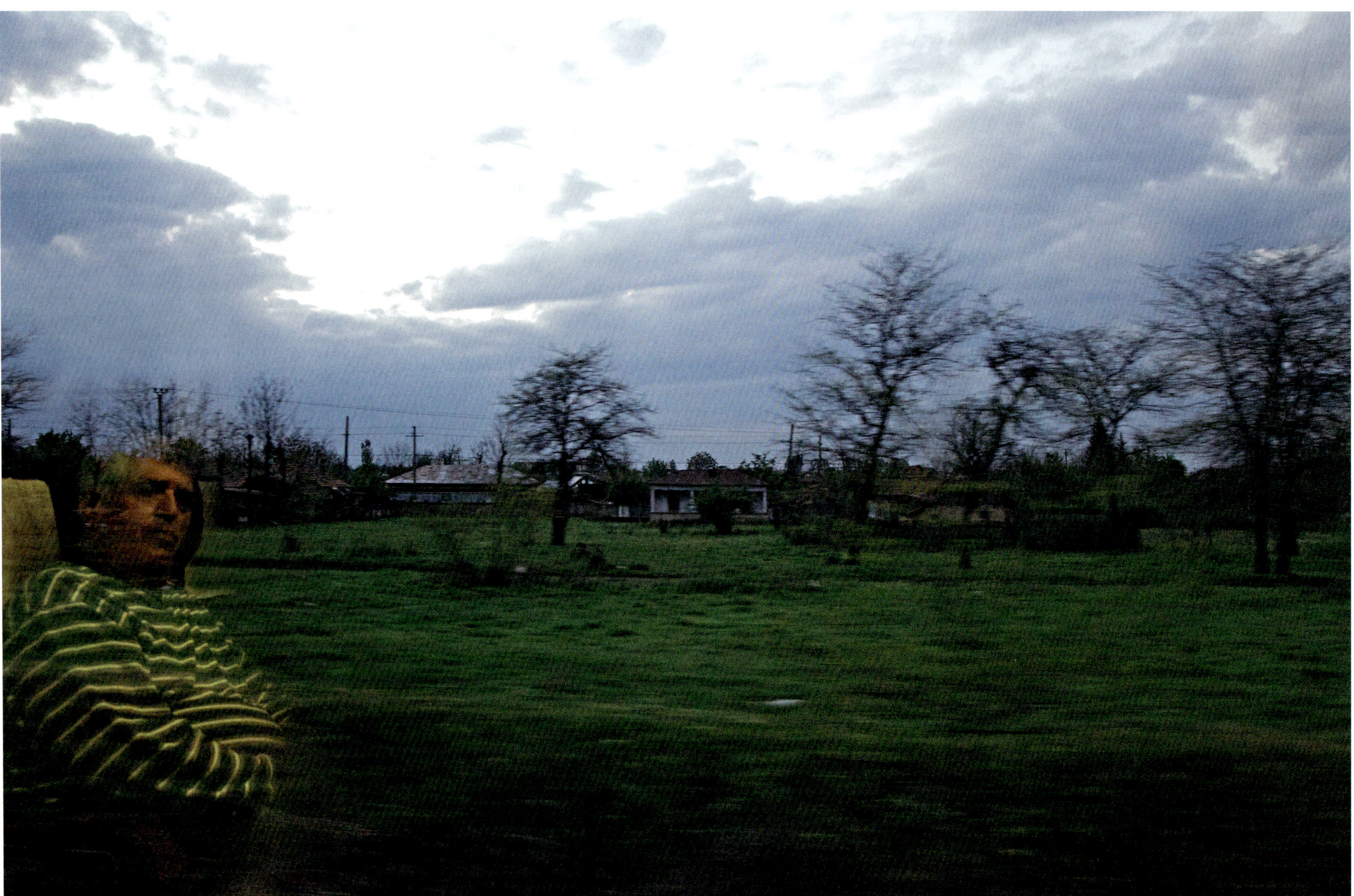

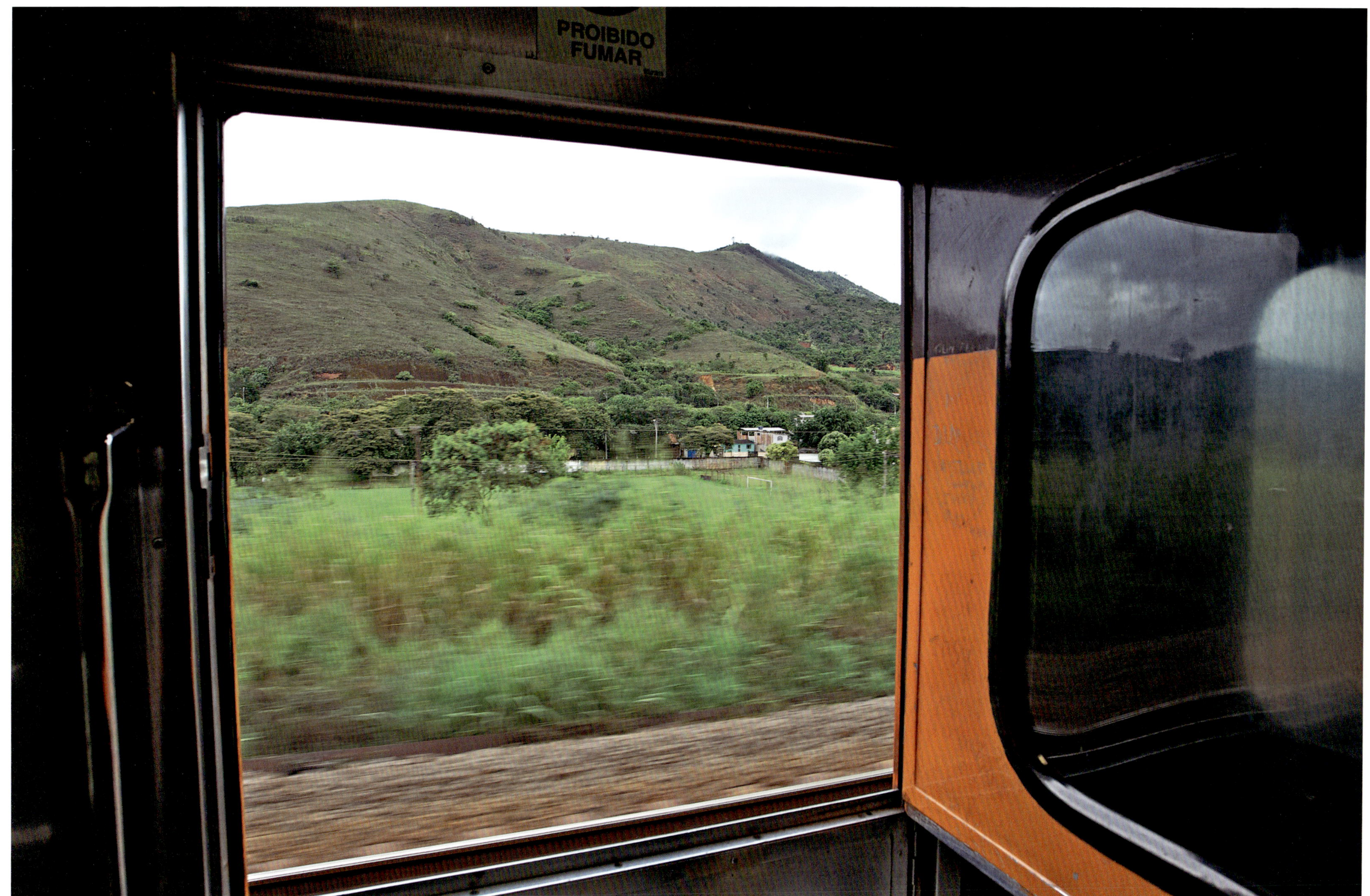

Brazil

Launched in 1964 in Japan and today carrying more than 150 million people a year, the 'Shinkansen' line, or Bullet Train, is considered to be the most advanced rail system in the world. The 515 km / 320 mile Tokaido Shinkansen Line connecting Tokyo and Osaka runs at an average speed of 274 kph / 170 mph. With a train every 20 minutes, it has so far carried almost five billion passengers. Today it is still the flagship for high-speed rail, as well as the most heavily travelled high-speed passenger train line on the planet.

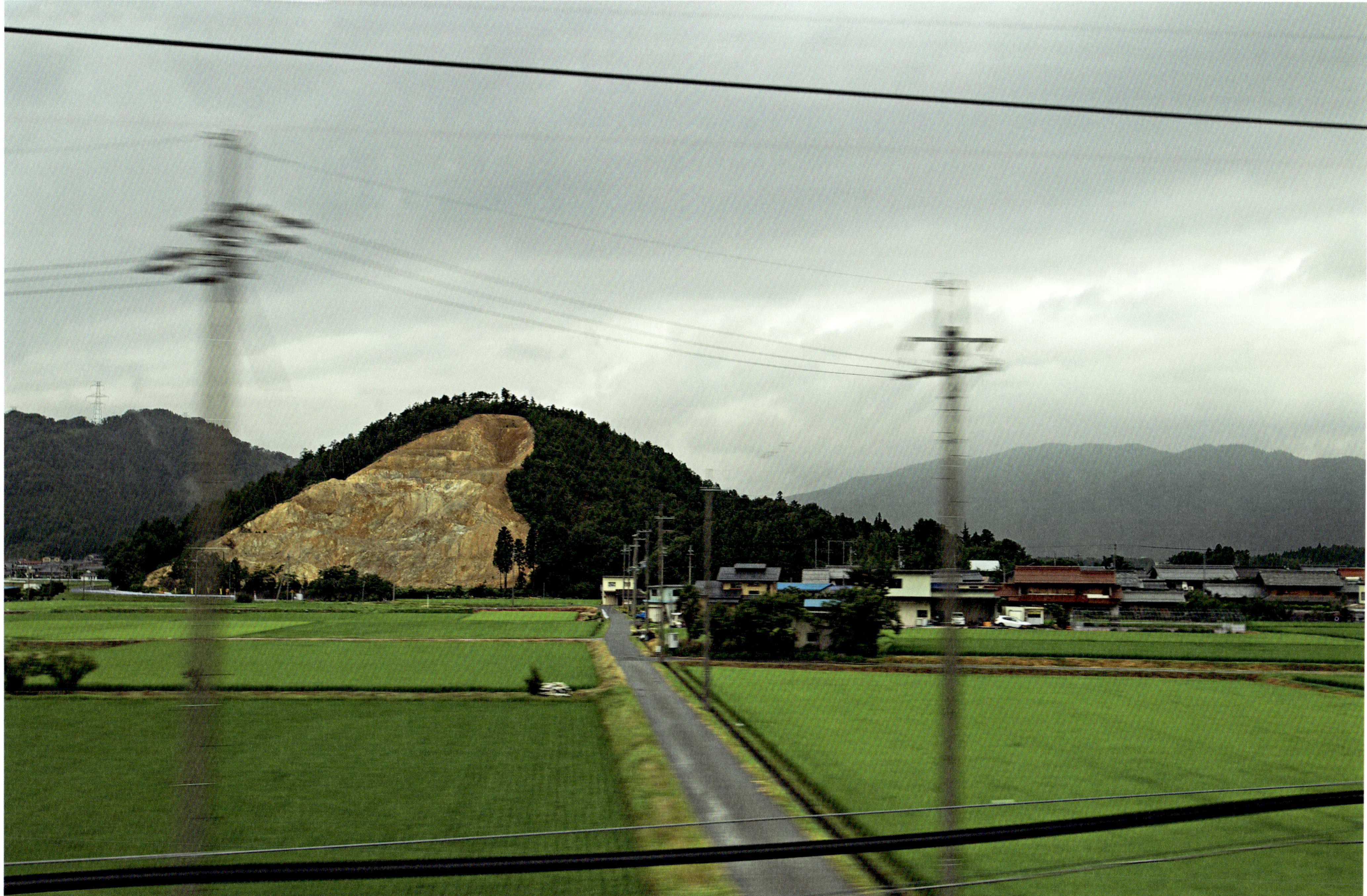

Following pages: United Kingdom

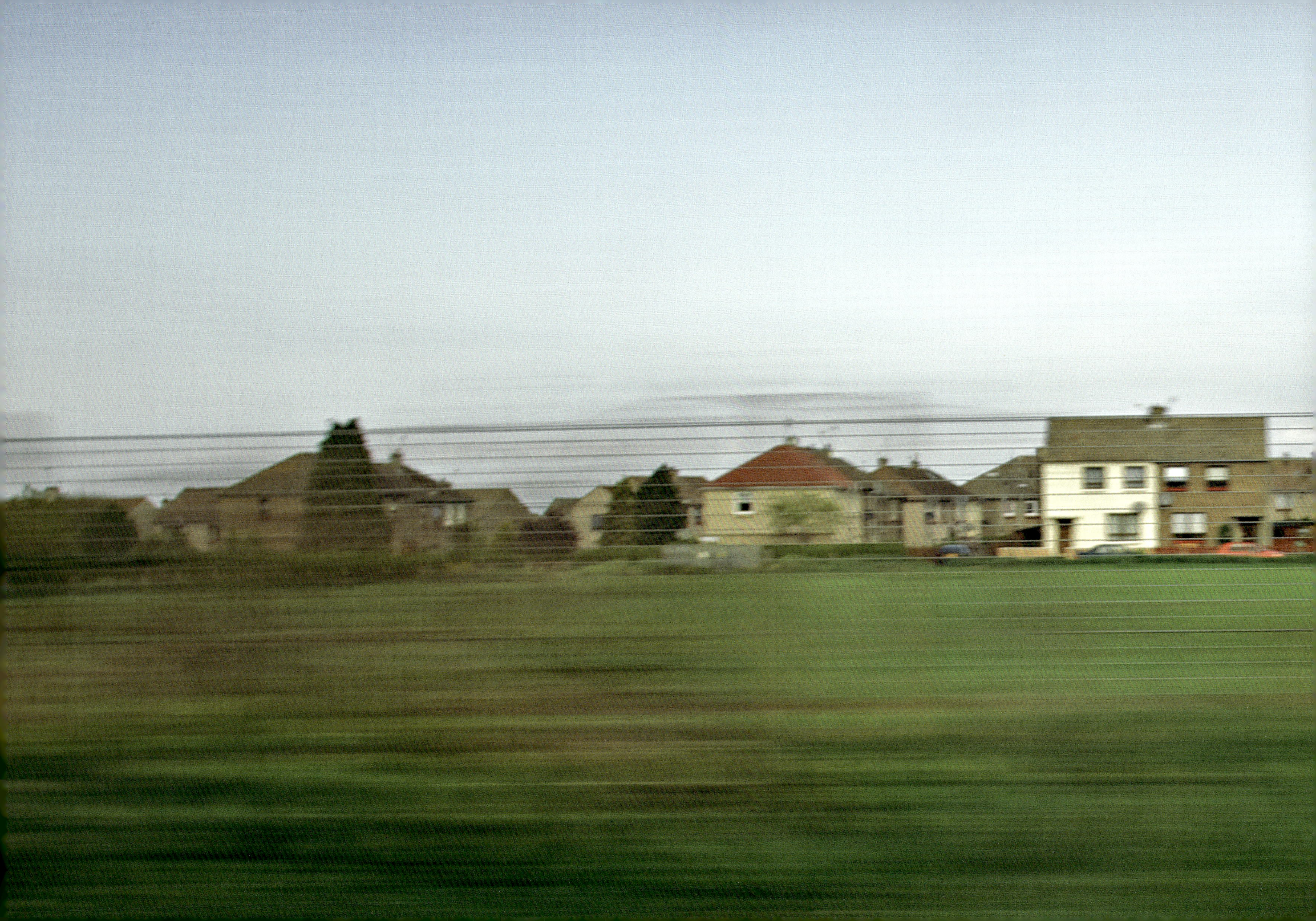

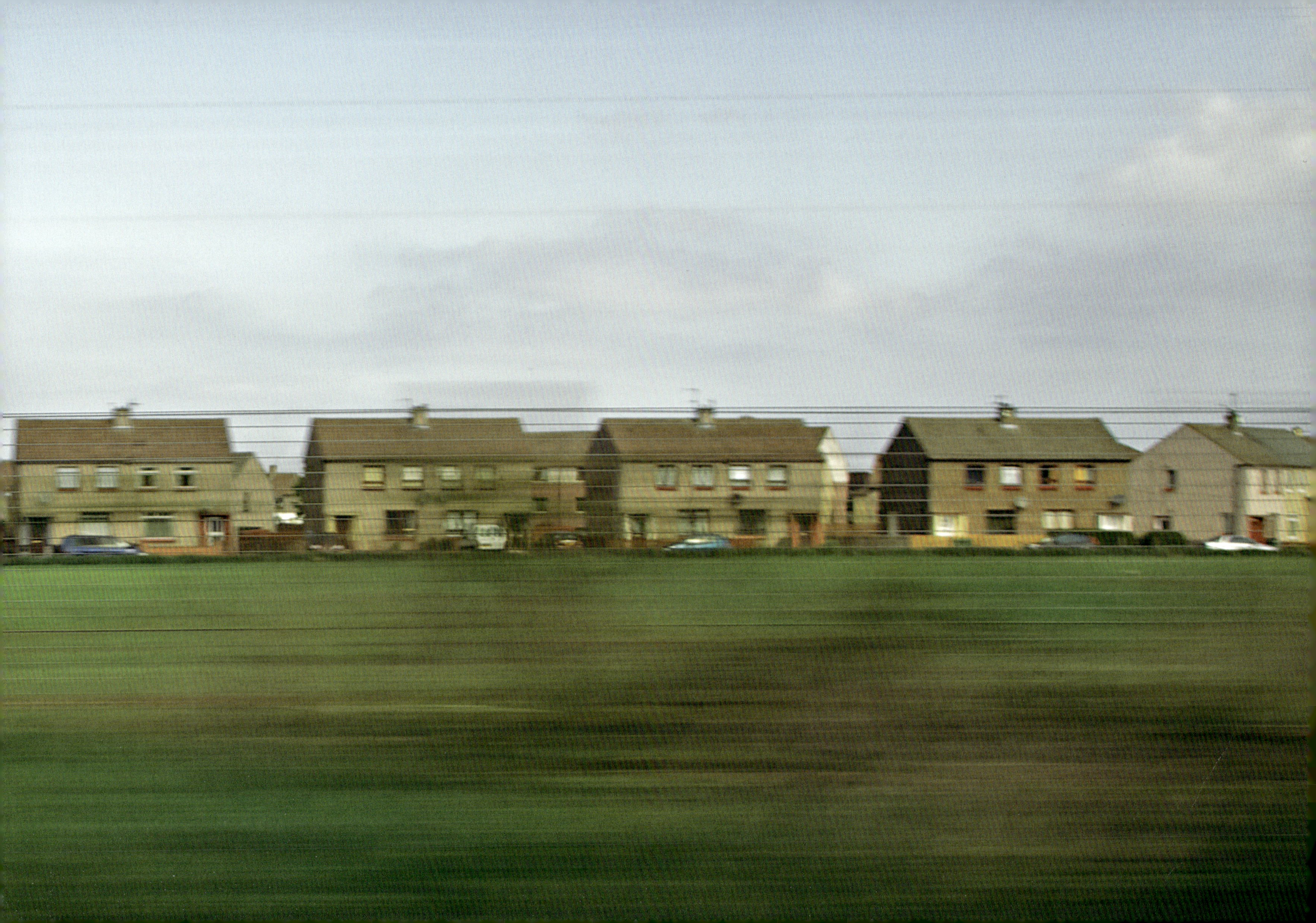

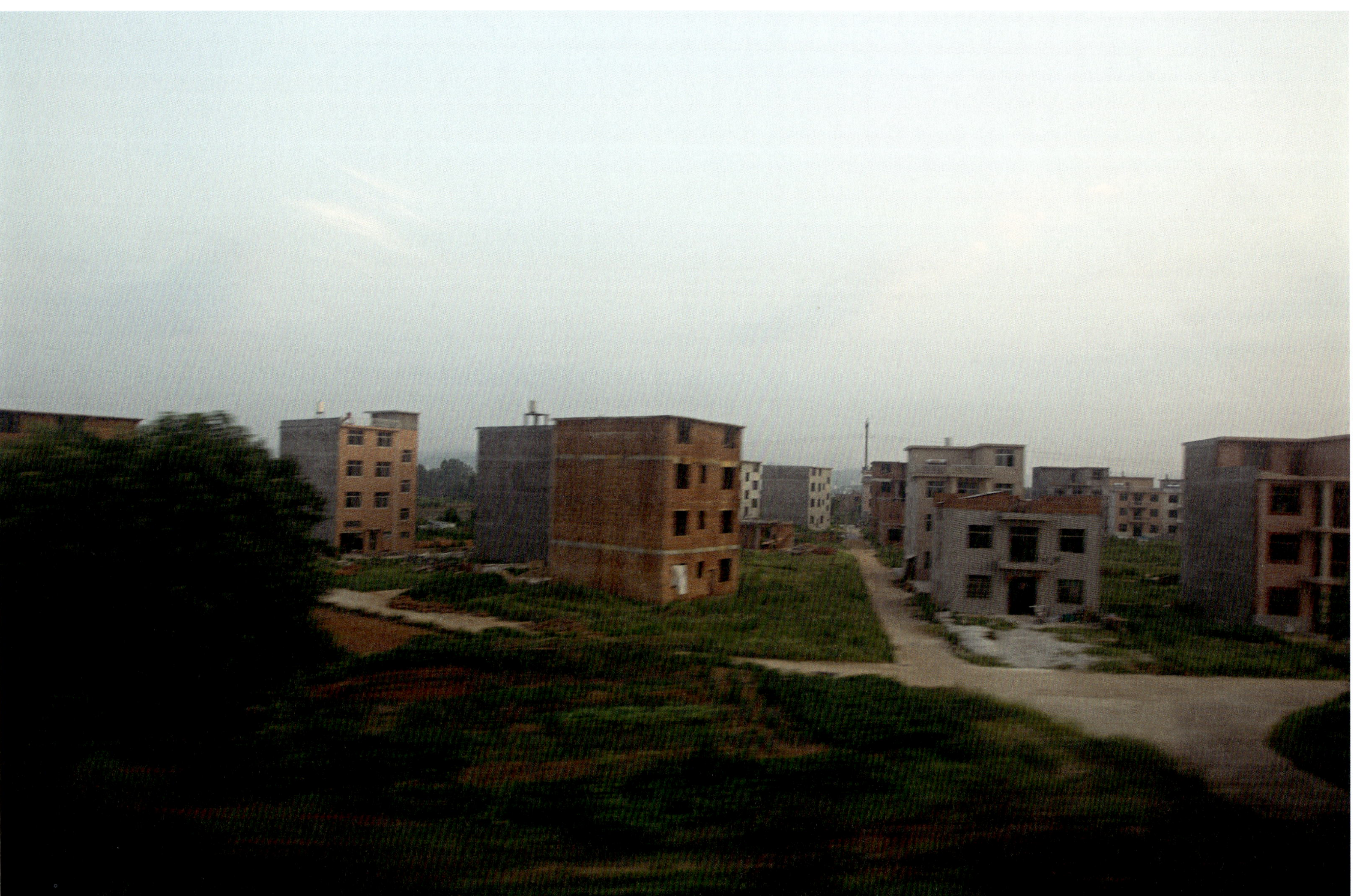

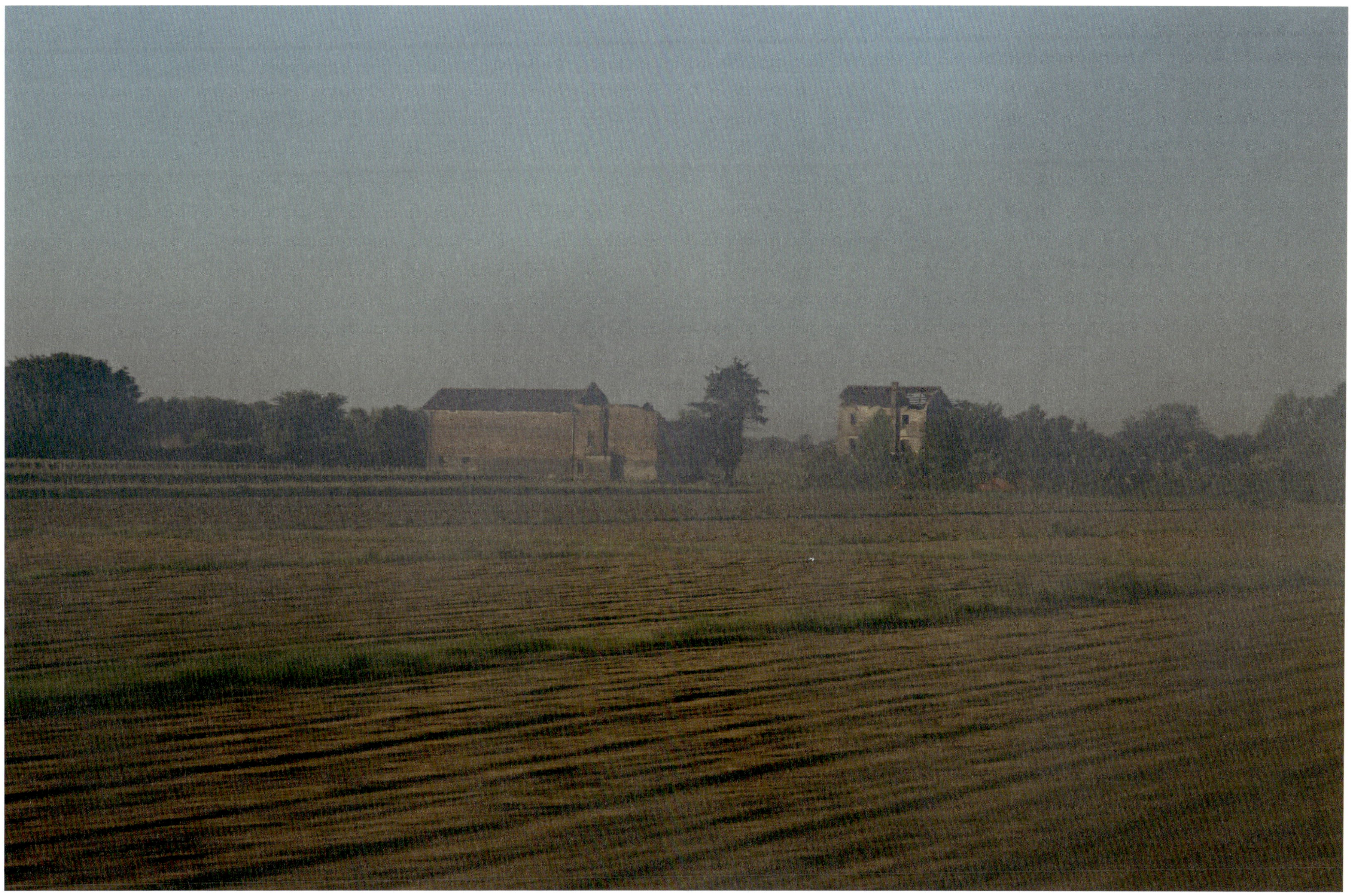

Italy

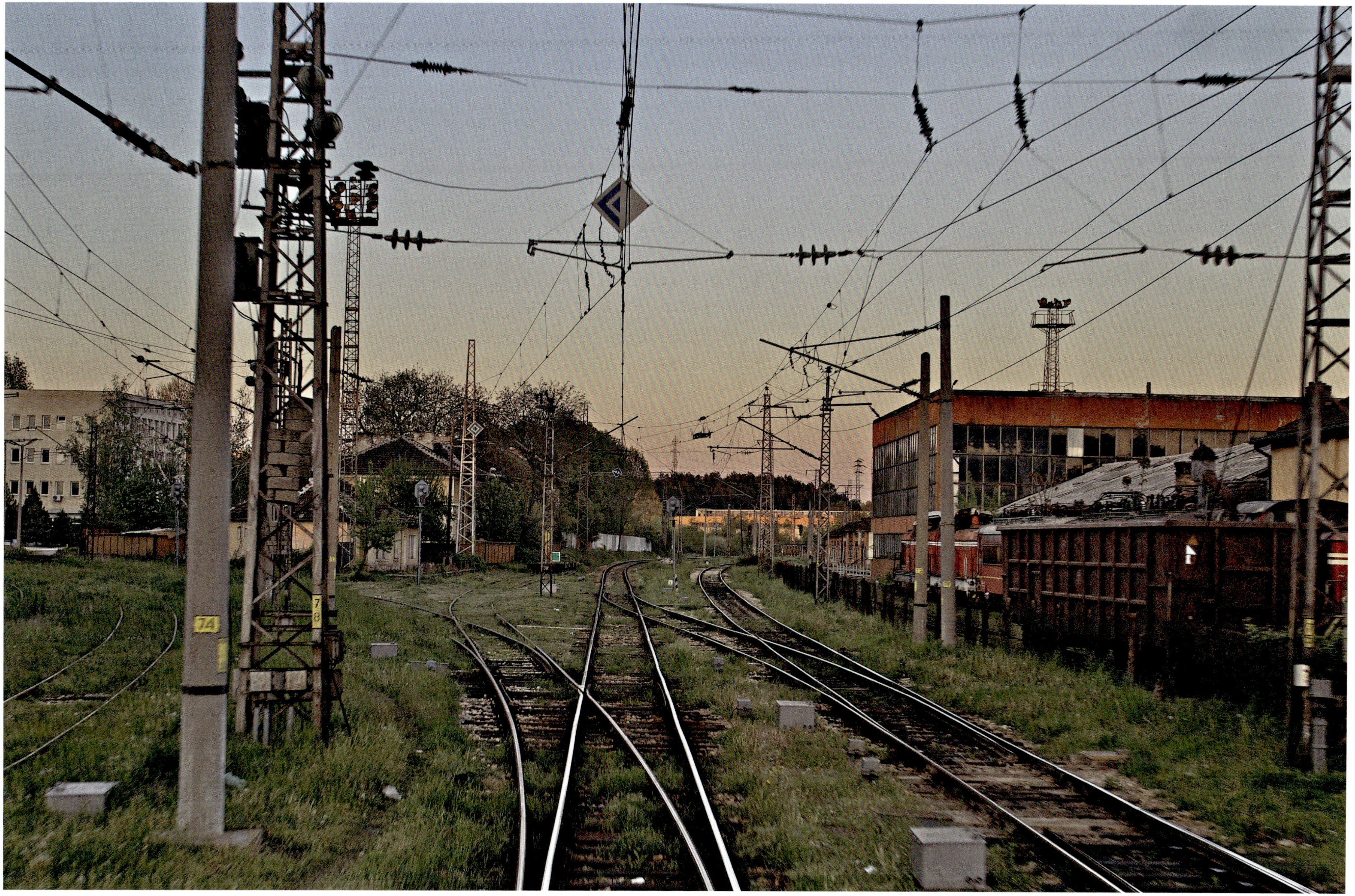

Bulgaria

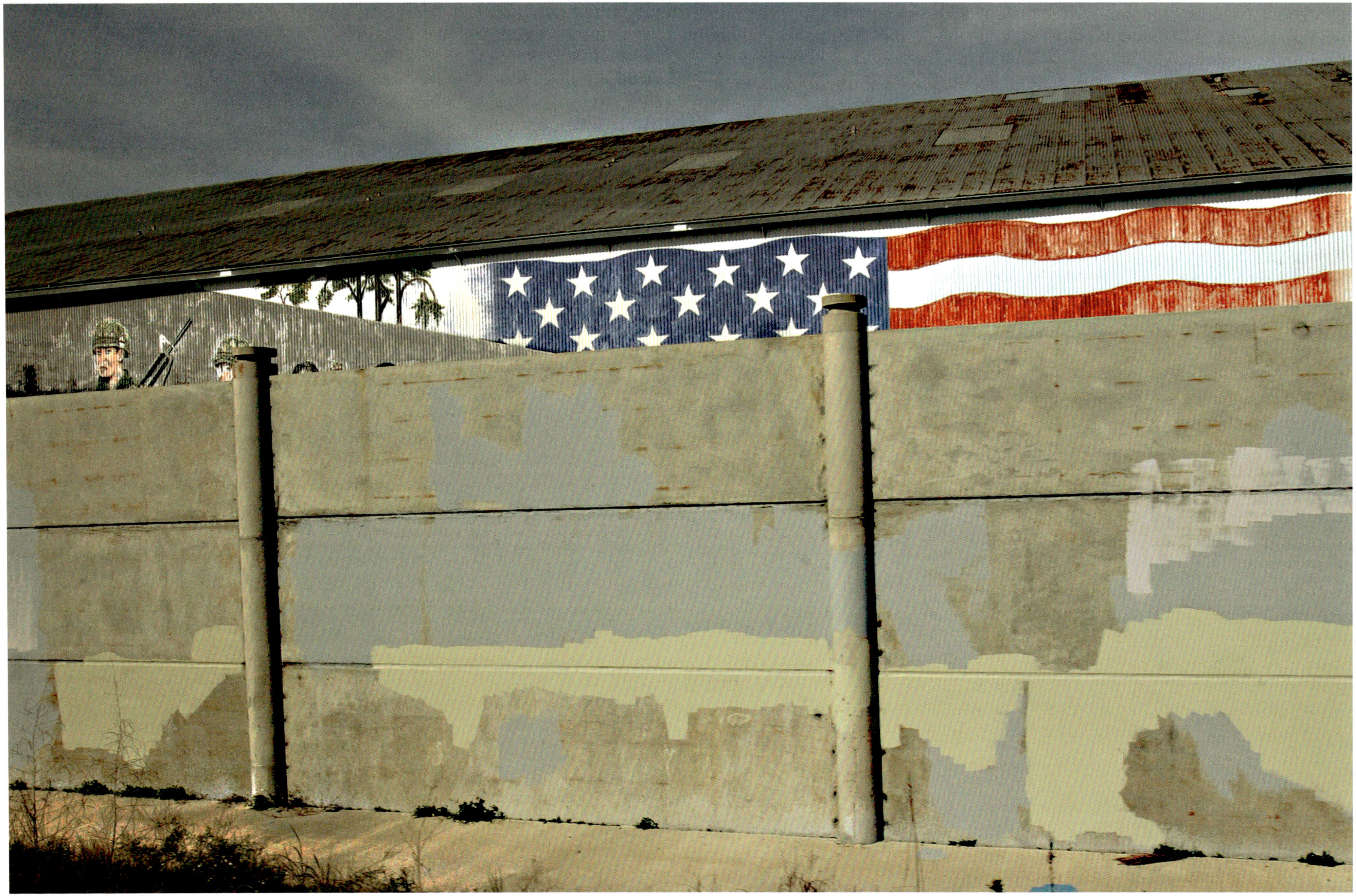

New Orleans, Louisiana, USA

Venice, Italy

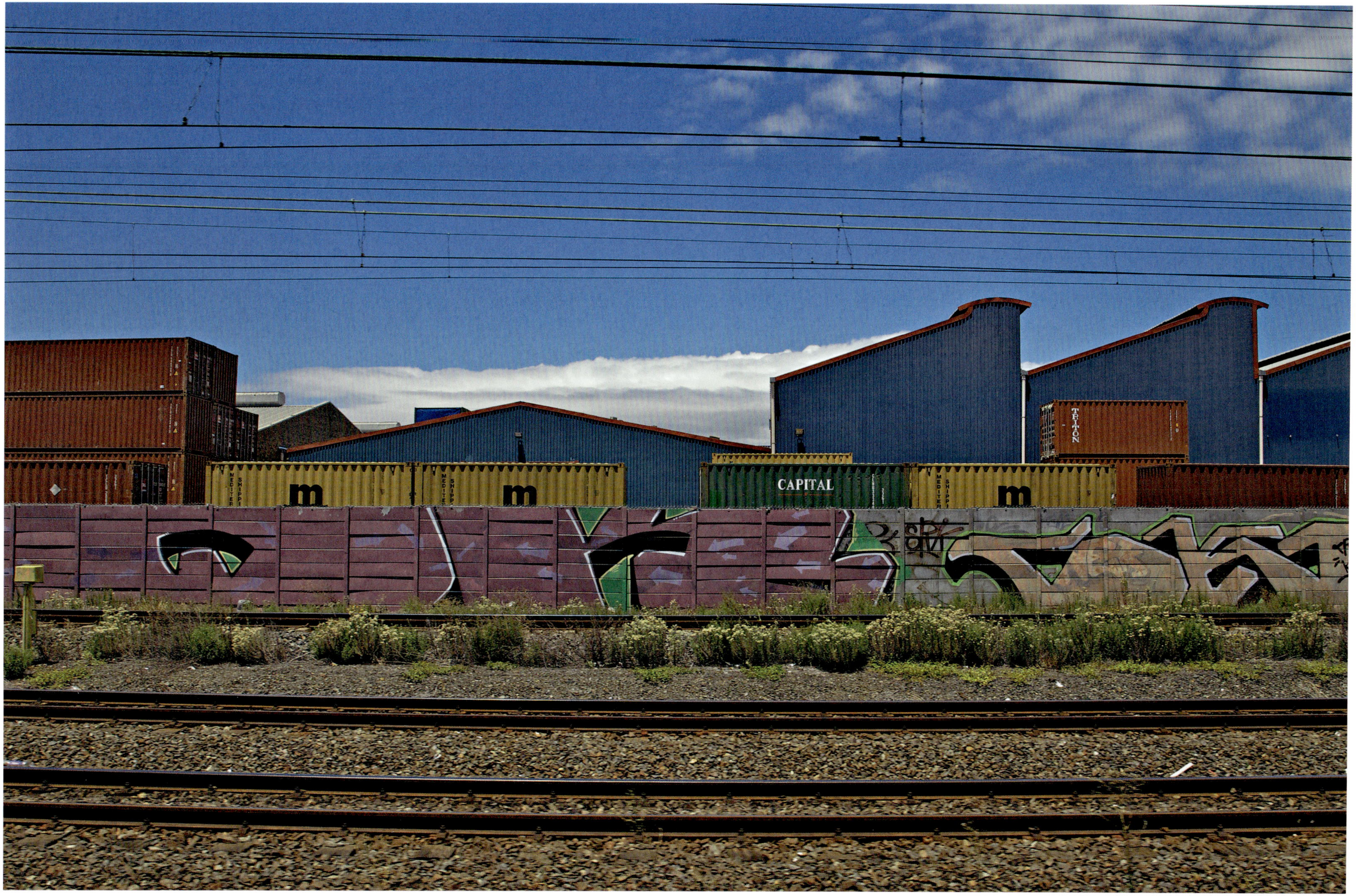

Cape Town, South Africa

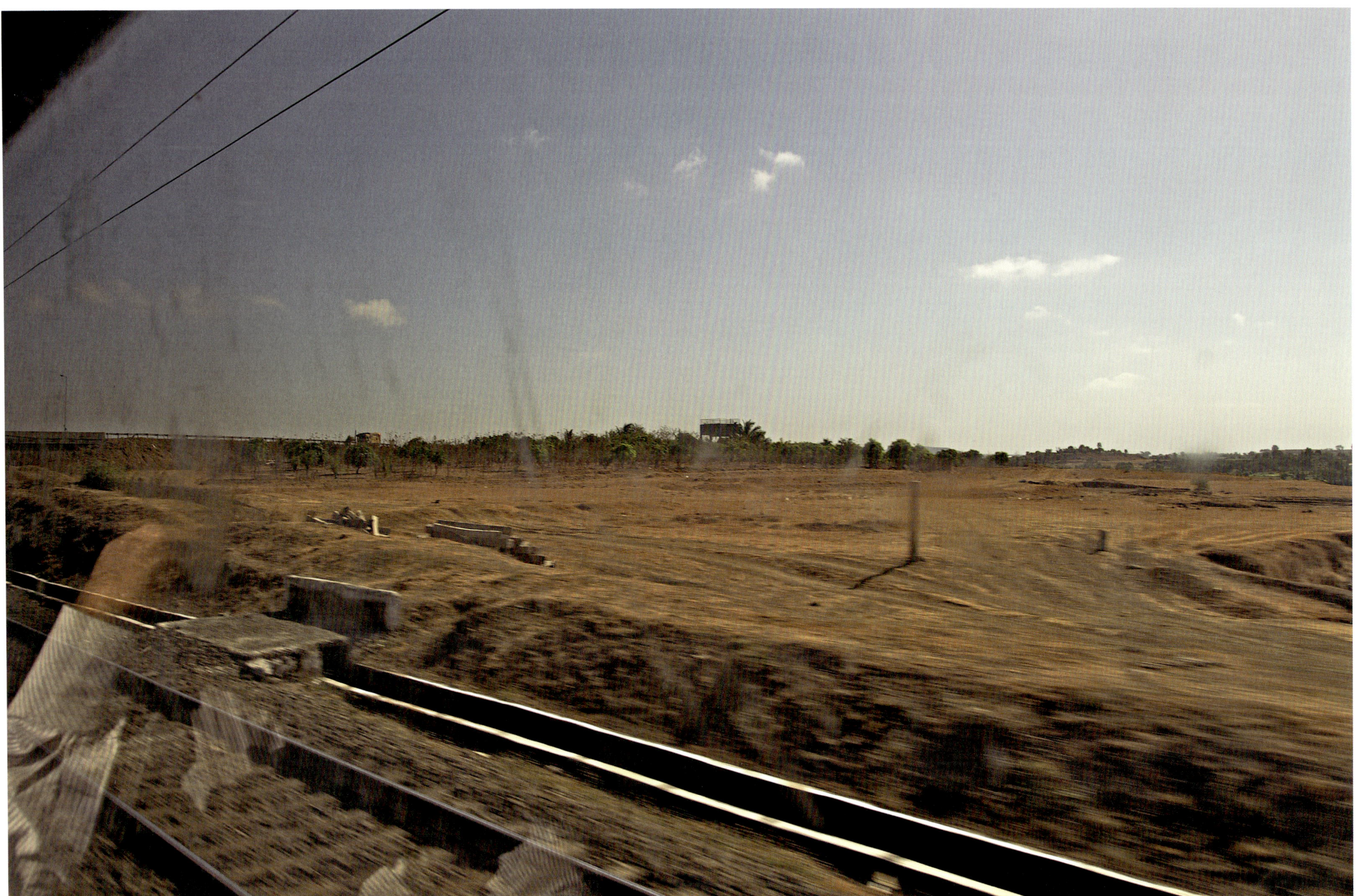
India

The longest station name in India is Sri Venkatanarasimharajuvariapeta.

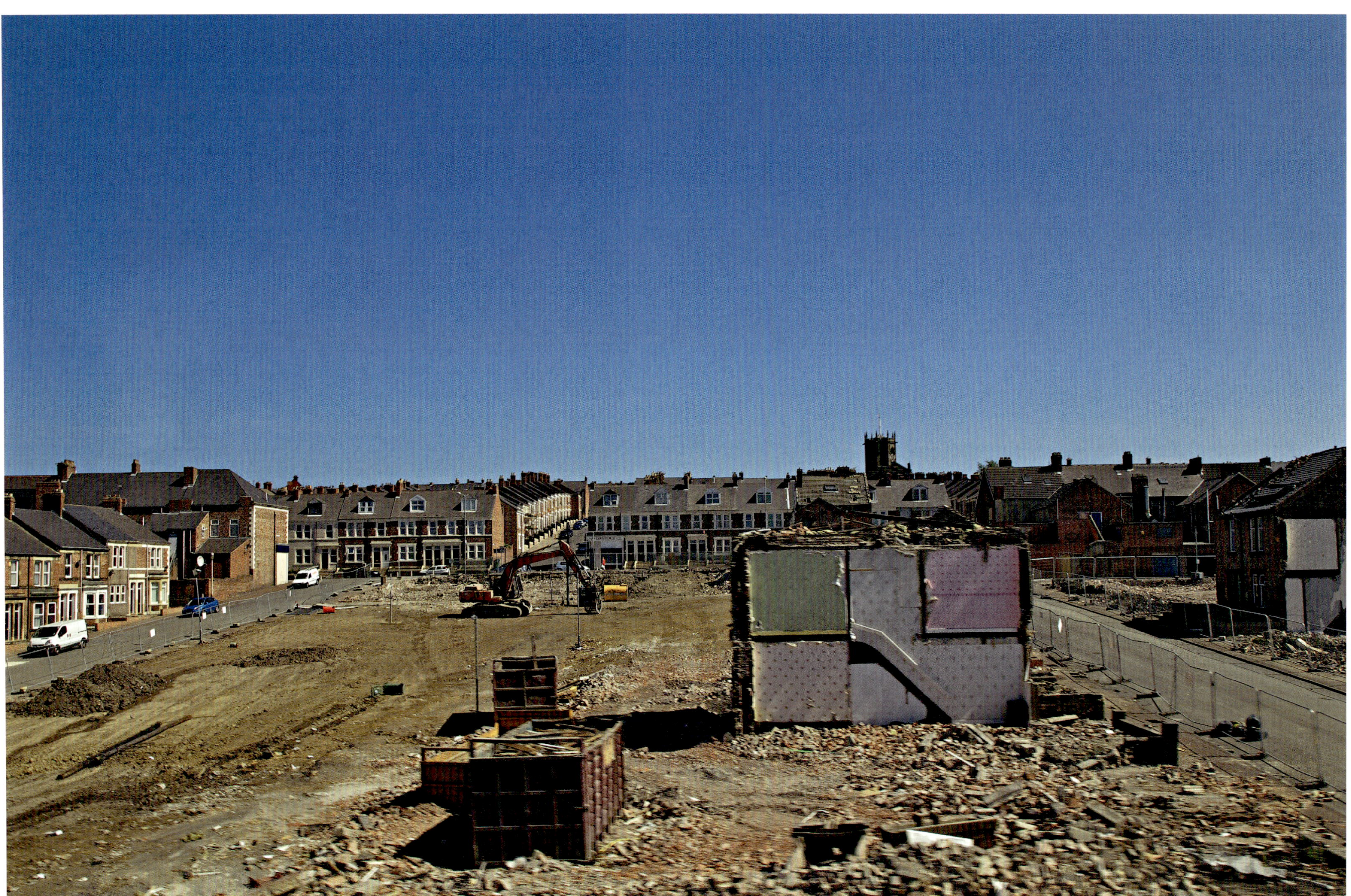
United Kingdom

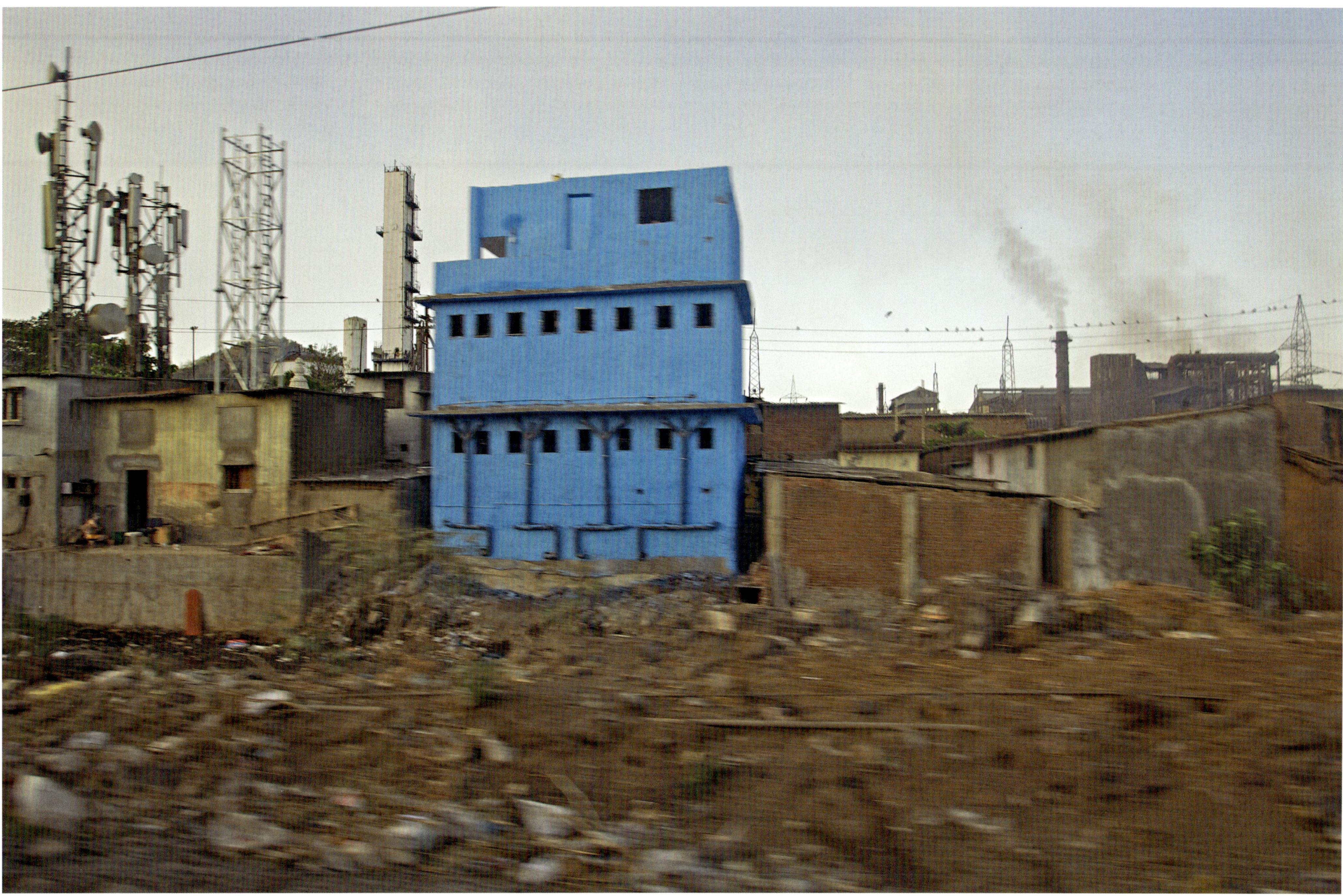

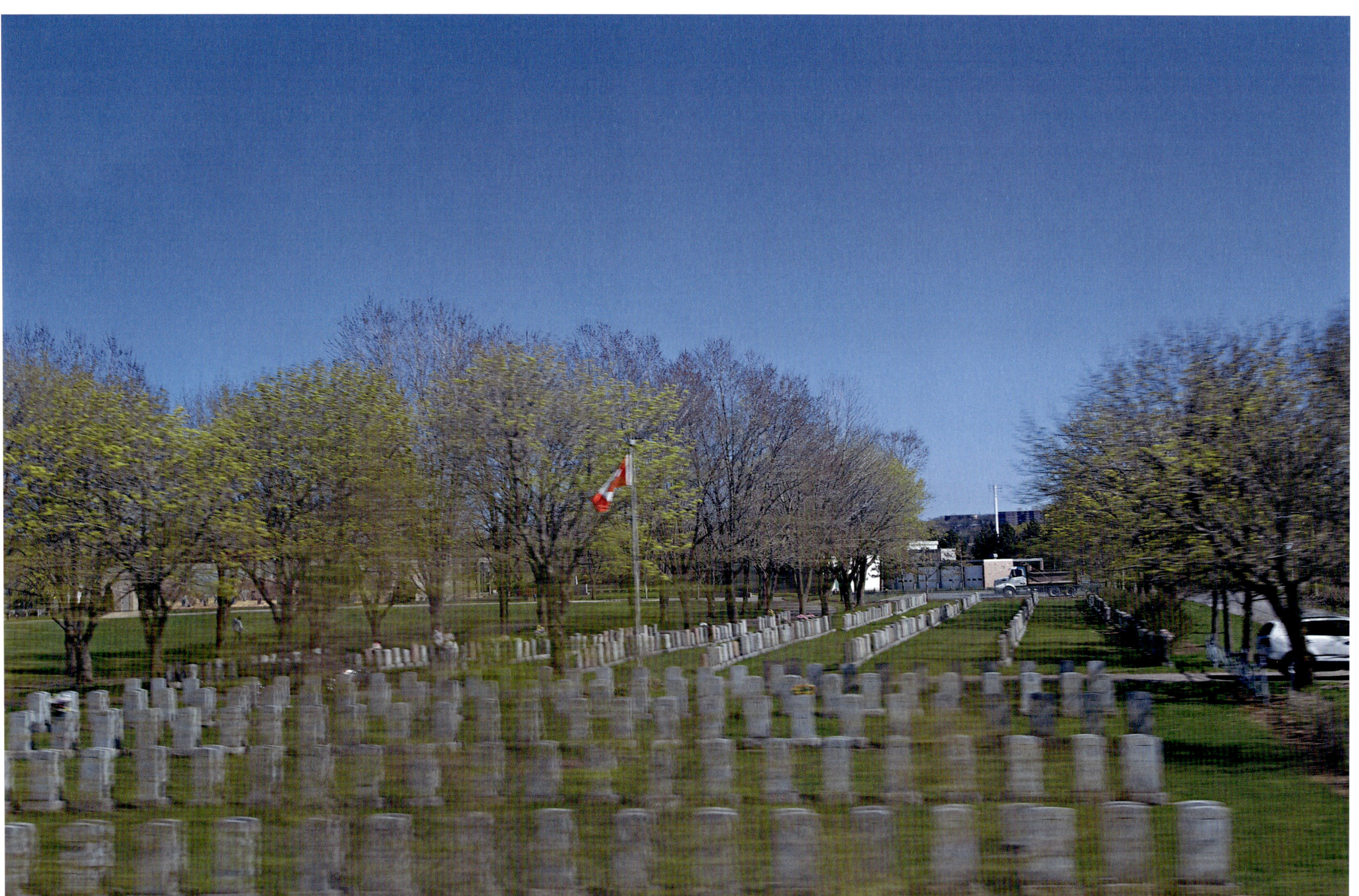

Bologna, Italy

Private rail companies in Canada are owned directly by tens of thousands of investors, including thousands of their own employees, and indirectly by millions of Canadians through savings and pension plans.

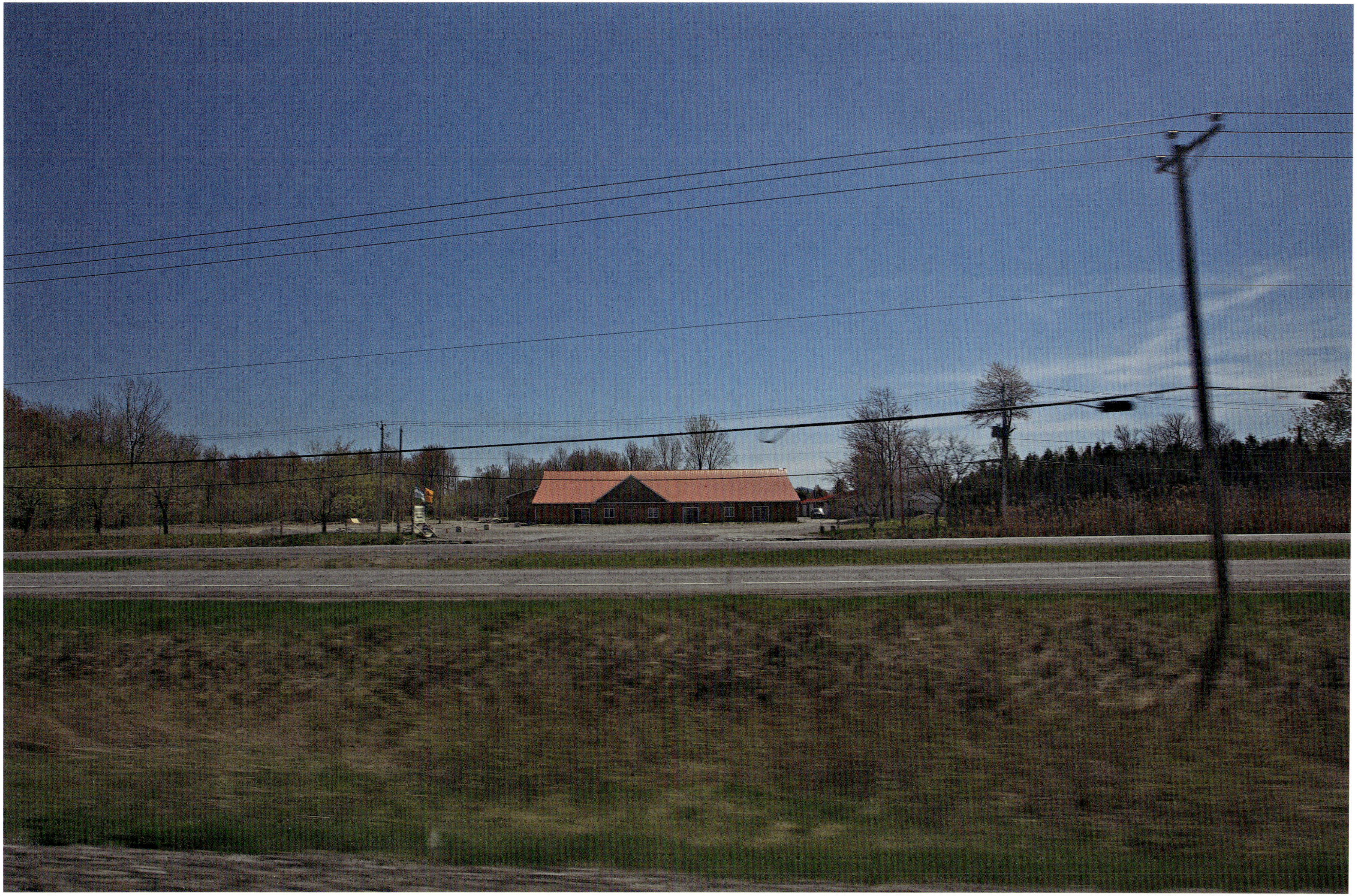

Quebec, Canada

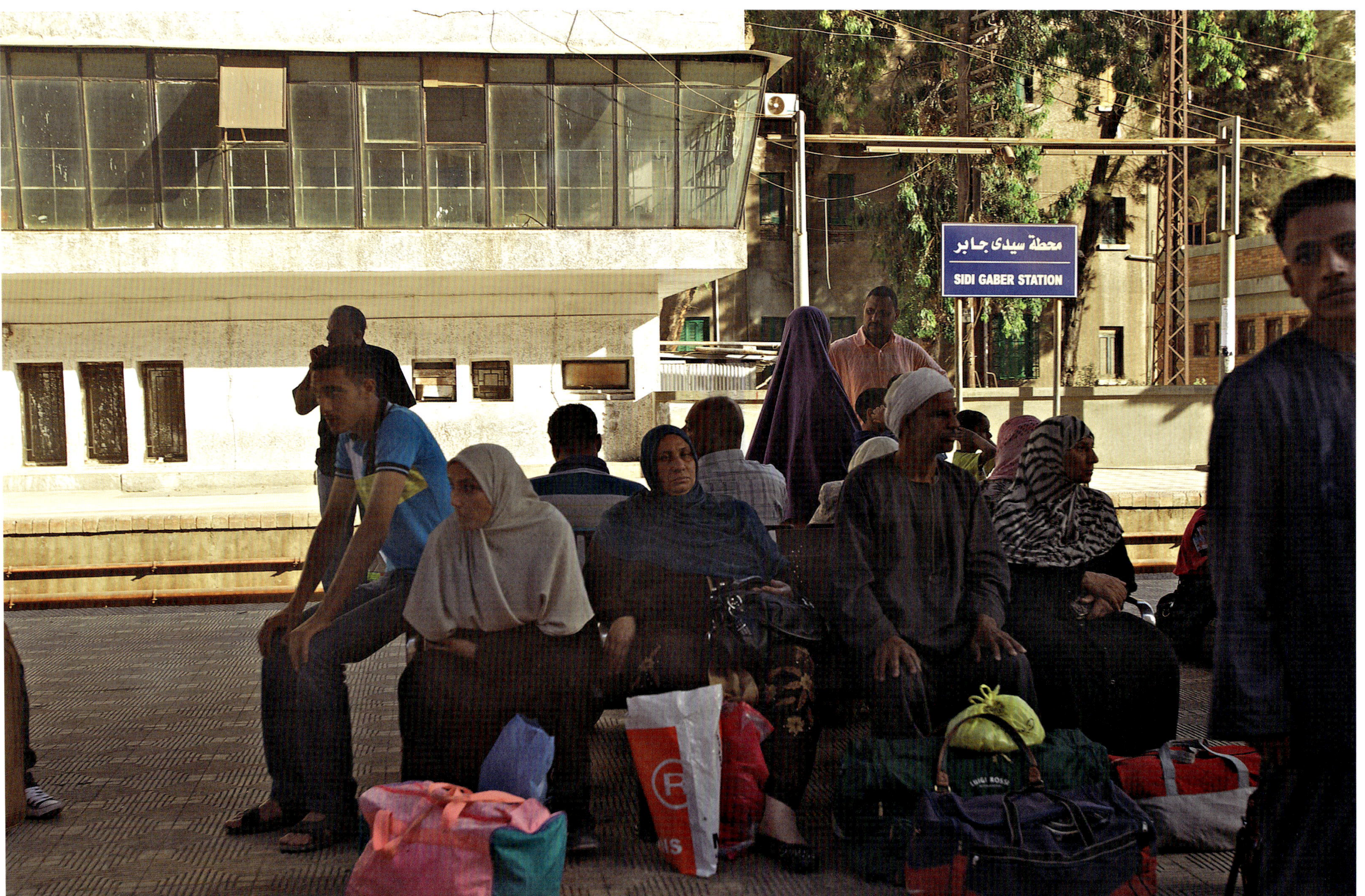

محطة سيدى جابر
SIDI GABER STATION

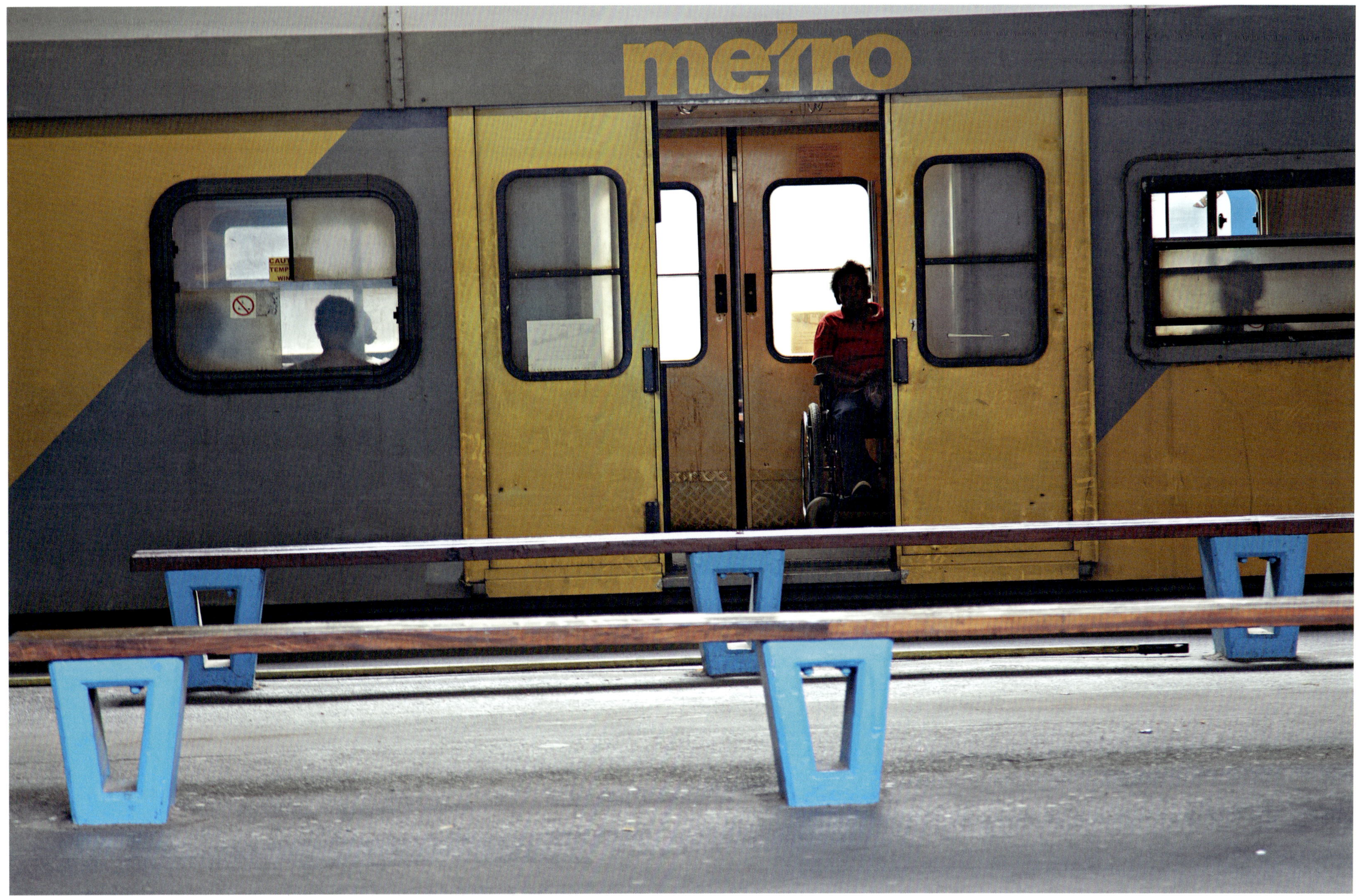

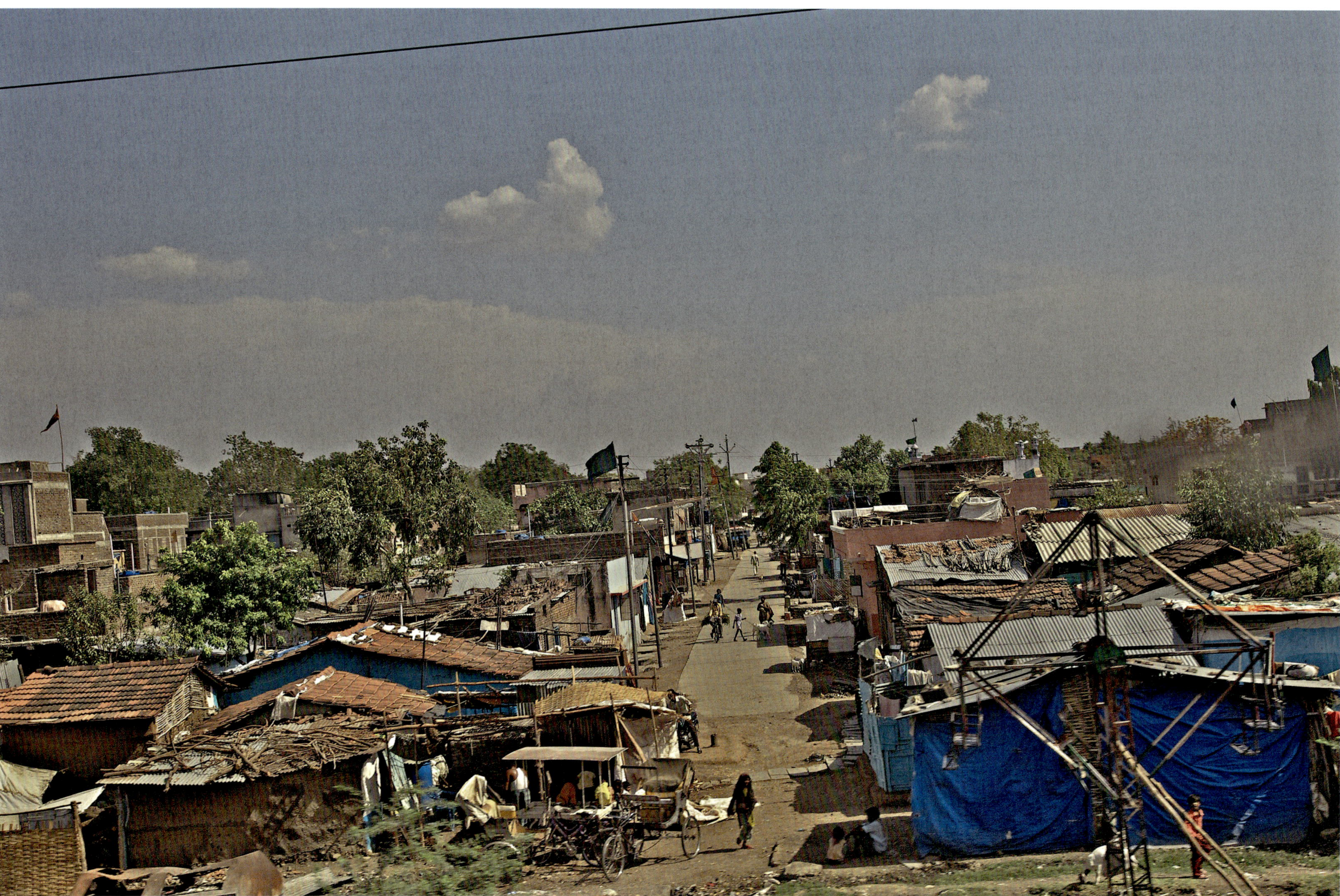
India

Indian Railways has 7,500 stations, comprising of 115,000 km / 71,000 miles of track over a route of 65,000 km / 40,000 miles. As of December 2012, it transported over 25 million passengers daily.

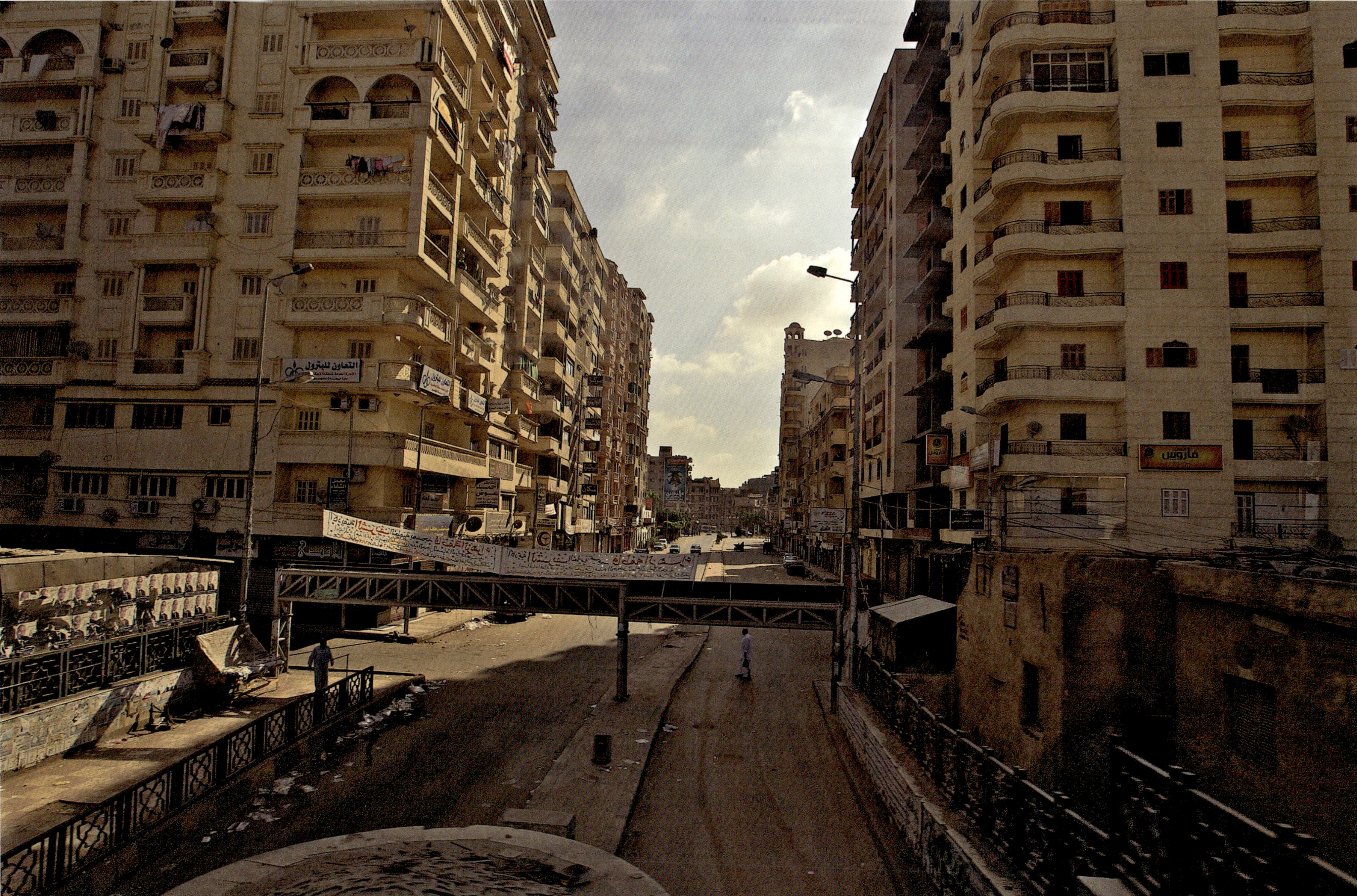

Alexandria, Egypt

Following pages: Canada

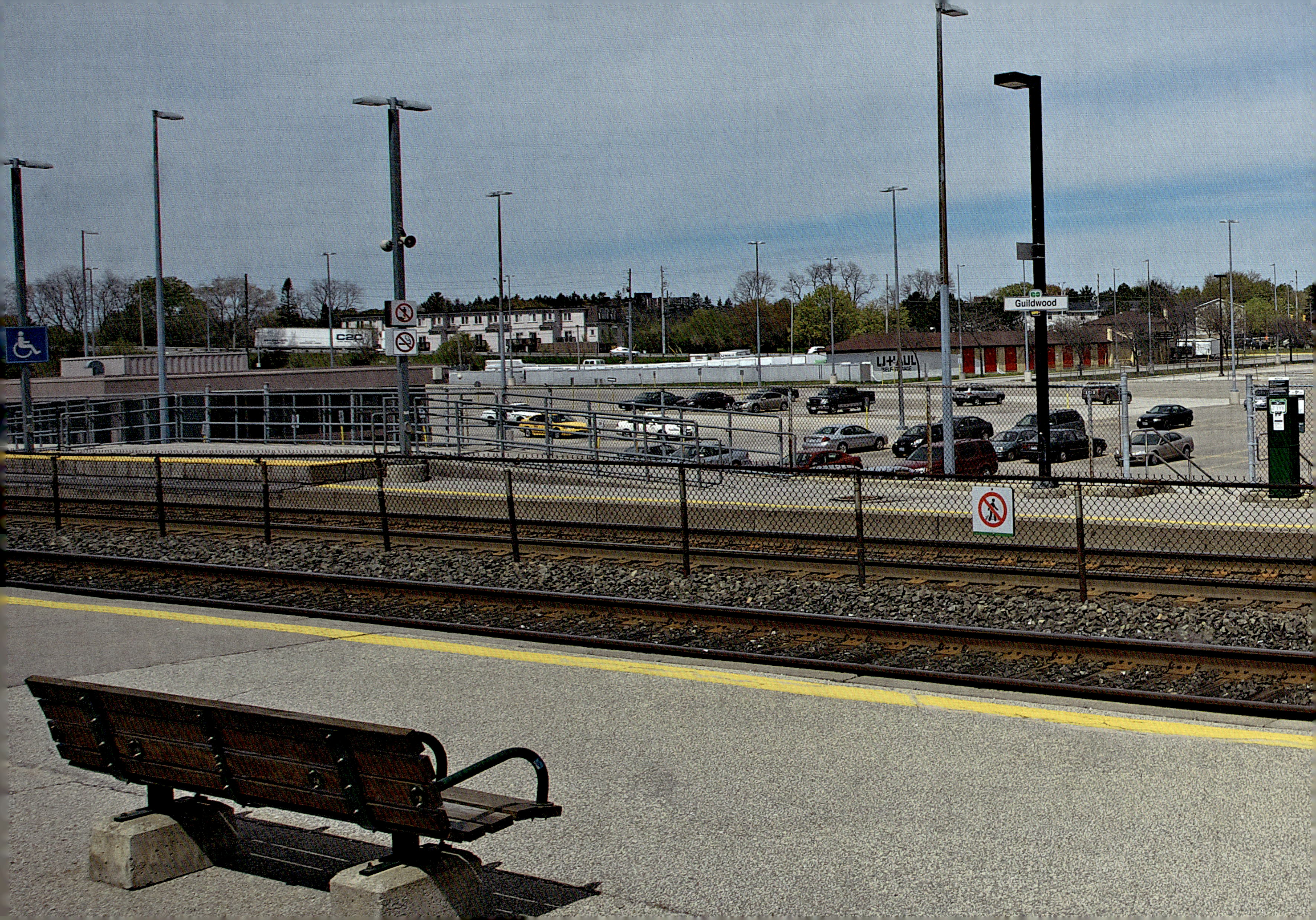

Guildwood

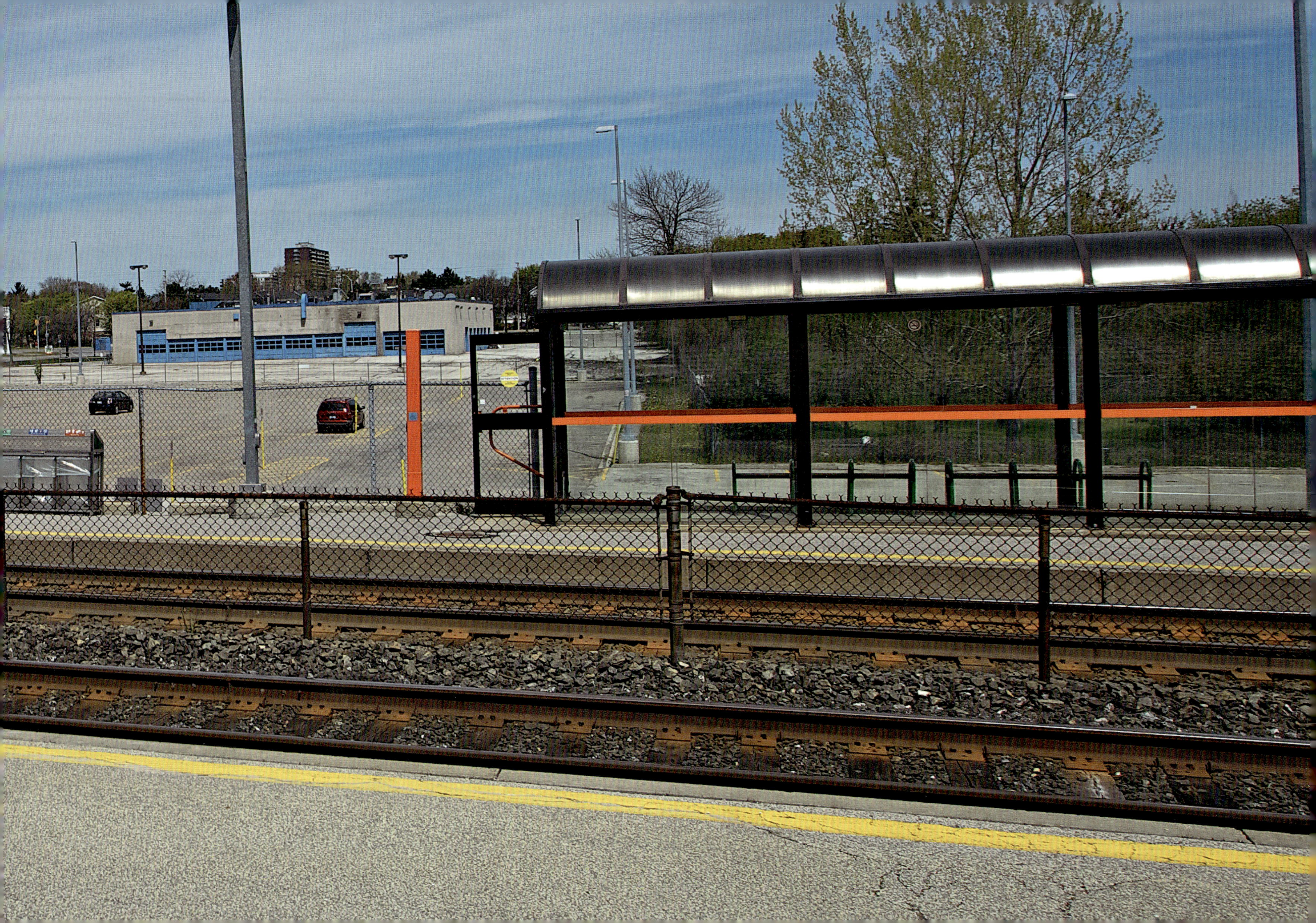

In November 1994, Eurostar's high-speed rail service was launched connecting Paris and Brussels, on one side of the English Channel, with London on the other. The Channel Tunnel holds the record for having the longest undersea section anywhere in the world, as well as being the second longest rail tunnel in the world. In September 2007 a record-breaking train left Paris Gare du Nord and reached London St Pancras in 2 hours 3 minutes 39 seconds.

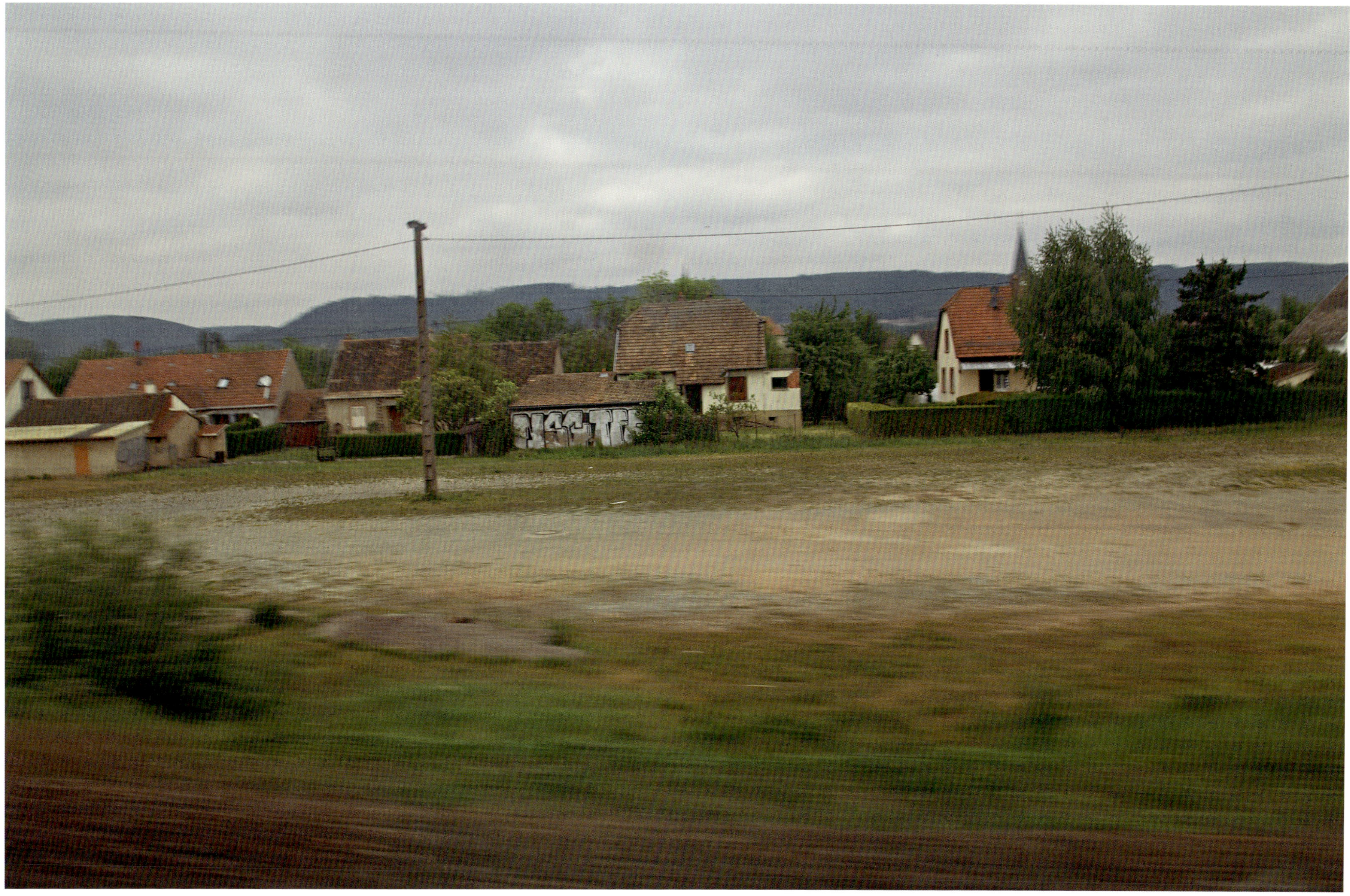

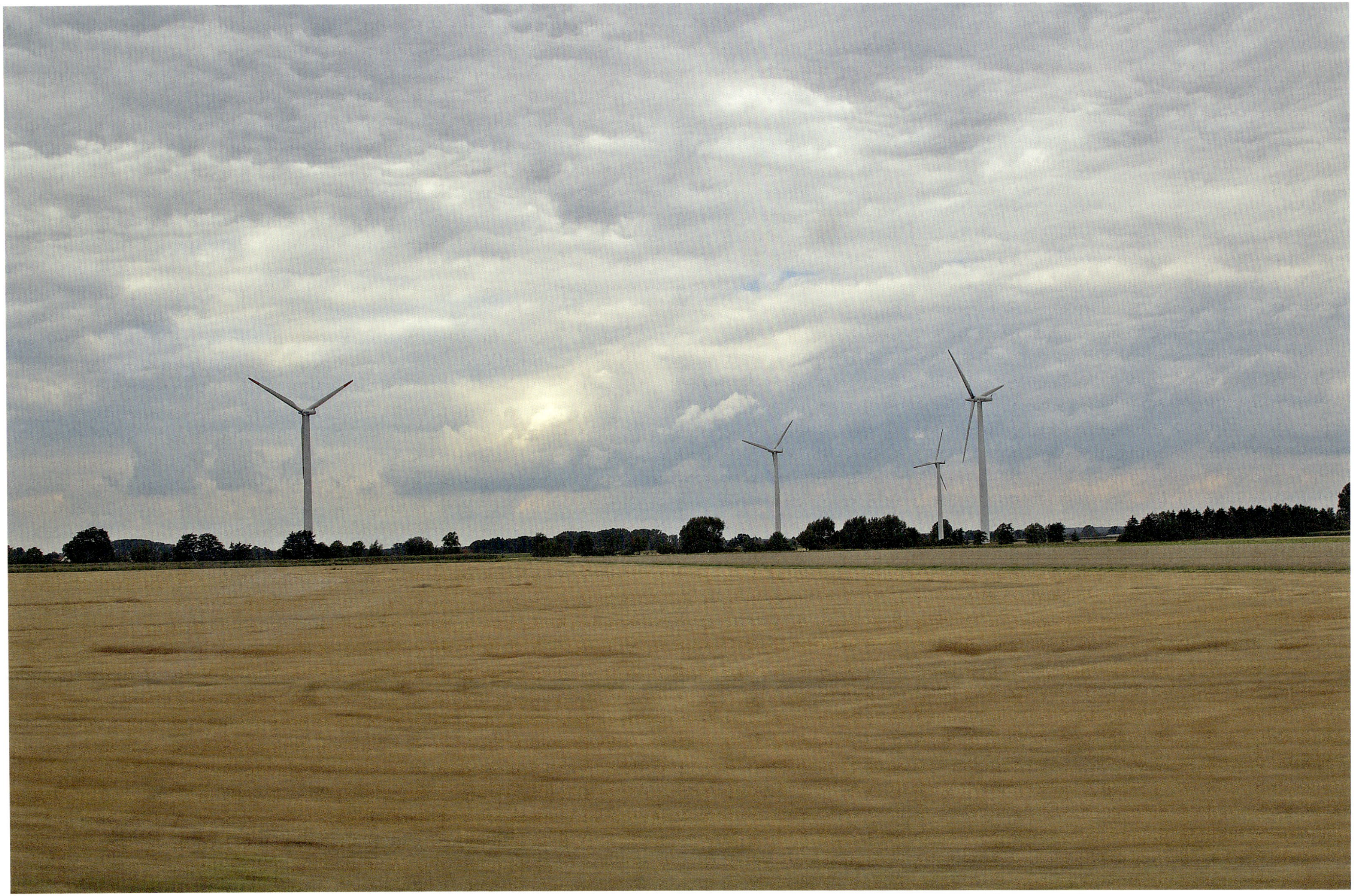

France

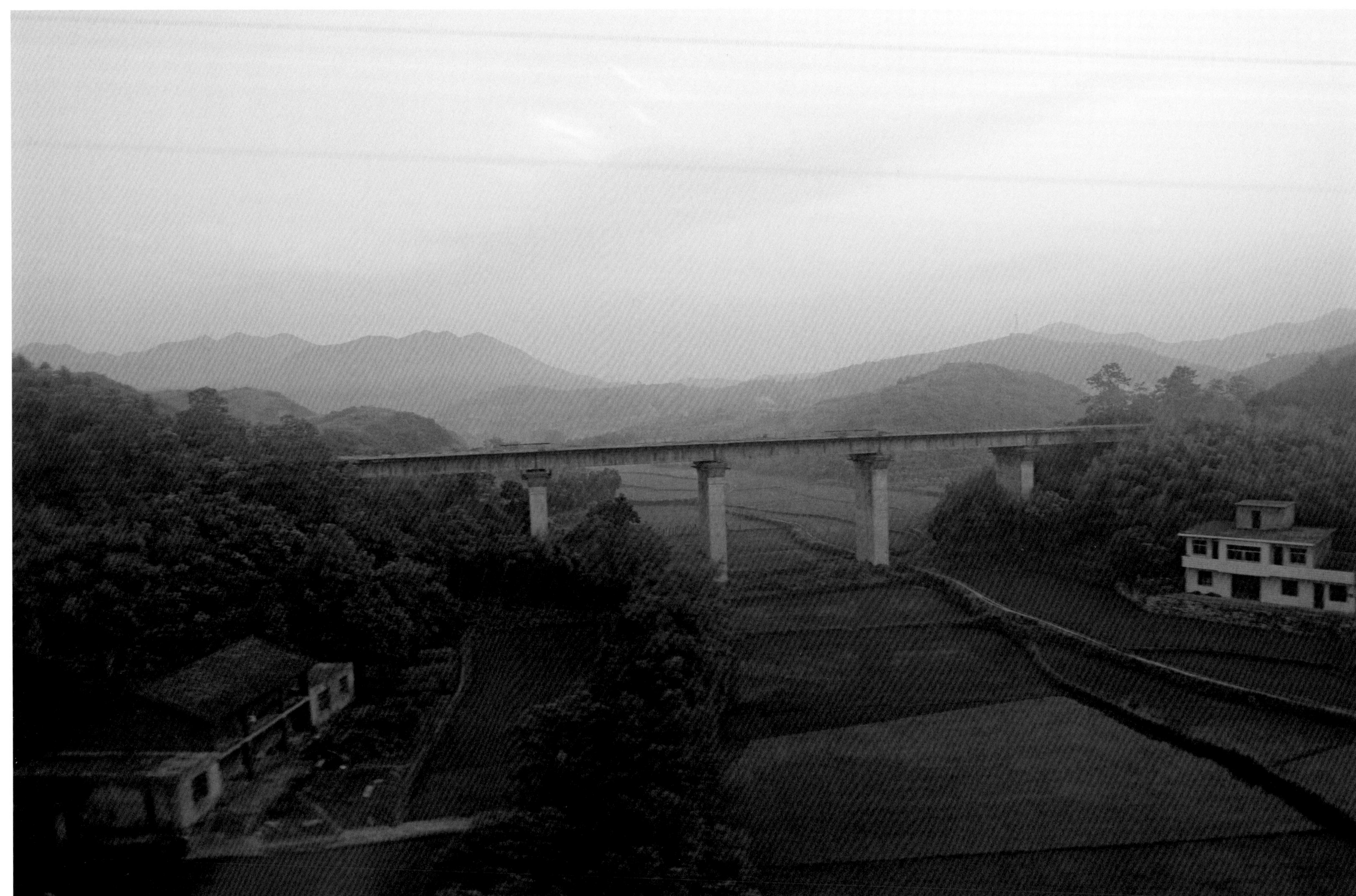
China

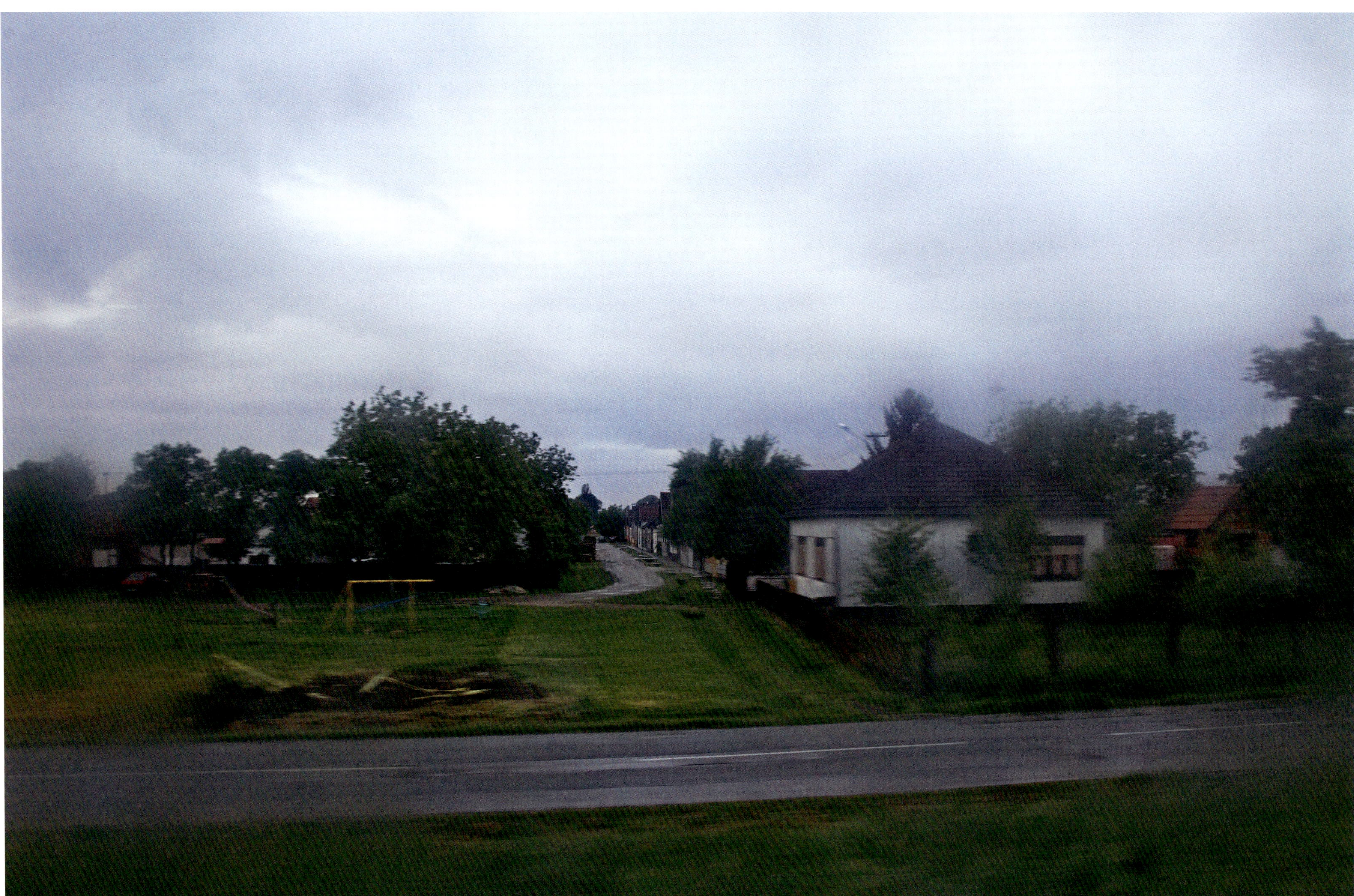
Serbia

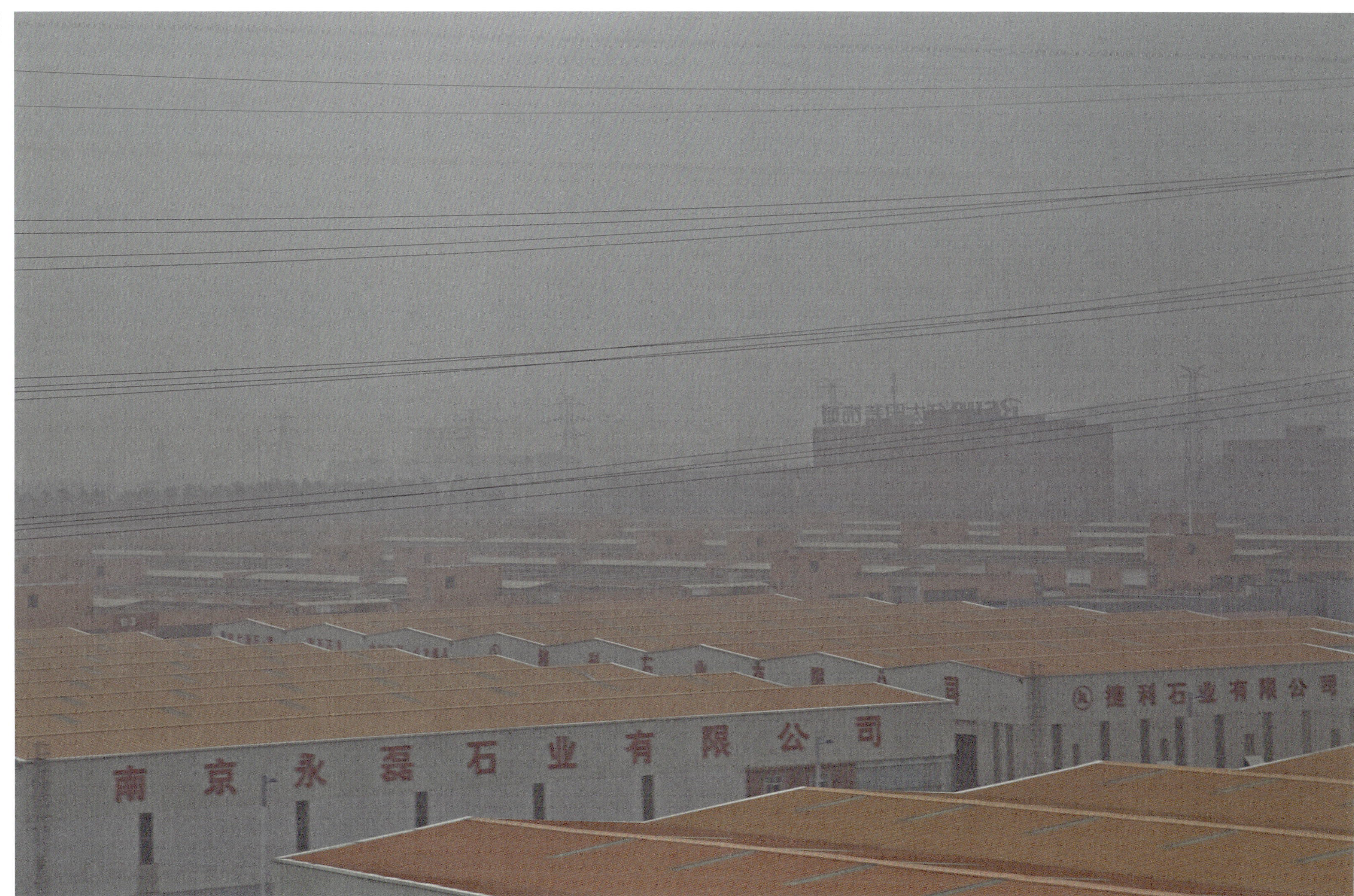
南 京 永 磊 石 业 有 限 公 司
德科石业有限公司

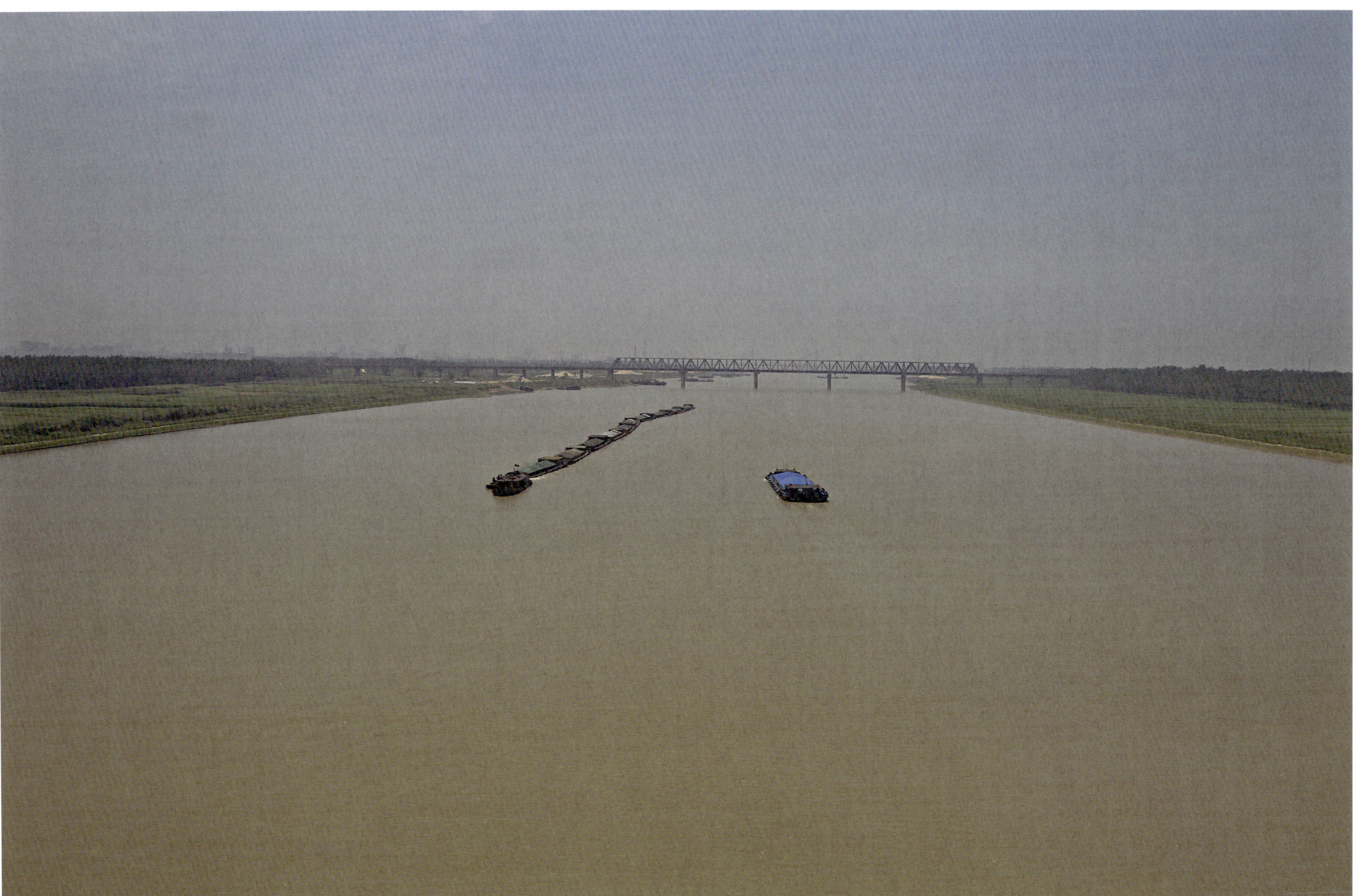
China

Trains are the most popular means of long distance travel in China. They carry twice as much freight and passengers as Russian trains and three times as much as the US trains. China's railways carry more than 1.4 billion passengers a year.

SOURCES

JAPAN

Page 122 - 'The world's busiest train stations', *railway-technology.com*, August 9 2012, accessed March 12 2013, http://www.railway-technology.com/features/featureworlds-busiest-train-stations

EGYPT

Page 73 - Gary Goldfinch, *Steel in the Sand, the History of Egypt and it's Railways* (Dorset Press, 2003)
Social and Economic Development Group Middle East and North Africa Region, Restructuring Egypt's Railways: Egypt Public Expenditure Review.
www.mof.gov.eg/MOFGallerySource/English/policy-notes/Restructuring Egypt's Railways - Augst 05.pdf

Page 78 and 84 - 'Egyptian National Railway (ENR)', http://www.ide.go.jp/English/Data/Africa_file/Company/egypt03.html

EUROPE

Page 58 - 'The Worlds Most Beautiful Railway Stations' Travel and Leisure, http://www.travelandleisure.com/articles/worlds-most-beautiful-train-stations/2

Page 150 - 'Eurostar', Wikipedia http://en.wikipedia.org/wiki/Eurostar

SOUTH AFRICA

Page 46 - 'Facts About Railways', http://www.thomascooktours.com/blog/facts-about-rail-journeys/

SouthAfrica Page 55 - 'Shosholoza Meyl', *Wikipedia* http://en.wikipedia.org/wiki/Shosholoza_Meyl

BRAZIL

Page 10 - Marc Johnson, 'How Britain is helping build Brazil's modern railways', *Rail* January 15 2013, accessed March 1 2013, http://www.rail.co/2013/01/15/how-britain-is-helping-build-brazils-modern-railway/

INDIA

Page 27 - Edgar Thorpe, *The Pearson General Knowledge Manuel 2012* (Pearson Education India, 2012)

Page 135 and 145 - 'Indian Railways' http://www.iloveindia.com/indian-railways/index.html

CANADA

Page 22 and 140 - 'Rail Facts', *Rail Canada* http://www.railcan.ca/education/facts

CHINA

Page 32 and 157 - 'Trains in China: History, Train Life, New Lines and Great Leap Culture' *Facts and Details*, http://factsanddetails.com/china.php?itemid=315&catid=13&subcatid=86

RUSSIA

Page 43 and 66 - 'The Trans-Siberian Railway', *Wikipedia* http://en.wikipedia.org/wiki/Trans-Siberian_Railway

ACKNOWLEDGMENTS

Thanks to: Martin, Wai, Hannah, Jessie, Darrow, Diana,
Francis, Marvin, and Marian

Very Special Thanks to: Gigi

Published in Great Britain in 2013
By Trolley Ltd
www.trolleybooks.com

Photography © Jarret Schecter
Text © Jarret Schecter
Design: Fruitmachine
Text Editing: Hannah Watson, Jessie Ramsay

ISBN 978-1-907112-44-7

Printed in Italy 2013 by Grafiche Antiga

Also in this series:
America Off Track (Trolley, 2008)
Russia Off Track (Trolley, 2011)